EMBRACING THE CROSS

EMBRACING THE CROSS

Life, the Law, and Loving the Lord
in the Lone Star State

Travis Bryan III
and
Tim Gregg

Faith in Resurrection Ministry
Bryan, Texas
www.faithinresurrection.org

Faith in Resurrection Ministry, Bryan, Texas, United States of America
©2020 Faith in Resurrection Ministry
Printed in the United States of America.

ISBN-978-0-578-71151-5

Library of Congress Control Number: 2020911952

The source of scripture quotations can be found in the Index of Scriptures in the back of the book.

Dedication

I dedicate this book to my wife Becky (Rebecca Wood Bryan). She has been my lover, my "Coach," my best friend, my encourager, the greatest mother of my three children I could ever have found. She is part of me and part of everything positive that has happened in my life since the day we were married. She is truly my "better half" and a wonderful gift to me from God.

Travis Bryan III

Table of Contents

Foreword

I'm honored to have called Judge Travis Bryan III a friend and client, fellow Aggie, and spiritual brother for almost fifty years. I am humbled to have the opportunity to introduce him to you here. He's a special kind of person.

Simply put, Trav—as his family and friends call him—is a wonderful human being. From the first time we met, I knew he was someone to be taken seriously. He's a very thoughtful man and a very Godly man. At his core, he's one of the most decent people I've ever known because he cares about people, every single one of us.

Trav and I share a lot when it comes to the nature of our upbringing. Next to God and our families, our greatest affection growing up was for the hallowed institution of Texas A&M. Both of us were raised by Aggie fathers, who completed their educations after serving our country during World War II. We were both "vaccinated" with Aggie Spirit long before we set foot on the campus with a mind to play college football. Travis is a year older than I am, so we missed being teammates for Coach Gene Stallings. I attended a junior college before walking on at A&M, thus I also missed the Aggies' Southwest Conference championship season of 1967. I did eventually earn a scholarship and now, all these years later, I continue my affiliation with our school as a member of the Texas A&M University System Board of Regents.

While Travis grew up the son of a wonderful mother and a terrific father, who was both a bank president and community leader, I was raised in the South Plains of Texas, in the small town of Tahoka. Despite the difference in our formative geography, Trav and I were instilled with the same basic beliefs. We were fortunate to grow up in homes filled with love and where a premium was placed on solid Christian values like hard work and discipline. There's a little less of that now in this world, I think, so a story like Trav's, one filled with challenges met and adversities overcome, has meaning for readers from all walks of life.

Unlike me, Trav is a scholar and a well-read man. He has a tremendous intellectual capacity and, as with any good trial lawyer, he's adept at research. For many years, he was an outstanding criminal defense attorney, and his legal training was an asset in his quest to find the truth in God's holy word.

Judge Travis Bryan III's story is important because it is a testament of how a common man found and became intimately familiar with God. I hesitate to use the word "common," but Trav has never seen himself as anyone special, nor tried to be anything other than a child of God. His story is important because it's one written by an individual willing to reveal his heart, his soul, and his mind to readers. What makes this book important is that, in Trav, each of us will see a bit of our own sometimes-flawed human selves.

In reading his story, I found that Trav's humanity—one of the things that makes him a dear friend to me—comes through on almost every page of this book. I was captivated to learn how his trials and tribulations eventually brought him to The Cross of Jesus Christ. Through years of study, reflection, and prayer, Trav learned to trust God completely. By immersing himself in the Word, Trav discovered the transformative power of The Cross, where healing, redemption, and salvation all await those willing to die for God's mercy.

The Almighty has blessed Trav with a wonderful family and a remarkable career. His story is both amazing and compelling. No matter your station in life, whether man or woman, old or young, there's a powerful message contained within the pages of this book.

I know of no better way to sum up my friendship and fellowship with Judge Travis Bryan III than to say that he makes me feel worthy. Rich or poor, black or white, innocent or guilty, Trav has the unique ability to see inside the soul of each and every individual he encounters. All of us have worth to him. All of us, Trav knows, are children of God and recipients of God's endless love. It is through that understanding that he makes everyone feel worthy. And I love him for that.

Phil Adams
Texas A&M Class of '70

Introduction

I'm not much for dwelling on the past, so the concept of telling my life story seemed a little unappealing to me at first.

After all, I'm not sure I've lived a noteworthy enough life to assume my story is worth your precious time.

I am not a politician, nor an actor, nor a chef, nor a business guru.

I've never flown into space–although the wife of my collaborator on this project has done so...four different times. Now that's a story I'd be interested in reading!

What I am is a Texas judge whose ancestors date back to the very beginning of our state's history. Thus, my hometown and I share a surname, and my great-great-granduncle sort of started the whole Texas thing.

I'm also a son, a brother, a husband, a father, and a granddad. I'm a staunch conservative–not unusual around these parts–but some of my views may surprise you.

But at the core of my existence, I'm a believer in God, a disciple of Christ, and a student of The Word.

So why does my story matter?

Well, like you and like everyone in this world, I've experienced my share of ups and downs. A lot of you may be plagued with occasional self-doubt, hopelessness, despair, or bouts of depression.

I know I am.

We're all a little flawed, "only human," as they say. I look back on my life and think, "I wish I would have done some things a little differently." That notion used to consume me, but God finally convinced me that the past cannot be changed.

In the book of Isaiah 43:18, it says clearly, *"Forget the former things, do not dwell on the past."* (Note: for any of my readers unfamiliar with the Bible, the first number refers to the chapter of the book being referred to, while the second number is the verse.)

Of course, we can learn from what we've done in days gone by. On occasion it's okay to look back on the past and ponder its meaning, especially when the intent is to find someone to write your story in a manner which might be of interest to some.

Especially when you want to share a thing or two that just might make a difference moving forward in someone else's life.

With your permission—which I suppose is implied, given that you've either purchased this book or borrowed it from a friend—I wish to offer here one man's perspective on Faith and Grace and God's Love and Redemption, and do so in a way that doesn't come across as "preachy."

Because I am not a preacher.

As an aside, I do believe the Gifts we receive from our Heavenly Father—like Grace and Love and Forgiveness—are worthy of capitalization, as are His attributes and processes, as well as the fruit of the Spirit, and even articles (The, A, An) when they modify special nouns, so you'll find that I apply that rule liberally throughout this book. I also capitalize the pronouns "referring to Deity," as it says in some dictionaries. Call me old-fashioned, but I think that reflects respect, as well as clarifies any confusion that might occur when talking about God and His creatures. Or call it "artistic license," if you will.

Even though I am a Believer, and I am a Follower, I've sometimes questioned contemporary Christian doctrine. One of the things that keeps me from regularly attending church is my discord with what I often hear preached from pulpits today. Particularly troubling to me is what some call the "prosperity gospel," which preaches material entitlement as a reward for believing in God. In the Bible, Paul promises the spiritual blessing of salvation, not the material blessing of wealth.

I believe that my own lengthy study of the Bible, coupled with a personal immersion in the views of Biblical scholars over the last couple hundred years, have given me a grasp of how God works in our lives. I describe that Divine interplay as "Embracing The Cross," thus the title of this book.

Jesus, it turns out, wasn't the only one to experience "death and resurrection."

"I have been crucified with Christ and I no longer live, but Christ lives in me," says the Apostle Paul in Galatians 2:20.

"Death"—in the guise of failure, hardship, sickness, and heartache—occurs regularly in all our lives. But, like our Savior, we too can experience a type of "resurrection," a personal renewal which leads to forgiveness, healing, contentment, and joy.

In assembling this story, I've found numerous examples of this death-and-resurrection dynamic which has played out, not only in my own life, but also in the lives of others I have known, respected, and loved.

Let me give you one example:

Before becoming a judge, I spent some twenty-five years as a criminal defense lawyer. Before that, I served my fellow citizens as a district attorney. I've seen a lot when it comes to practicing the law, but as a Christian, one case stands out for me: that of a fifteen-year-old juvenile accused of murder.

When I first met him, this boy was sitting alone in the detention center of the courthouse trembling like a leaf. His fear emanated both from what he was charged with, as well as from the fate which potentially awaited him.

When I became his court-appointed attorney I told him not to worry because "worry is the devil's tool."

In fact, I may have quoted from the book of Matthew 6:34: *"Do not be anxious about tomorrow, for tomorrow will be anxious for itself."*

The young man was eventually convicted of murder, but, given his age and the extenuating circumstances of his case which I presented during his trial, he was sent to a juvenile home for eighteen months.

There, for the first time in his life, he had time to reflect, and in those reflections I believe he opened his heart to God. Upon release, he returned home, we became friends, and he did his best to find a new way. I was proud of the great strides he took into manhood.

But I also saw that old demons continued to haunt him, and he was ultimately arrested again in his early twenties on charges of domestic violence.

For the second time in a court of law, I stood by this young man's side.

And for a second time, he was found guilty of his crime.

Now, it might appear that I had failed my young friend, but as a defense attorney my job isn't always to keep people out of jail. In his case, I believe I could have done so, but when the time came to argue what constituted a fair punishment for his crime, he did not choose the easy path.

He chose the way of God's Truth.

At his sentencing, he admitted his wrongdoing and spoke of how God had assured him that in prison he would find his "resurrection." In that moment, I knew the young man had taken to heart my encouragement that he Embrace The Cross.

That troubled young man is now nearly forty years old. He is as dear to me as one of my own children.

He will tell his own story later within the pages of this book.

Through my work in America's criminal justice system, God has used me to touch the hearts of men and women headed toward or already mired in the ways of the devil. Not all have been able to soften their hearts in acceptance of the Love of Jesus Christ, but some have.

And, in those moments of Reformation, I have experienced my own Salvation.

After working many months on this book, I've come to realize that my story may not be half bad. Like every good story, it's a tale of Redemption—mostly my own.

But my story also contains tidbits and tales different from others within the Christian genre. In these pages you'll find reflections of football fortunes and golfing passions, both good and bad, as well as accounts of crime, punishment, and a wedding-day donnybrook involving yours truly.

As the subtitle of the book suggests, here you'll find one sinner's story about "Life, the Law, and Loving the Lord in the Lone Star State."

Let's get started.

1

Speaking The Truth

I'm fairly certain I don't have a lot in common with the late artist Andy Warhol. I'm not too sure about his political or religious views, and I can't say I'm all that familiar with his work, save for those "soup cans" he painted.

I'm a political conservative and a God-loving Texan in a politically conservative state. Norman Rockwell is more my artistic cup of unsweetened tea.

To Warhol's credit though, I will say that my life is proof of his most often-quoted adage: Everyone is destined for fifteen minutes of fame.

I would humbly suggest that, in my case, the same goes for "infamy," as well.

My biggest brush with notoriety came in the early 1980s, long before some of you were even born. At the time, I was a young prosecutor here in Texas. I made unintentional national headlines for my opposition to the nomination of Sandra Day O'Connor as a justice on the United States Supreme Court.

If you're old enough, you may remember that episode, and you might even remember me.

Let me recap this somewhat "dark" period of my life.

During his campaign for the presidency in 1980, Ronald Reagan promised American voters that he would seek to place a woman on the Supreme Court, the constitutionally mandated judicial panel which up to that point in our country's history had been the exclusive domain of the American male. I supported Reagan in his presidential run and mostly admired the man during his eight years as our nation's chief executive.

After Reagan entered the White House, I didn't give much thought to the matter of a woman on the nation's highest court. In the summer of 1981, I was busy in the courts myself as the thirty-four-year-old district attorney for Brazos County, working in the Central Texas town of Bryan.

And, yes, I share the same name as the city in which I've spent my entire life. My great-great-grandfather, William Joel Bryan, sold land to the railroad which eventually became this place, and the city is named in his honor.

William's uncle brought the first American settlers to this part of what is now Texas in 1825. At the time, the region was controlled by Mexico.

Even if you're not a Texan, you may have heard of that now-famous *impresario* and pioneer.

Stephen F. Austin is known today as the "Father of Texas," and to those of us bearing the Bryan name, we are kin to the man.

Austin eventually led Texas to declare its independence from Mexico in 1836. The capitol city of Texas is named in his honor, as are buildings, parks, and thoroughfares in pretty much every county of the state, including the high school I attended here in Bryan.

While Stephen Austin is universally beloved where I come from, such wasn't the case with Sandra Day O'Connor, at least when it came to her 1981 Supreme Court nomination. Many conservatives here in Texas, as well as across the country, expressed concern about her pro-abortion record as a member of the Arizona State Senate. I was pro-life then and remain pro-life now, but that wasn't my principal reason for opposing Mrs. O'Connor.

My take was more of a "fundamental" nature.

The news media broke the story about Reagan's decision to select O'Connor as a Supreme Court nominee more than a month before the announcement became official. On that summer afternoon—July 10, 1981, to be exact—the courthouse reporter for *The Bryan Daily Eagle* newspaper stopped by my office to chat. In the process, she asked me what I thought of the impending O'Connor nomination.

Before I answered, she asked me, "Can this be on the record?"

"Sure," I replied, certain what I had to say would be no cause for alarm.

I am aware today that some people here in my hometown of Bryan, Texas, think that I grew up with the proverbial "silver spoon" at my ready disposal. Both my grandfather and father, whose names, like mine, were "Travis Bell Bryan"–I'm the third– were presidents of the First National Bank of Bryan and influential pillars within the local community.

Their good standing around here probably helped get me elected as local DA.

"TB," as we called my granddad, was a friend to American presidents. Daddy, whom everyone in the family called "Big 'Un," was an influential man, too. The school board here chose to rename the local high school in Daddy's honor.

In his professional life, my father was a great practitioner of diplomacy and decorum. Unquestionably, his demeanor was key to his business success.

As a teenager, and like a lot of young people that age, I looked at life in very literal terms. "Nuance" and I were not yet acquainted…and I can't say that we've ever been particularly close friends. Some of the things Daddy felt necessary to do in his business dealings didn't seem quite right to me. I was always proud of him, and I loved my father dearly, but I didn't yet understand the importance of getting along with people to make it in this world.

To me it seemed that Daddy sometimes could be a little full of himself, and maybe, on rare occasions, the fact of the matter is he could fudge on the truth a little. An incident during my senior year of high school–which I'll get to later–sort of affirms what I mean.

At some point in my formative years, I decided that I would always stand for the truth. And not just "the" truth, but in a foreshadowing of my future career, I stood firmly committed to "the whole truth, and nothing but the truth," as well.

So help me God.

I hung onto this idealistic conviction well into adulthood. And, as you might expect, on more than one occasion, my version of the truth reached up and bit me right in the butt.

So when that reporter from the local newspaper asked me my thoughts on Sandra Day O'Connor's worthiness to become a Supreme Court judge, I spoke from the heart, if not from the head.

"I believe in the Bible and that God created woman to be man's helper," I was accurately quoted in *The Eagle* the next day. "Men are more capable of being judges. It has been my experience that women have a hard time being objective."

As if that wasn't bad enough, I went on to say, "The world is a better place because of women. But there are too many women competing with men for jobs."

I'd suggest you take a moment or two to let those words soak in a little. Trust me, I've had a long time to think about them.

By the next day, my story was everywhere. This was long before the internet, but the public shaming associated with my remarks was sizable and widespread. My brother, Tim, who was working in Houston at the time—about two hours from Bryan—learned about my insertion of foot into mouth on the radio of his car, via Paul Harvey's nationally syndicated *News and Comment* show.

Tim later told me when he heard the story, he nearly drove off the road.

When Tim tried to call me at my office, he couldn't get through. Nobody could. My phone rang off the hook for much of the rest of that week.

"What did you do???" my only sibling queried incredulously when he finally reached me.

"I said what I thought," I told him.

In response, Tim laughed at my misfortune. His attempt to console me ultimately amounted to these few painfully obvious words: "You'll be in hot water for a while until all this simmers down."

When I got home from work that evening, my dear, sweet wife Becky was waiting for me at the front door. Becky has been a constant source of comfort and reassurance for the entire span of our nearly fifty years of marriage.

From the look in her eyes that fateful day, I could tell she already knew I'd been raked through the coals.

"I guess I've proven to the world that I'm a 'male chauvinist pig,'" I said as she welcomed me into her arms.

"You're no male chauvinist," she whispered into my ear. "You're a good, decent man, and you prove that every day in every way."

"I think I screwed up big time," I said, retreating from her embrace. I held her out at arm's length, searching for the look in her eyes that would tell me what she really thought.

Fortunately, her love for me was unconditional. Truth be told, I'd tested that love many times before.

When I talked to my parents later that evening, Daddy said he couldn't have been prouder of me.

"Trav, you said the right thing!" he insisted. "A lot of my customers at the bank have expressed similar views about the O'Connor nomination."

"That a *woman* wasn't fit to be a judge?" I asked.

"Well, not exactly," Daddy replied, "but, dammit, someone has to tell it like it is!"

Mama, like Becky, was mostly concerned about the beating she knew I was already taking in the court of public opinion.

According to an Associated Press story that ran nationally soon after, Elizabeth Cowan, assistant to the president of Texas A&M University, my alma mater, called my remarks "very sad."

The A&M campus was and is about a mile from my home in Bryan.

Another important voice from the school, that of Irene Hoadley, the director for A&M's Library Services, posited that I was "living in the past century," and that she was "shocked" by what I had said.

Paul Harvey, as Tim told me, had not been kind to me, either. The list of those with a dissenting view to mine was long and, in many cases, extremely vocal.

It took me a good while to come to terms with that episode of my life. At the end of my term as DA, I chose not to seek reelection. Despite my accomplishments in the office, I truly believed that my reputation as a "chauvinist" made me a poor candidate.

Not until perhaps twenty years later, in the midst of my years as a highly-successful criminal defense attorney and during an intense period of personal inquiry seeking Biblical truths, did I realize that in the aftermath of my remarks pertaining to O'Connor, I had experienced what amounted to a personal "crucifixion" and presumed career burial.

I found solace from God's Word.

"Blessed is the one who perseveres under trial because, having stood the test, that person will receive the crown of life that the Lord has promised to those who love Him" (James 1:12).

Both Healing and Salvation can be found through the act of Embracing The Cross.

This book is a testimony to that premise.

Ask anyone who knows me, and they'll tell you I'm serious about my faith with a strong commitment to both my God and my Savior, Jesus Christ. Politically, I have a conservative-minded view of the world, but socially, I believe in compassion, fairness, and Love for all people. It took those years of intense study of Scripture for me to realize that we are all equal in God's eyes.

"Then Peter began to speak: 'I now realize how true it is that God does not show favoritism...'" (Acts 10:34).

I'm a changed man and a better person for having reached those conclusions, but I still have a long way to go.

O'Connor's nomination was approved unanimously by a U.S. Senate body composed of ninety-eight white men like me and two women—all of whom were a little more open minded about things than I may have been at the time. O'Connor served twenty-five years on the Court. As a district judge myself now, I respect how she interpreted the laws that govern our great nation.

Most of the time.

Roe v. Wade, the 1973 Supreme Court ruling affirming a woman's legal right to abortion in this country, remains the law of our land. I am still opposed to abortion, but as someone who has sought and sentenced individuals to be put to death for their crimes, my "pro-life" stance has broadened, as I will explain later.

I realize now it was wrong for me to oppose O'Connor strictly based on gender. For most of you, that may seem pretty obvious. You'll be glad to know, I hope, that I've had a hand in placing several women on the bench in my time as a Texas judge. I'm proud to say they've all been exceptional stewards of justice.

As you read ahead, be forewarned: I am not perfect. I am no better, nor worse, than anyone else. I believe that Jesus Christ is the only way to Eternal Salvation, but that Salvation is not "earned." It is received through Grace and affirmed through Embracing The Cross.

In Mark 8:34, Jesus states that whoever wants to be His disciple must deny themselves and take up their cross and follow Him.

If there's one thing I've learned having spent decades working with the people accused of crimes, it's that the power of Love unceasingly makes the critical difference at the crossroads of life. We either accept that our lives are marked with a death-and-resurrection continuum ordained by God, or we succumb to a hardening of the heart and a rejection of the cornerstone of the Love that is the embodiment of God's Goodness.

I hope you'll find that my story reflects that.

Ironically, my name does.

"*Travis*" is a Middle English name of French origin which roughly translates to "keeper of the crossroads."

Let me take you to one of those crossroads now.

2

The Court of Law

In my career as an attorney, I've played all three major roles in the courtroom drama that is the focal point of our American judicial system.

Once a jury trial begins, the victim and the accused are secondary players. It is the prosecutor, the defense attorney, and the judge who dominate the proceedings. Their influence on the outcome of a case is undeniable.

Some have compared a jury trial to a chess match, but I think it far more resembles a basketball game. Perhaps that's why basketball is played on a "court."

Preparation is important, and the rules of engagement must be followed, but an attorney, regardless of the client's point of view, must excel at both offense and defense in order to earn a winning verdict.

Occasionally, but not very often, a trial goes into "overtime." In our legal system, that's known as a "mistrial," which comes about as a result of an error in proceedings or when a jury is unable to reach a unanimous verdict.

One case in which I was involved as a defense attorney went into "triple overtime," which turned out to be the most enthralling experience of my nearly fifty years as a lawyer and a judge. I'll write about that in the chapters to come.

But the single trial which shaped me most as an attorney and, although I was unaware of it at the time, began to mold my current Christian convictions, took place in the aftermath of one of the most vicious murders in the history of my Texas town.

Unlike many of my legal peers, I gave virtually no thought to becoming an attorney when I was young.

I received my undergraduate schooling at Texas A&M University, just a few miles from my parents' home in Bryan, and as the son and grandson of bankers, dutifully pursued a major in finance.

I give credit to my father for pointing me in a different direction.

One night on a visit to my parents' home during my senior year at A&M, Daddy and I got into a bit of a fuss about something or another. While my father and I may have shared different outlooks on what it took to become successful in life–his way was proven, mine was mostly idealistic at the time–we both possessed a sizable stubborn streak.

Thus, we squabbled occasionally, which led to words from Daddy which altered the course of my life.

"Trav," Daddy said, using the foreshortened version of my name which everyone who knew me used at the time, "you like to argue so much, why don't you become a lawyer?"

Truth be told, I didn't have a lot passion regarding the financial future which seemed to be my destiny. Entering Texas A&M, I had joined the school's Corps of Cadets, and with the Vietnam War raging in southeast Asia, I figured I was destined to wind up there.

Surprisingly, Daddy's emotionally charged suggestion struck an immediate chord within me. Since I was fairly certain I didn't really want to spend my life behind a desk working at a bank, maybe he was right.

And it did seem I liked to argue.

I never did make it to Vietnam, but I had friends from the Corps that did and died in service to country.

The Vietnam War was one of the most divisive times in our nation's history. I still have strong feelings about that period, but my thinking on the matter has changed dramatically through the years.

More on that later.

I attended Baylor Law School in nearby Waco, Texas. My attendance there provided my military deferment. After graduating and passing the bar exam–a "death and resurrection" story I'll get to later–I returned to Bryan with a new wife, ready to put my legal expertise to work.

And I did so, at least for starters, at Daddy's bank.

I knew, even before I took the job, the bank couldn't offer me the kind of experience I craved. My work had mostly to do with such things as contracts and foreclosures, but Daddy had put me through both college and law school, and I felt I owed him at least a little bit of my time and new-found legal talent.

In addition to my work at the First National Bank of Bryan, I entered into private practice with another young local attorney by the name of Neeley Lewis. Neely had grown up in College Station, son to an A&M professor. He had gone off to the University of Virginia to get his undergraduate degree, but returned to Texas to study law at Baylor, where he was a year ahead of me.

In working professionally with Neeley, I discovered a hunger to become a criminal attorney.

One case in particular whetted that appetite.

I was hired to represent a young solider stationed at Fort Hood, southwest of Waco.

He had been returning to his post one night, speeding through the small town of Belton, Texas, when he ran a red light and hit a woman who had stepped into a crosswalk.

She died from the injuries she received in the accident.

The ensuing trial was basically a "no contest" case.

Given my lack of experience, the prosecutor walked all over me. The judge also did a rookie like me no favors, siding with the prosecution at almost every turn.

My client was found guilty of vehicular manslaughter and sentenced to five years in prison. In hindsight, that was probably the best outcome he could have expected, but I came away from the experience feeling like I had done a poor job.

Still, I was eager to learn from the experience and try again.

Eventually, I decided to do the illogical thing: run for the office of Brazos County district attorney. I was still incredibly inexperienced as a trial attorney, but I loved being in a courtroom and the challenges the setting provided.

A lawyer once told me that trying a criminal case is like "capturing a speck of dust floating in the sunlight."

That guy was a lot more esoteric than I am, but his point is well taken. Both defense attorneys, as well as prosecutors, have to be sensitive to many things. Everything you do is done to persuade the jury to take your side of a case. How you dress, how you move about the courtroom, your tone of voice in the moment, and how and when you make eye contact with the jury matter greatly during proceedings.

The goal is simple: Get the jury to like *you* as a counselor, whether or not they agree with your side of the case. A favorable opinion of an attorney can often influence the verdict a jury renders.

I knew none of that as I took my legal beating in Belton, but the outcome helped me get focused on my future.

I split time for almost six years doing legal work at the bank and honing my skills as a trial attorney. I paid my figurative debt to Daddy, while slowly improving as a defense attorney. Still, neither Neeley nor I were setting the world on fire in private practice.

By the time I turned thirty, I knew I needed something that would offer me both job satisfaction, as well as a paycheck big enough to support my wife and children. So, in 1978 I officially took a plunge into politics, entering the race for district attorney.

As a DA, I felt I could really practice the law, the key word, I suppose, being "practice."

To do that though, I had to get elected. While I knew I couldn't run on my "record," I did have one advantage: the Bryan name.

The DA position opened through a "musical chairs" scenario which involved, of all people, my own cousin–although he came from the non-Bryan side of the family.

I'm going to write about Bill Davis a lot in this book. While Daddy's "encouragement" prompted me to consider entering the legal profession, Bill's example as an attorney and judge inspired me not only to want to become a lawyer, but also to be a good one. I went to Baylor Law School because that's where Bill had gone.

Bill was a first cousin to my father through my dad's mother. Bill was an outstanding attorney who, for a time, served as district judge for Brazos County.

The same position I hold now.

When Bill was named to the Court of Criminal Appeals in Austin, his departure from the Bryan legal scene opened up his district judgeship. The county's DA at the time, Tom McDonald, was appointed to fill Bill's vacancy. Roland Searcy, the county attorney and the natural pick to move up the ranks, filled the vacancy in the district attorney's office until elections could be held.

Roland was my opponent in the 1978 Democratic primary for local DA.

Does the fact that I ran as a Democrat and am now a conservative Republican surprise you? Well, if you know anything about Texas political history, it shouldn't.

When it comes to people of a certain age, most every conservative in Texas was once a Democrat. While I still have friends in the Democratic party today, ideologically, I'm just not able to get on the same page with those who possess a more liberal point of view.

There was a time in Texas, a long time in fact, when Republicans were sort of a political afterthought. Today's Republican mindset was once the domain of conservative Texas Democrats.

A bunch of us eventually changed party affiliation, including big names like John Tower, Phil Gramm, Kay Bailey Hutchinson, Rick Perry, and Ted Cruz.

Lloyd Bentsen was the last Democrat elected to the U.S. Senate from Texas. Bentsen served as a senator in Washington from 1970 to 1993. He gained his seat by upsetting another long-standing Texas conservative, Ralph Yarborough, in the 1970 Democratic primary. In that year's general election, Bentsen easily outdistanced a young Texas Republican by the name of George Herbert Walker Bush.

By the time Bush and his presidential running mate Dan Quayle defeated the Democratic ticket of Michael Dukakis and *Lloyd Bentsen* in 1988, I had been a Republican for a number of years.

Let me say that I'm proud that President Bush later chose Texas A&M as the site of both his presidential library and final resting place.

During my campaign for DA, my father thought it would be a good idea for me to visit the bank and meet a few of his customers. "You'll get support that way," he said. "Just go out, be yourself, and ask for their vote."

I agreed to do so.

One of the first people I met at the bank seemed interested in my message. After I was through, or maybe "seemed finished" to him, he told me, "You're the first person who ever asked me to vote for them, and I appreciate that.

"I'm going to vote for you just because you asked."

Campaigning was easier than I expected.

Soon, I walked up to another customer, an older woman with a bitter look on her face. I shook her hand, introduced myself, and without seeking to exchange pleasantries, I launched into my election spiel.

I didn't get the same positive response as I had with the gentleman before. In fact, I wasn't eliciting any sort of reaction, but I plowed through to the end.

"You know," she said after I stopped talking, "you've never spoken to me before"–she didn't look familiar at all–"and now that you're running for office, you come up and talk to me like a used-car salesman."

Ouch.

"I wouldn't vote for you for anything."

Knockout blow.

As she walked off in a huff, my first thought was that she had taken such offense to me, she might yank all her money out of Daddy's bank.

As far as I know, she did not do so. After her rebuff, I left the bank filled with discouragement. I was able to eventually put the episode behind me and regain my enthusiasm for the race. I won my primary by a margin of just a couple hundred votes, out of more than 13,000 cast.

I then easily swept to victory in the general election…because I had no Republican opponent, and just like that, I was the Brazos County district attorney.

I officially took office on November 20, 1978.

And just three weeks later the brutal killing of a local twenty-seven-year-old husband and father set into motion events which would stretch my legal expertise to the breaking point and strain the confidence I had hoped to build between myself and my constituency. "These trials will show that your faith is genuine. It is being tested as fire tests and purifies gold—though your faith is far more precious than mere gold…" (1 Peter 1:7).

3

Good Samaritan

One of my first duties as Brazos County's new district attorney was to attend a conference in Wimberley, Texas, put on by the Texas District and County Attorneys Association. The meeting was an orientation session for me and my peers, held in the picturesque Texas Hill Country, north of Austin.

At the conference, prosecutorial newcomers were affectionately known as "baby DAs." We were all enthused by our political victories and eager to enforce the law.

On my return to Bryan from that two-day gathering, I stepped into my new office located in the Brazos County courthouse ready to tackle just about anything. I'd barely had time to unpack my briefcase that morning when my one-and-only assistant prosecutor, Bill Torrey, rushed in with some bad news.

"There's been a real bad murder," he said.

A couple years younger than me, Bill had served under my predecessor in the DA's office, Roland Searcy. Thus, he had a lot more prosecutorial experience than I did.

What Bill went on to tell me about the local murder shook me to my core. The Wimberley gathering had bolstered my professional confidence and, while matters relating to murder cases had been covered, to actually be facing such a case less than a month on the job unleashed all the insecurities which had plagued me throughout my run for the office.

Bill is now the DA in Milam County, Texas. His office is located in the small community of Cameron, located about an hour's drive from Bryan. Bill still loves his work and he gets to do it in one of the most beautiful old county courthouses you'll find anywhere.

Bill and I met in Cameron not too long ago to discuss our first Brazos County murder case. It came to be known as the "Good Samaritan murder," and it caused quite a sensation around town.

Frank May was *The Eagle* staff writer assigned to the case. Frank and I spent considerable time together during both the investigation of the crime and the trials which followed.

Here are excerpts from a few of the early stories Frank wrote about the murder.

Driver found dead after apparent try to start vehicle

(Dec. 12, 1978) Authorities are bewildered over the Monday night killing of an unidentified young man who apparently was being a Good Samaritan for motorists having car trouble on Sandy Point Road, one-fourth of a mile east of FM 50 in Brazos County.

The man, described as a white male, 20 to 30 years old, was found lying in a ditch with massive head injuries in front of a home on Sandy Point Road early this morning.

Man's beating death may be linked to robberies

(Dec. 13, 1978) Investigators of the Monday night killing of Tim Merka, 27, of Mumford, speculated Tuesday that the death may be connected to recent armed robberies in Brazos and two surrounding counties.

The persons described as waving down Merka while he was driving along Sandy Point Road near FM 50 Monday night were two black males, one wearing a knit stocking cap. Two black females were with the two men, according to witnesses.

Witnesses said they saw Merka's pickup drive past the four persons who had been stranded on the roadside with car trouble and were waving him down.

Helpful habits probably led to killing

(Dec. 14, 1978) Tim Merka was a happy, easy going young man who was devoted to his work and always wanted to help people, especially those in trouble.

*But his attitude of giving others needing aid may have led
to his own downfall.
That is how shocked friends and co-workers described
Merka's life Wednesday.*

Mumford, Texas, is an unincorporated township a few miles
northwest of Bryan. At one point in its history, the community
thrived, but that all changed in 1899 when the nearby Brazos River
flooded, devastating the locale.

Tim Merka's death devastated Mumford, too, as well as the rest
of Brazos County. Merka was a young man with a seemingly bright
future and a family who loved him. He did not deserve to die.

It was the job of local law-enforcement agencies to find the
killers and my job to ensure that justice would be served.

Forty years ago, violent crimes were a rarity in Brazos County.
It wasn't that people didn't get into arguments and shoot each
other from time to time. Among a certain element of society, those
things are more commonplace than you might think.

And unfortunately, from time to time, very bad things
happened to good, law-abiding citizens, too.

Tim Merka, father to four children and a former student at
Texas A&M, died after being bludgeoned to death with a tire jack.

Given the brutal circumstances of Merka's death, the manhunt
to find his killers was unprecedented for the time and place. Less
than two days after the crime was committed, two young men
turned themselves in. Shortly thereafter, another man and a
sixteen-year-old girl were also arrested.

With four suspects in custody, I began preparation to
prosecute the cases. In the end, we tried the three men arrested:
James Charles Manuel, nineteen; Danny Ray Harris, eighteen; and
his brother, Curtis Paul Harris, seventeen.

I was haunted by just how young the accused were. While they
would be tried as adults, they weren't really men yet. They were still
boys.

But the evidence in the case was overwhelming.

A local man, Elmore Green, told investigators he was home,
living on the outskirts of Bryan, when he witnessed Merka stop
and offer assistance to a group of motorists in need.

According to Frank May's reporting, Green said, "It was about 10:30 (at night) and I saw them wave him down on the road. I saw him helping someone get a boost off his pickup."

Green went on to tell May he had gone to bed shortly thereafter and the next morning as he was leaving for work, he discovered Merka's body.

"I figured he was dead and (I) wasn't going to go near him," Green said. "I called officers right away."

Sheriff's deputies found Merka's body in a ditch next to the vehicle he had tried to start. His own pickup had been stolen, probably providing the motive for the crime, along with a shotgun Merka kept in the cab of his truck.

A grand jury indicted the three men on capital murder charges. The girl was held in custody and eventually offered damaging testimony against her friends.

While it was abundantly clear this was a capital murder case, the local citizenry went out of their way to make sure I understood that. I received calls, letters, and "man on the street" advice demanding the harshest possible penalty for the perpetrators.

Some even wanted to take matters into their own hands.

"Is this Travis Bryan?" a caller asked after I picked up the phone in my office in the days following the initial arrests.

"Yes, it is."

"I'm not going to tell you my name"—this was decades before Caller ID– "but now that you have those criminals in jail, all you have to do is let them out and let me know when you do.

"They'll be dead within a day. You won't have to try the case."

My startled response came out something like, "Man, are you kidding me? I can't do anything like that. Who is this?"

The anonymous vigilante hung up.

It was clear the community demanded a swift and just punishment for the killers of the Good Samaritan, but as the evidence in the case mounted, so too, did the pressure on the "baby DA."

I began to hear voices in my head.

"You can't do this." "You don't know how to do it." "You're too inexperienced to get the outcome this case deserves."

My insecurities had a hold on me, and, to my detriment, they weren't about to let go.

One especially fitful night, I woke up my wife.

"Why are you tossing and turning like that?" Becky asked, not amused that her restful slumber had been disturbed. "What's wrong?"

"I'm scared," I told her. "I'm scared I can't do this case."

The first of the three trials for the accused had wound up in Judge Tom McDonald's courtroom. McDonald wanted to make my district-attorney predecessor, Roland Searcy, James Manuel's public defender. As is the case for many former prosecutors, Searcy had become a local defense attorney when I defeated him in the race for DA. He ultimately declined to represent Tim Merka's accused killer because Merka had been a friend of his.

As the new district attorney, I didn't have the option of saying "thanks, but no thanks."

"Nobody believes I can do this," I told my wife in bed. "Now I'm convinced I can't do it, either. I'm at a complete loss."

Becky tried to console me, but after I made it clear I wasn't willing to listen to reason from anyone, she finally gave up. My wife kissed me on the cheek, turned out the light, and quickly went back to sleep.

Laying there in the darkness, my mother's voice popped into my head from out of nowhere. Her words reminded me of something she had always told me as a child.

"When in doubt, pray it out," she would say.

So, I tried.

"God, I can't do this case," I whispered in the middle of the night, my prayer more resembling a complaint than humble supplication. Realizing this, I made a quick course correction.

"Father, while I may not be worthy, I believe with all my heart that You can ensure justice is done for those who knew and loved Tim Merka. And I believe You can do that through Bill and me."

My assistant seemed to have a lot more confidence in our abilities than I did. As we headed toward the trials, Bill was handling his duties in a workmanlike and responsible fashion. While I was trying to put on a positive front, my worries were getting in the way of my work.

"God, please lead the way," I beseeched. "I have to answer for this crime. This community demands that answer."

I fell silent before adding one last request.

"My Father in Heaven, can You help me?"

The thought of that night still brings me to tears, given my doubts and hopelessness at the time and how God then restored me in answer to my prayers.

In the days and weeks which followed, as preparations in the case intensified, things began to click between Bill and me. More and more, I became confident that I could achieve a just result for Tim Merka, his family, and his friends.

By the time of the first trial in 1978, Bill and I had a pretty good understanding of what had happened that night on the edge of town. Merka had paid the ultimate price for being a Good Samaritan.

We tried Curtis Harris first, knowing he was the principal actor in the perpetration of the crime. After Harris was convicted of capital murder, we tried his older brother, Danny, and their friend James Manuel together, also seeking the death penalty. The teenage girl at the scene of the crime testified against both Manuel and the Harris brothers.

On my recommendation, convinced that he was not aware of the Harris brothers' intent, I recommended against the death penalty for Manuel. He received a twenty-five-year sentence as an accessory and was released on parole after serving four years of his prison term.

He would go back to prison in 2008 for staging an armed robbery of a Bryan-area restaurant to cover money stolen by his then-wife who was a manager at the establishment.

In their ensuing trials, both Harris brothers were convicted of murder in the first degree and sentenced to death, but both verdicts were overturned, due to procedural issues separate and apart from how Bill and I prosecuted the cases.

Given the furor in Bryan that the killer's verdicts had been rendered moot, due to legal "technicalities," the subsequent trials for both were moved to Montgomery County, north of Houston.

In their retrials, Danny and Curtis Harris were again found guilty, and I succeeded in making my case that both deserved to die for their crime. Once the trials were all gaveled to conclusion, Judge McDonald sought me out to offer his congratulations.

"I was wondering whether you could do this case," he told me. His words confirmed my earlier suspicions that some had doubted my ability to get the job done.

"Not only did you do it, Trav," Judge McDonald continued, "you did as fine a job as I've ever seen."

From the beginning, it was clearly established that the older brother Danny had handed Curtis the tire iron, which he then used to beat Merka to death.

To drive home that point in Curtis Harris' first trial, I brought the actual tire iron used to end Tim Merka's life with me as I approached the jury during my closing statement. It was my intent that they get one more look at the murder weapon.

While describing the horror of Merka's death, I knew words alone couldn't convey what must have been going through the victim's mind as he lay prone, facing his extinction.

Reviewing the pivotal events of the crime in front of the jury, I slowly raised the tire iron high above my head. The tone of my voice remained measured as I calmly recounted Curtis Harris's actions that fateful night.

"He raised up his arms like this," I said.

In the next moment, mustering up all my strength, I hammered that tire jack onto the courtroom floor. My action created an awful noise that reverberated throughout the entire courthouse and shocked the men and women sitting in the jury box. My office would later pay for the damages I inflicted, but it was a small price to unleash the emotions I felt and wanted each of those jurors to feel.

Fourteen years later, Danny and Curtis Harris were put to death at the Huntsville Prison Unit, known for decades as "The Walls."

On July 1, 1993, Curtis, thirty-one, was executed by lethal injection. Danny, who would die twenty-nine days later at the age of thirty-two, was allowed to spend a final hour with his sibling shortly before Curtis entered the death chamber.

"I wanted to cry, but God wouldn't let me," Danny Harris told Jim Hiney of *The Eagle*.

"It was like He was assuring me that Curtis was alright, that Curtis was at peace, that Curtis was with Him out of this world."

Of his own eminent death, Danny said, "My life isn't about me, I'm not stuck on my 'selfish' self. No one should be stuck on their selfish self. That's why people are the way they are today."

Later in my life, I would study the Bible for years before reaching that same conclusion.

Like the Apostle Paul, Danny Harris had to face death to Embrace The Cross.

Curtis and Danny Harris were two of the seventeen men executed by the state of Texas in 1993. In 2018, thirteen more men died in Texas for their crimes.

As a state district judge here in Brazos County now, I do not have the power to inflict the death penalty on an individual. A jury does that. I have presided over juries which rendered a punishment of death, and I have pronounced that sentence to the court. My role in the matter is "ministerial."

I am sworn to uphold the law, but I am not empowered with determining whether someone should live or die.

As a Christian my views on the death penalty have matured through the years, and I am no longer in favor of capital punishment. I believe that the taking of another human life is wrong, whether it be in the womb or from death row.

In the gospel of John 10:10, the Bible tells us Jesus came into this world to bring life so that we might "live life more abundantly." God is not a killer. Some people accuse me of blasphemy when I say that. The Old Testament contains many accounts of death as result of "the wrath of God."

The real blasphemy is to say that God kills people.

God does not kill people. God is Love.

Satan kills. Satan is evil.

What the Harris brothers did to Tim Merka was evil and the work of Satan.

As Christians, we should never do the bidding of the devil.

4

The Father of Texas

Okay, time for a brief history lesson and a look at the Bryan family tree.

Chances are if you're not from Texas, you've probably never heard of Moses Austin.

Well, he wasn't from Texas, either.

The story of Texas, though, begins with Austin, a Connecticut-born, three-time financial failure.

In an unceasing, life-long quest for wealth, Moses Austin tried his hand at dry goods in Pennsylvania, mining in Virginia, and banking in what would come to be known as the State of Missouri.

Austin's dry-goods business never took off, and his bank near St. Louis failed. In between, he became a fugitive from justice when mounting debts forced his sudden exit from the lead mines of southwestern Virginia, a livelihood into which he had married.

Moses Austin's marriage to the former Mary Brown did last. The couple had five children, two of whom died as infants. Their oldest child was named Stephen Fuller Austin, who ultimately succeeded in life where his father did not.

Although Stephen Austin never married, nor had children of his own, he did give birth to the state of Texas, a dream that began with his father.

Less than a year after the Panic of 1819 closed the doors of Moses Austin's financial institution near the banks of the Mississippi River, he envisioned a completely new enterprise: leading a band of frontiersmen and speculators into the unsettled part of New Spain north of the Rio Grande River, an area known for more than 175 years since that time as Texas.

In his quest, Austin traveled to what today is San Antonio. There, he made a persuasive presentation to Spain's provincial governor, Antonio María Martínez. Although he was initially turned down, Moses persisted and was ultimately awarded permission to settle 300 Anglo-American families in the agreed-upon region in what is today south central and southeast Texas.

Within a year, though, Austin was dead in Missouri, and Martínez was removed from power. Mexico declared its independence from Spain on September 18, 1821.

Three months earlier, Mary Austin conveyed to Stephen her husband's dying wish: the colonization of a portion of what had become the Mexican state of *Coahuila y Tejas*. Reluctantly, Stephen agreed. He traveled back to San Antonio where eventually he secured a revised land grant from the new Mexican government.

The territory Austin had been given permission to settle—mostly to help the Mexican government keep the indigenous population ensconced there in check—stretched from the Gulf Coast to the Brazos River Valley.

"*Tejas*," incidentally, is the Spanish spelling of the Caddo Indian word pronounced "tay-sha" which means "friend."

Austin proved a compelling salesman and gained commitments from hundreds of settlers interested in joining him in the new territory. Under the terms of his "empresarial" grant, married males among his contingent would receive a league of land, 4,428 acres, at a price of $30 payable over a six-year period.

That was $30…total.

Payable over a six…year…period.

Terms like that you can't find today.

Austin brought his first group to Texas in late 1825. That contingent, including my forefathers, is today known as the "Old 300." From what I've read, they actually numbered 297, both families and "partnerships" of unmarried men, who secured a total of 307 parcels of land.

That amounted to an area a little smaller than the state of Delaware.

There are countless books written on how Austin and his fellow "Texians" eventually gained their independence from Mexico. To this day, some of my neighbors and friends still proclaim, "Remember the Alamo!" That phrase commemorates the historic 1836 Texian defeat in which my namesake, William Barret Travis, and his small band of insurgents were killed by

Mexican forces at the Alamo Mission, now a world-famous tourist attraction in present-day San Antonio.

I'm still not happy that Hollywood cast a British actor, Lawrence Harvey, to play Travis in the 1960 film, *The Alamo*, which also starred John Wayne as Davy Crockett and Richard Widmark as Jim Bowie.

In the 2004 cinematic remake of the Alamo story, Billy Bob Thornton played Crockett. While Thornton isn't the Duke, I thought he did a good job with the role. A young actor by the name of Patrick Wilson–an American born, like Stephen F. Austin, in Virginia–handled the role of Travis well, in my humble opinion.

Six weeks after the actual Alamo engagement, General Sam Houston ended the Texas Revolution at the Battle of San Jacinto near the present-day Houston suburb of LaPorte.

That melee did not last long. Houston's victory over Antonio López de Santa Ana–both general of the Mexican army and president of the country–took about eighteen minutes to secure.

The date was April 21, 1836.

April 21 also happens to be my birthday, a fact of which I'm very proud.

So, you're probably asking, "How do the Bryans fit into all this Texas history?"

While Stephen Austin had no offspring of his own, he did have a sister named Emily, two years younger than he was. In 1813, two months after Emily's eighteenth birthday, she married James Bryan in Potosi, Missouri. Two years before, Bryan had become acquainted with the Austin clan when he bought one of Moses Austin's Missouri mills from eighteen-year-old Stephen, who had assumed responsibility for liquidating his father's business assets in the aftermath of the financial downturn.

James Bryan intended to take Emily and follow Moses to the riches promised in the proposed new Texas colony, but Bryan died on July 16, 1822 at the age of thirty-two. He left behind five children, including daughter, Mary Elizabeth, born just two weeks before her father's death, and son, William Joel Bryan, age six at the time of his father's passing.

Emily remarried in 1824. Her new husband was James Franklin Perry. In 1832, and with nine children in tow–including fourteen-year-old William–James and Emily joined her brother in Texas, settling on Stephen's Peach Point Plantation in today's Brazoria County, located near the Texas Gulf Coast.

Many of my distant relatives are buried at Peach Point, including, for a time, my great-great-great uncle Stephen Austin, who died on December 27, 1836. His body was exhumed in 1910 and moved to the Texas State Cemetery in Austin.

My great-great-grandfather William Joel Bryan, who died in 1903, remains interred at Peach Point.

After Texas declared its independence in 1835, but before that independence was won, William joined his uncle Stephen on the fields of battle. The two took part in the siege of Béxar near San Antonio. William also fought under the command of Sam Houston in several skirmishes across the region. Unfortunately, he missed the deciding Battle of San Jacinto due to a case of the measles.

After the Texas revolution, William became owner of the Durazno Plantation, not far from Peach Point. He married his stepfather's niece, Lavinia Perry, and the couple had seven children.

Texas maintained its independence until 1845. At that point the Republic peacefully joined the Union, becoming its twenty-eighth state. One important condition of that agreement was that Texans would be allowed to own slaves. Thus, in the years leading up to the Civil War, Texas sided with the South.

With the South's secession from the Union and the advent of civil war in 1861–some in my family continue to call it the "War of Northern Aggression"–William took command of a company of Confederate troops. Given his wealth, derived from Stephen Austin's original landholdings, he was able to fund his own command.

Four of his sons fought with him against Northern forces. A fifth son, Erin, my great-grandfather, was merely a boy, born in 1852.

Ultimately, as most of you may know, the Confederacy was vanquished.

While the war resulted in considerable devastation throughout much of what we call today the "Old South," Texas was spared. The state soon became an attractive destination for retired Confederate soldiers whose homes and livelihoods had been extinguished in defeat.

For many, Texas again represented a new beginning. The fledgling Houston and Texas Central Railroad offered newcomers a means to a fresh start in the rich farmlands of the Brazos River Valley.

For several years the railroad's northern-most terminus from the ever-growing township of Houston was Navasota, about twenty miles south of downtown Bryan today. With the great demand for pastureland in central Texas–and cotton would be a lucrative cash crop in the region–William sold the railroad a small swath of his property east of the Brazos to locate a water station.

That stop ultimately became the City of Bryan, established in 1866, incorporated in 1871, and named for William Joel Bryan, my great-great-grandfather.

Both William and his brother, Guy Morrison Bryan, became influential political figures in Texas. The two helped persuade the state's legislature to accept terms of the Morrill Act, which ultimately led to the creation of what today is Texas A&M University.

The Morrill Act was put forth to Congress by representative Justin Morrill of Vermont in 1862. It was enacted into law by President Abraham Lincoln in early 1863, two years before the end of the Civil War.

The Morrill Act established the creation of land-grant colleges across America–so named because they were funded by the sale of federal lands owned in states throughout the Union.

The idea had been a point of contention for southern states before the Civil War. Their fear was that land seized by the federal government and sold in the South would be principally used to establish schools in the nation's more populous north.

The state of Texas's land-grant college and its first public institution of higher education was ultimately located five miles south of Bryan and called the Agricultural and Mechanical College of Texas, thanks in part to the persuasive powers of my ancestors. The school was opened in 1876, far enough from Bryan proper to keep its young ladies at a safe distance from the college's all-male student body, and those same young men out of Bryan's notorious downtown saloons.

Texas A&M remained an all-male military school until shortly before my arrival on campus as a "fish" in the fall of 1965.

"Fish" was a "term of endearment" given to incoming freshman in the A&M Corps of Cadets. I was a member of the Corps during my four years of undergraduate education, although I did not receive the "full treatment" that others in my class endured.

Some, in fact, did not endure and left the school.

More about all that later.

Because of my affiliation with the former Agricultural & Mechanical College of Texas–now Texas A&M—I am an "Aggie." I want to make that abundantly clear.

It should be obvious where that nickname comes from. You'll also find Aggies at New Mexico State and Utah State universities, which are also land-grant schools.

So are Ohio State, Penn State, and the University of Florida. None of those schools, though, is home to Aggies.

Today, Texas A&M University is one of the most highly regarded schools in the country, with an enrollment of more than 60,000 students, both men and women. It's located in what is now known as College Station, Texas, Bryan's sister city to the south.

A depot along the Houston and Texas Central Railroad line was built to serve the needs of the newly established A&M College in the late nineteenth century. The local postmaster referred to the locale as the "college station."

And, simply put, the name stuck.

In my time serving the people of Brazos County, including the citizens of both Bryan and College Station, I have seen the occasional dispute erupt between our neighboring communities. These were sometimes worthy of the bad blood made famous, if not by the legendary Hatfields and McCoys, then at least the equal to the conflagration that once marked the intercollegiate football rivalry between Texas A&M and the University of Texas.

Let it be known that I hate the University of Texas; not the people, just the institution…and that damned shade of orange they call their own.

That extreme animosity toward Longhorns is a common sentiment among many Aggies, and the feelings run mostly mutual.

The two school's football teams no longer meet on the college gridiron. And in my mind, that's not such a bad thing. While we were first, A&M was conceived as sort of an afterthought, thanks to the windfall of the Morrill Act.

The University of Texas was mandated by the Texas State Constitution, and they've had a proverbial you-know-what up their you-know-where ever since.

I take comfort in knowing the Lord forgives me for these thoughts.

It's an ironic twist of fate, I think, that dissolution of this great intrastate athletic clash was actually foreseen in my school's fight song, called the "Aggie War Hymn," composed in 1918.

> *Good-bye to Texas University.*
> *So long to the orange and white.*
> *Good luck to the dear old Texas Aggies,*
> *They are the boys who show*
> *the real old fight.*
> *The eyes of Texas are upon you.*
> *That is the song they sing so well—*
> *SOUNDS LIKE HELL!*
> *So, good-bye to Texas University,*
> *We're goin' to beat you all to --*
> *Chig-gar-roo-gar-rem!*
> *Chig-gar-roo-gar-rem!*
> *Rough! Tough!*
> *Real stuff! Texas A&M*

Those words were written by former A&M student Pinky Wilson in a letter home during a lull in the action…of World War I.

5

TB and the Guys

The original Travis Bell Bryan, my grandfather, once wrote an eight-page, single-spaced letter to the president of the United States. In the letter, composed on Mother's Day, 1948, he explained to Harry Truman the value of reactivating the World War II airbase that had been opened just outside of Bryan in the spring of 1943.

As president of the First National Bank of Bryan, my grandfather knew that when his customers were happy, his business was good.

Bryan Army Air Field, as the installation was known during World War II, pumped a sizable amount of money into the local economy, and the city prospered because of that.

With the base's proven economic impact to the Bryan area, "TB," as my grandfather is known in the Bryan clan, was eager to see airplanes circling the local skies again. Before initial construction of the airfield was completed, he led a local fundraising effort to purchase a P-51 Mustang for the war effort.

America's patriotic pride was rampant back then. Public financing of war machinery–airplanes, tanks, and even battleships– outside the usual military-industrial complex was a fairly common occurrence during World War II.

Granddad's bank sold more than $5 million in war bonds during World War II. That translates to about $73 million today and helped bring the Axis to its knees.

TB was a persuasive businessman and his P-51 fundraiser met its $50,000 goal. A fair-sized portion of that sum came out of his own pocket.

For reference, that $50,000 price tag would equal nearly three-quarters of a million dollars today. At least I think so. I meant to get my brother, Tim, the banker in the family, to check my calculations.

My grandfather officially presented the plane to the commanding staff at Bryan Field on the day the base was dedicated: June 6, 1943. In fact, he asked that those ceremonies be delayed to allow for the arrival of the aircraft.

My grandfather called the plane the *Spirit of Bryan Field*, a name which echoed that of Charles Lindbergh's famous trans-Atlantic flying machine, the *Spirit of St. Louis*. The young daughter of one of the base's administrative officers christened the aircraft with a bottle of water taken from the nearby Brazos River.

My grandfather spoke of the significance of this gesture:

"Those who drink from the Brazos are destined to someday revisit it," he told the Bryan Field gathering of nearly 20,000 people. That number may have been an exaggeration by the local media covering the dedication—"fake news," if you will. There weren't close to 20,000 people living in the entire Brazos Valley region at the time, but maybe they came from parts near and far.

Spirit itself never returned to the Brazos Valley or to Bryan Field. In fact, according to its service records, it never left the continental United States.

It was sold for scrap before a final peace was reached with Japan.

My grandfather would not have been pleased with that news.

His letter to President Truman also did not get the hoped-for results.

In that lengthy correspondence, TB suggested to Truman that a sizable number of Texas A&M cadets, obligated to military service after completing their education, could receive post-graduate training at Bryan Field, thus providing the newly formed United States Air Force a steady stream of young pilots.

When nothing came of the notion, my granddad found another potential opportunity two years later to save the base and bring jobs back to Bryan. He oversaw the creation of a one-hundred-page brief promoting Bryan Field as the ideal location for a proposed Air Force "air academy."

West Point, New York; Annapolis, Maryland; Bryan, Texas: To my grandfather, that wasn't a far-fetched notion at all.

The Air Force Academy eventually found a home in Colorado Springs. My grandfather was reportedly told that Bryan had finished "in the top five."

By that time, though, the pressure was off. Business was booming at the old airbase once again, thanks to the onset of the Korean War.

Perhaps, just perhaps, Bryan Field was reopened in the summer of 1951 thanks to TB's annual gift of a Stetson hat to President Truman each Christmas. Records preserved at the Truman Presidential Library in Independence, Missouri, confirm those "tributes."

My grandfather was a "bigger than life" figure for me as I was growing up. I was born in 1947, and my first memory of Granddad was probably when I was three or four years old, just about the time he got Bryan Air Force Base back up and running.

He took me out there a few times and told me someday I might become an Air Force pilot.

Sadly, that did not happen. Nor was I ever really wild about the idea.

As I've related, my relatives are spread all over Texas. The descendants of Moses Austin settled throughout the vast land-holdings Stephen Austin received from the Mexican government.

William Joel Bryan, Stephen's nephew, had seven children, all born at Durazno Plantation, the location of which is today a two-and-a-half-hour drive from Bryan, near the shores of the Gulf of Mexico.

William's youngest son, Erin, is my great-grandfather.

Even though his father was the namesake for Bryan, Erin Bryan never really spent much time there. He and his wife, the former Nannie Walderman, settled on a farm outside of Giddings, Texas, about sixty miles southwest of Bryan. That's where TB was born on September 5, 1892, the sixth of seven children.

In Bryan, the legacy of the founding brothers, William and Guy M. Bryan, was being furthered by Guy's son, Guy III.

"Wait!" you say, "Guy's son was Guy III? How does that make any sense?"

We have a sometimes-complicated system for naming children in the Bryan family. My two boys are Austin and Joel. Technically,

Joel is William Joel Bryan VI. My daughter is Becca...and my wife is Becky.

When you've got a rich family history from which to draw names, you sort of look the other way on originality.

 Let me explain about the "Guys."

In 1843 William and his wife Lavinia had a son they named Guy, in honor of the original Guy Morrison Bryan, William's brother.

Thus, William Bryan's son was Guy II, not Guy, "junior."

Nearly thirty years later, in 1871, the original Guy finally got around to having a second son, whom he also named Guy.

William married at twenty-five. Guy the First didn't tie the knot until he was thirty-seven. His son, Guy, came along when Guy the First was fifty. Guy the First's thirty-seven-year old wife, Laura, did not survive the experience of giving her husband a fifth child, the second Guy.

So, by the time Guy II was in his late twenties, he had an infant cousin also named Guy.

We call him Guy III for clarity.

Got it?

I'll admit, the Bryan genealogy gets pretty confusing at times. I have a book called *Descendants of Moses Austin* that is three inches thick. I'm glad to have that book and happy to try to set my part of the family record straight here, as confusing as it may seem.

While the original Guy Bryan was the family's first attorney, Guy III became the family's first banker, who helped start what would become the First National Bank of Bryan. An ambitious man, Guy III left the bank–and Bryan–around the turn of the century, circa 1900, for Houston and the greater opportunities in banking that existed at the First National Bank there.

My brother Tim sort of followed that same path.

With Guy III's departure, leadership of the First National Bank of Bryan fell into the capable hands of a man that would become my other great-grandfather, Hannibal Osgood Boatwright.

Throughout his life, Boatwright went by simply "H.O."

H.O. Boatwright was a son of the South. Born in South Carolina, he moved with his family to Bryan, Texas, when he was about eight years old. He spent more than fifty years as a Bryan banker and was partners with Guy Bryan III in the venture that became the First National Bank of Bryan.

Meanwhile, TB's parents, living on the farm outside Giddings, Texas, wound up divorcing, a rarity in those days. Going their separate ways, they ultimately died a month apart in 1910 when my grandfather was eighteen years old.

Although he was a Bryan, TB did not enjoy the largesse of other lines of his family. He was a self-made man, and it is that stock to which I like to lay claim.

My grandfather may or may not have finished high school. Farm kids often did not have that luxury. He did not attend Texas A&M. Instead, he enrolled in the McKenzie-Baldwin Business College in Bryan. Oak Oral McKenzie ran the school with his wife, the former Ruth Baldwin.

McKenzie's story is an interesting one. He grew up in Illinois and studied law at Illinois Wesleyan College. After admittance to the Illinois bar, McKenzie moved to Texas in 1911 and became an auditor for the railroad. It was in Yoakum, Texas, that he met and married Ruth.

After securing a license to practice law in Texas, Oak and Ruth moved to Bryan in 1917. In 1922, he was elected Brazos County Attorney and served one term in that office.

Given that McKenzie ran the business school with his wife as an equal partner, my guess is that he would have had a more accepting public stance on women in the workplace than I had "back in the day."

Come to think of it, my grandfather himself may have been a "gender trailblazer" just like Sandra Day O'Connor.

Or, maybe not.

There was a time when business colleges served as "secretarial schools." The term, as it turns out–at least on the early side of the twentieth century–referred to the development of the clerical expertise required in business and was not particularly gender based.

In all honesty, my grandfather's attending a "business college" in his youth would not have been out of the ordinary for a young man wanting a future in the business world.

At McKenzie-Baldwin, TB learned a skill that re-opened the door for a Bryan to be involved with the First National Bank of Bryan.

My grandfather always relished time in front of a typewriter. After all, how many successful bank presidents spend a good part of a Mother's-Day Sunday hammering out an eight-page, single-spaced letter, even if it was intended for the President of the United States?

Bryan family lore suggests that Guy III put in a good word for TB when the latter applied for the position of stenographer at the First National Bank of Bryan. And thanks to his typing prowess, TB got the job at H.O.'s bank

From there, Granddad steadily rose up the corporate ranks.

Ultimately, in a savvy business move, he married the bank president's daughter, my grandmother Ruth.

The original Travis B. Bryan was the real deal. At the outset of World War I, he resigned his position from the bank and enlisted in the U.S. Army. He was trained and sent to France for active duty.

Unfortunately, TB came down with a case of double pneumonia which nearly took his life. It was during his convalescence that he was able to watch in wonder what was taking place in the skies overhead. Aerial dogfights between aviators representing the Allied forces and Central Powers ignited his lifelong infatuation with the Army Air Corps, which later became the Army Air Forces, before morphing into the United States Air Force.

I wish TB could have landed the Air Force Academy for Bryan. Instead, the city eventually named a municipal golf course in his honor, which was a pretty big deal for him and my family.

We're a clan of golfers, and my daddy was the best of our bunch.

6

Mama and Daddy

I got caught up in my grandfather's love affair with the Stetson hat at an early age.

For some of you, a Stetson may seem like a very "Texas" thing. The Stetson company actually was started in Philadelphia, and for many years the hats were made in St. Joseph, Missouri.

Only recently have the hats become a product of the Lone Star State. They're made now in Garland, located half an hour northeast of downtown Dallas.

Stetsons have adorned the heads of many famous cowboys, including John Wayne, the Lone Ranger Clayton Moore, and singer Gene Autry. More recently, another country and western artist, Garth Brooks, famously favored a Stetson.

And while I don't think he wore a Stetson, there's another "singing cowboy" we're going to talk about a bit later in the book, and since he was kin to my grandfather, my guess is he may have wound up with a Stetson, too.

And, perhaps most "infamously," actor Larry Hagman's "J.R. Ewing" character on the long-running television show *Dallas* conducted his dastardly business deeds and illicit romantic relationships peering from beneath the brim of a Stetson hat.

In fact, J.R.'s Stetson now resides in the Smithsonian Museum.

I am not sure if one of Harry Truman's "Travis B. Bryan" Stetson models ever made it into the collection at the Truman Presidential Library located in Independence, Missouri, but Truman is known to have worn the hats which my grandfather gifted him.

While we're on the subject of presidents and their Stetson hats, President George W. Bush once presented a black Stetson to the president of South Sudan, Salva Kiir, on a visit to the White House in 2006. Kiir was so enamored with the gift that, to this day, he rarely allows his photograph to be taken without wearing the hat, or one of the many ones he has had made to look just like the original.

Check it out online. It's a little strange.

Me personally? I'm not much for hats in general, unless it's a sunny day on the golf course, or I'm helping my son, Joel, coach his Little League baseball team here in Bryan.

When I was about ten years old myself, a Stetson representative visited my grandfather and father at the bank. After college, Daddy went to work for his dad, and TB groomed his only child to become his successor as head of the bank.

Given that my granddad had handed out a lot of Stetsons to important people over the years, the Stetson folks wanted to say thank you by giving all of us hats, too.

I'm sure my brother Tim got a hat, but he's kept quiet about it through the years.

The last thing I wanted to do with a precious day of my summer vacation from school was to spend it getting fitted for a stupid hat, even if it was a Stetson.

My grandfather would not have been happy if he knew I felt that way.

Hats look good on other people, but they don't look good on me.

I particularly felt that way as a ten-year-old, which was why I threw a pretty good fit when Mama told me I would be going to work with my dad to receive a hat.

"Just like the one your grandfather likes to wear," she told me.

In Texas, we call the kind of fit I threw with my mother that morning "raising hell." I'll confess now to getting a little worked up over things on occasion in my youth.

Okay, maybe my parents did spoil me just a little as a kid. As I continue to tell my story here, I'll let you be the judge…which will make two of us!

Get it? You be the "judge," while I am a judge, a *real* one!

Ha, ha!

Forgive me for slipping in a little judicial humor.

To tell the truth, I've never been a much of a joke teller. And in my youth, I never did have much luck trying to persuade Mama when her wishes opposed mine.

So, it was with minimal enthusiasm that I accompanied my father to the bank to get my hat.

The Stetson folks made a big production of handing out their hats, not only to members of the Bryan family, but also to key bank employees and to some of my grandfather's best customers. They eventually found me lurking in some darkened corner and yanked me up in front of a camera where a hat–a few sizes too big, as it turned out–was placed on my head and a photograph was taken.

"Here, kid. Enjoy."

When I saw the picture a week or so later, I looked like a moron, but I still have that picture.

The hat? Uh, I'm not sure what happened to it.

Contrary to the opinion you may be forming here, I wasn't really a bad kid. I never did any of the things usually associated with a problem child. I didn't grow up and become a teenager who drank or smoked or did drugs.

And, in all honesty–and my wife, Becky, knows this–I wasn't much of a ladies' man growing up, either. As you might sense by now, anxiety played a good bit into that: anxiety stemming from the acne I suffered from for most of my high school years.

The fact I was a Bryan living in Bryan added a little extra constraint to my social life, too.

There's a reason Moses Austin got his family out of "Austinville," Virginia. I'm sure Stephen F. rolls over in his grave regularly after being dug up from the family estate in Brazoria County and hauled halfway across Texas for re-interment in Austin, Texas.

Who needs that?

Trust me, there's a lot of pressure when you're a kid and your family is the namesake of the town in which you live. My parents never suggested I was special because of my ancestry or that I had to toe a higher line because of my last name. I guess my hope as a child was to do something important in life and make my family proud.

Maybe something important enough to write a book about.

Well, I'm writing one anyway.

Both my parents, Travis B. Bryan, Jr., and the former Norma Norman–her friends called her "Nonie"–were good people. We attended the First Baptist Church of Bryan. My dad taught Sunday school there and was a deacon at the church.

In his letter to Harry Truman, my grandfather, in the litany of details he chose to share with the president about his personal life, called himself a "Scotch-Irish Presbyterian of a very poor caliber." As I was growing up, every Sunday morning on our way to church, Daddy, Mama, Tim, and I would drive past my grandparents' house–they lived on the same block we did–and TB would usually be out watering his lawn.

When I finally mustered up the courage to ask him why he picked Sunday to do his yard work, he replied, "The preacher told me it was a sin to play golf on Sunday. I wasn't willing to stop doing that, so I stopped going to church, instead."

TB never minced words. Maybe I picked up that habit from him.

My granddaddy did love to play golf. As I've told you, the municipal golf course in Bryan for many years was named in his honor.

Sadly, it's now closed, although there is talk of turning the property into a spectacular public park. Our family fully supports that idea.

Like my grandfather, I love the game of golf, too. In fact, I think golf serves as a framework towards achieving a more Godly life.

I really do believe that, and I'll share with you why and how later in the book.

In fact, I'll be devoting an entire chapter to "The Spiritual Nature of Golf."

When I was a kid, I was always impressed when Daddy got up in front of the church congregation. With his commanding voice and his impassioned words, Daddy could slay an audience. He taught a Sunday school class to twelve-year-olds, and I was in that class when I was twelve years old. I don't remember a lot about that experience, but people still tell me they remember the positive impression Daddy made on them.

Most people thought Daddy was this tremendous Christian believer. He was a regular fixture in church, but in hindsight, I don't think he depended as much on God as he did himself and his own earthly devices.

Daddy was not someone who truly Embraced The Cross, but that's okay. He, like many of your own fathers, was a product of the times. More Ward Cleaver than the Apostle Paul.

Don't know Ward Cleaver? He was a famous TV dad from the late fifties and early sixties on *Leave It to Beaver.*

Daddy was an only child of what you might call a "blue-chip" family. While his dad, my grandfather, didn't go to church a lot, Daddy's mother, Ruth, was a very spiritual woman. In fact, what she instilled in my father in the way of Faith in God helped get him through World War II.

My dad graduated from Texas A&M with the class of 1949, but he didn't begin college there. He initially enrolled at Baylor. He went there, I think, to follow in the footsteps of his cousin, Bill Davis.

Bill was not only my mentor in the law, but also one of the finest people I've ever known. He was a dutiful student at Baylor. My father was not.

In fact, Daddy flunked out of Baylor in 1942. Later in life he told us he couldn't get serious about college after the bombing of Pearl Harbor drew the U.S. into World War II.

My father joined the Navy and reported to Farragut Naval Training Station near Coeur d'Alene, Idaho. He was assigned to the Pacific Fleet and attached to the command of Admiral Chester Nimitz

Daddy served his country as a radio man, second class. He was fortunate to travel within Admiral Nimitz's carrier group in that they almost never sailed into the height of naval battle. My father said he only saw one Japanese Zero during the war, and it flew harmlessly overhead.

His biggest skirmish came against Mother Nature, and it nearly cost him his life.

Charting weather conditions fell, at least partially, into Daddy's area of responsibility as a radio communicator. Still, according to him, keeping abreast of weather conditions was very much a hit-or-miss proposition.

"Nobody in their right minds," he said, "would intentionally sail into a typhoon, unless they were unaware it was there."

Daddy's group had the misfortune of doing just that.

"Biggest waves I ever saw."

According to my father, the storm drove his ship deep into ocean waters, and then raised the boat into the sky, as if being thrust toward the heavens by a giant leviathan.

Just as there are no atheists in foxholes, that storm, according to Daddy, made Believers out of a lot of men.

During the war, my father was open about his Faith. "I tried to be a good Disciple," he said. "In letters home, I wanted my mother to worry a little less about me, knowing that I had put myself into God's hands."

That was particularly the case, he said, during the typhoon.

"Those that knew I was a Christian kept asking me how they could get saved like me."

The tempest eventually passed, and after four years of service God brought Daddy safely home from the war. I was born two years later, in 1947, while my father was a student at Texas A&M. Tim came along in 1950 after Daddy had graduated and started working at the bank.

Like a lot of businessmen of his time, Daddy wasn't home a lot when I was growing up. As the breadwinner of the family, he was at work during the day and often attending work- or civic-related functions at night. On the weekends, he usually headed to the golf course if the weather permitted play.

My mother was the real rock of our family. But, unlike my dad who seemed to have life in the palm of his hand, Mama had demons.

Looking back, I know now she went through her own death-and-resurrection numerous times.

Mama was frequently at odds with other people. We had one neighbor, a real down-home Southern lady named Mrs. Davison. She was, I think, one of the sweetest people I've ever known. She just loved Tim and me, and was good to both of us, as well as being a trusted friend to Mama.

And then one day, that all ended.

With others, including my father, Mama was becoming more and more moody and unforgiving, but with Tim and me, she was constant in her love and parental compassion.

One evening years later, when I was maybe sixteen or seventeen, Daddy called Tim and me into the living room to tell us Mama had gone to a hospital and "wouldn't be home for a while." The "hospital" turned out to be a mental-health facility in Waco, and Mama stayed there, under her own volition, for nearly a month.

Nobody ever mentioned the word "depression" in association with her absence from home.

Today there are numerous pharmaceutical treatments to lessen the effects of depression in people. I know because I've tried a few myself. I was an overly sensitive child who grew up into an adult who has struggled with depression,

As I understand it, depression can be caused by a wide variety of things: a chemical imbalance in the brain, genetic predisposition, stressful events, health problems, reactions to medication, or a combination of these factors.

As someone who has dealt with depression much of my life, I want to make clear that the disease is nothing to be ignored or embarrassed by.

Modern medicine looks at depression much differently now than when Mama sought help.

She was a little better when she got home, but it's difficult to know whether they ever got to the root of her problems.

Mama had good reason to be depressed.

When my mother was young, probably about seven or eight years old, her father committed suicide in the house where his family lived. Mama discovered the body.

Of course, she never talked about the episode, nor did she speak much about her childhood. Whenever someone brought up the subject of her youth, she would emphatically try to change the subject. If she couldn't do so, she would leave the room.

Mama and Daddy argued a lot as I was growing up. I suppose some of that could have stemmed from the fact Daddy left her home alone a lot. Their disagreements, like Mama's falling out with Mrs. Davidson, probably also stemmed from her untreated depression. Despite the friction, there was never any doubt or concern in my mind whether or not my parents loved me or that they wouldn't always be together.

God blessed me in that regard, and in her quest for inner peace, Mama led me to what became her source of Great Comfort.

After my mother's return home from the hospital, I saw her spending more time with her Bible. As she sought solutions there to the problems which plagued her, I think she began to put her Trust in God in a way that she had never been able to trust people.

Looking back now, I understand it was her Faith which began to heal her.

I was fortunate that both my parents lived long lives. Daddy died on September 28, 2009, when I was sixty-two. Mama passed away six months later on March 3, 2010.

There's not a day still that I don't miss them both.

7

"Victory or Death"

The house that I grew up in here in Bryan is once again for sale.

It's not a big home as homes of former bank presidents go. It's one story, about 2,100 square feet, bricked–painted gray–and includes a shaded interior courtyard, and a coach house and two-car garage out back.

It sits near the downtown area and is a block away from a grade school that didn't exist when I lived in the neighborhood. My elementary school was a few more blocks from home when I was a kid.

Across the street from my old house is a park which does a pretty good job of recapping the history of the city of Bryan. It's called Heritage Park. When I was a boy, it was a vacant pasture where my friends and I devised any number of outdoor games.

At the end of the block on Hutchins Street, between East 30th and 31st, is a two-story American Craftsman-style home that belonged to my grandparents when I was growing up.

That's where "TB," my granddad, would water his yard on Sundays, biding his time before he headed to the golf course.

When my grandparents moved into that house, they gave Daddy the home in which they had lived, the one where I grew up.

As it turned out, Daddy lived his entire life in that one place.

A woman well acquainted with our family bought the home a number of years ago and promised she would take good care of it. She has. When she decided to sell it, she gave us plenty of notice. I have to admit the thought has crossed my mind to bring the house back into the family.

My two sons, Austin and Joel, have moved back to Bryan in the last year. Could I envision one of them living in that house?

You bet! Might they be interested? Probably not. It's a little old now and lacks some of the amenities a modern family desires.

I'm awfully grateful to have my boys back in town. Both sought to carve out their own careers outside of Bryan, and I thought that was a good idea for both of them. But, now that they are both in their forties, successful businessmen with children of their own, it means the world to me that they've chosen to return to Bryan to continue our family's legacy here.

I can say their futures, and the future of our hometown, look very promising.

I'd like to take a moment here and offer an apology to all of my children, not just my sons, but also my daughter Becca who lives in Colorado with her family. In taking the time to look back on my life through the notion of this book, I realize more than ever that I possessed a few shortcomings as a father.

Some of these I've already discussed with my kids. I lived a bit too vicariously through their lives and accomplishments growing up. It's a mistake which many parents make, and if I had it to do over again, I would have pushed my children a lot less.

As to the cause of my sometimes-foolish parental behavior, a look back on my own upbringing is very revealing.

Not only did I grow up in Bryan, Texas, but as a boy, I attended Travis Elementary. Both the school and I were named for William Barrett Travis, the previously mentioned leader of the garrison which defended the Alamo during the Texas Revolution.

One of the most sacred documents of Texas history is known simply as the "Travis Letter." Its successful passage from the site of the Alamo to a nearby "Texian" outpost proved to be a rallying cry, not just in the aftermath of Travis's death, but for Texans ever since.

It's a stirring missive, to say the least. I have a framed copy of it on the wall of my office at the Brazos County Courthouse.

To the People of Texas & All Americans in the World-
Fellow Citizens and compatriots
I am besieged, by a thousand or more of the Mexicans
under Santa Anna - I have sustained a continual
Bombardment & cannonade for 24 hours & have not
lost a man. The enemy has demanded a surrender at

discretion, otherwise, the garrison are to be put to the sword, if the fort is taken - I have answered the demand with a cannon shot, & our flag still waves proudly from the walls - I shall never surrender or retreat. Then, I call on you in the name of Liberty, of patriotism and everything dear to the American character, to come to our aid, with all dispatch - The enemy is receiving reinforcements daily and will no doubt increase to three or four thousand in four or five days.
If this call is neglected, I am determined to sustain myself as long as possible & die like a soldier who never forgets what is due to his own honor & that of his country - VICTORY or DEATH.
William Barret Travis

My dad dramatically recited the contents of this letter to our family many times when I was a kid. He loved it, and both of us were grateful that our great-grandparents, Erin and Nannie Bryan, chose to name their son "Travis."

I was made familiar with the Travis Letter at an early age and "victory or death" became a figurative personal mission statement in my own life, as it was, I think, for both my father and grandfather.

But, as eloquent and measured as William Travis's last correspondence was before he died at the tragically young age of twenty-six, as a ten-year-old myself, I still lived life in the moment, completely oblivious to the consequences of my sometimes-careless behavior.

Riding my bicycle home from school one day when I was in about the third grade, I accepted a friend's challenge to race him to the end of the street. Given my highly competitive "victory or death" spirit, I quickly took what I thought to be a commanding lead. Peering back over my shoulder to see the size of my advantage, I swerved directly into the path of an oncoming car, hitting it head on.

Fortunately, we were in a residential neighborhood, and the car wasn't moving at a high rate of speed. The driver probably saw me and began slowing down.

Still, when the collision occurred, I flew off my bike, hit the windshield of the car, and rolled off to the side and onto the pavement. The driver's wife, Aquilla Conway, who would later become my seventh-grade English teacher, went into hysterics at the scene, certain that her husband had killed a little boy.

As it turned out, my Guardian Angel had protected me, and I wasn't hurt, other than the damage done to my bike and my pride. After regaining my senses and calming Mrs. Conway down, I left my twisted set of wheels at the scene and walked home, relishing the comfort and attention I was sure I would find in my mother's arms.

Unfortunately, she wasn't there. I had forgotten that Mama was at work.

Up to that point of her life, my mother had been a full-time homemaker and a dutiful and responsible parent to her two young sons.

Mama also had a wonderful touch when it came to home decor. The home I grew up in was a thing of beauty to me, both inside and out. Mama toiled incessantly to get everything "just right," and later worked with Becky to make the home in which we live a picturesque setting, too.

That shared love of domestic "burnishment" truly bonded my mother and my wife.

With Daddy gone so much during my childhood, Mama decided she, too, might want a life outside the home. She began working part-time in a small antique store. She tried to be home before my arrival from school, but on the day of my bicycle accident, she had not yet returned.

After she got home and discovered my bumps and bruises, she blamed herself horribly for not being there when I needed her.

While my parents usually tried to take the pressure off and convince me I could just be a normal kid, I had a hard time thinking of myself in those terms. The self-imposed burden of living up to the family name hung from my neck like the proverbial albatross.

Most of all, I see now, I wanted my parents to be proud of me.

I attended Lamar Junior High, a brand-new school on the then "outskirts" of Bryan. Today, there is no divide between Bryan and

College Station, but sixty years ago, there was still plenty of open land between the two towns.

Unlike at Travis Elementary where we spent all day in one room, each hour at Lamar brought a class change, and this idea completely flummoxed me. On the first day of school, I was certain I wouldn't be able to find my way around. To make matters worse, since I was also unfamiliar with the concept of a personal locker, I carried all my books with me and my school supplies in a cigar box.

Stop and let that image soak in.

I made it through almost the entirety of my first day without incident. Then, on my way to my last class, I was inexplicably overwhelmed by the traffic in the hallway. Suffering my first junior high panic attack while looking at room numbers to try to find my class, I inadvertently bumped into another student, and my books and the cigar box were knocked to the floor.

Before I could begin the process of collecting my belongings, a few passersby started kicking my things all over the place. I stood there paralyzed by my misfortune and waited until the hallway was clear to finally gather my things.

That little episode made me late for class on the first day of school. By the time I got into Mama's car after school, I was completely frazzled. I was confused and angry and on the verge of raising more than a little hell.

Before Mama could ask me how my first day had gone, I exploded.

"This has been a TERRIBLE day!" I screamed. "I HATE school here.

"I don't want to EVER come back again."

My meltdown not yet complete, I burst into tears.

We drove home in silence. I'm sure Mama was heartbroken at my sorrow, but she knew well my tendency to blow things out of proportion. When she parked in our driveway, I stormed into the house and threw my cigar box toward an empty chair, its contents again sent flying.

I slumped onto the living room sofa. It was there Mama joined me.

"Everything will be okay," she said. Perhaps Mama truly did understand the "death and resurrection" principle which took me so long to discover later in life.

"Things are going to happen to you, and you'll eventually be all right. You'll get up the next morning, and you'll be ready to go.

"Don't worry about it," she advised me. "Nobody's hurt. Well, your feelings are hurt now, but that will pass."

I watched as she patted me on the leg. She got up to make her way to the kitchen. As she did so, she turned and asked, "Can I get you anything?"

I shook my head, still in the midst of a prolonged pout. Before she was out of earshot, I finally spoke up.

"Do you have any of those good chocolate chip cookies?" I asked.

"No," she replied, "but I sure can make you some."

I had a pretty good rest of my seventh-grade year, at least for the next week or so.

Then, football practice began.

8

Bear Bryant and Doc Sprague

Football isn't just "king" in Texas, it's full-blown religion.
At least that's the way it used to be. Today, online stories
lament the demise in popularity of football in general and the
quality of football played in Texas, particularly on the college level.

The "Hatfield and McCoy" types separately sporting maroon
and burnt orange still bicker about Texas A&M's departure from
the Big 12 Conference for membership in the SEC, thus severing
the A&M-Texas football rivalry for the recent past and foreseeable
future.

To tell you the truth, I was all for the move. And my reasons
for that go back a long, long way.

My first time to Austin was in 1956. Daddy took Tim and me
up there for the A&M-Texas game. We'd seen the Thanksgiving-
week showdown at Kyle Field, but this was our first time to see
the contest on our rival's home soil.

Longhorns commonly abbreviate the name of their school as
"UT." Aggies refer to it as "tu," which rhymes with "pee-yew" and
the lack of capitalization is intentional.

To this day, nothing is more exciting to me than the pre-game
pomp and circumstance leading up to the kickoff of a college
football game.

That day in Austin, I was on sensory overload. I had on my
Aggie visor and my Aggie T-shirt, and I was bouncing around like
a kid on a sugar high, taking in all the sights and sounds.

I remember walking through a group of college guys dressed
in cowboy gear. That was something I had never seen at an A&M
home game, and I thought the cowboys were pretty neat.

They turned out to be the Texas "Silver Spurs," the group
charged with the responsibility of taking care of…

Wait. I cannot proclaim the name of the Texas mascot before telling you about the First Lady of Texas A&M.

Her name is Reveille. She is the finest, most noble, and inspirational mascot in all of college sports. Our current First Lady is Reveille IX, a purebred "rough collie." Her deceased predecessors are laid to rest outside the north end of Kyle Field. A more sacred patch of land on the A&M campus you cannot find.

Now to continue with my story.

I wasn't aware of it on my first trip to Austin, but the Silver Spurs were and remain the keepers of Bevo, the Texas Longhorns' live longhorn-steer mascot. On game days in Austin, Bevo stands, mostly docile, behind the north end zone at Memorial Stadium. His quiet nature amidst the frenzy of the Longhorn faithful is attributable, some say, to bovine sedatives.

Thus, like many Tea-Sips on football game day—the Aggie origin of that term stems from the notion that while graduates of Texas A&M were off fighting wars, Longhorn alums were home "sipping tea"—Bevo watches the proceedings in a drug-induced stupor.

My brother Tim wound up attending Texas for a year and a half, but like our father, he saw the "error of his ways" and completed his schooling at Texas A&M.

As I've mentioned before, I have no real animosity for those who support the Texas Longhorns. I have nothing against them as individuals. What I can't stand is their Longhorn culture, their Longhorn arrogance, and how on too many autumn afternoons, their Longhorns have beaten A&M on the football field.

My bitterness goes all the way back to that first trip to Austin with my brother and Daddy.

It turned out I made a grievous error walking through the group of Silver Spurs. One of them—out of sight of Daddy, I presume, otherwise there would have been hell to pay—put out a cigarette on my rear end, burning a hole through my pants and leaving a good-sized welt on my butt.

So immersed in the setting was I that day, I didn't really feel any pain. And by the time I did, it didn't really matter because, dammit, we WON THE GAME! The final score was 34-21, and the victory also gave Coach Paul Bryant's team a conference championship.

Most of you know Bryant by his nickname.

"Bear" Bryant's greatest claim to fame came during his twenty-five years as head football coach at the University of Alabama. He guided the Crimson Tide to six national championships there.

Before taking the Alabama job, Bryant coached the Texas Aggies for four seasons. In 1956, the win over Texas that I witnessed completed an undefeated season for Bryant's squad and gave the school its first Southwest Conference championship since 1941.

Usually, the Southwest Conference title came with an automatic berth into the Cotton Bowl game, but Bryant's '56 Aggies were ineligible for post-season play because of recruiting violations.

That happened a lot back in those days. In fact, a multitude of recruiting scandals brought down the entire legendary league after the 1996 season. For A&M, nothing was ever really the same again until the school moved to the Southeastern Conference in 2012.

In between, A&M played in the Big 12 Conference which ultimately dwindled to just ten teams. Texas remains a member of the Big 12 with no room on their schedule to renew their rivalry with the Aggies.

While Bear Bryant was in College Station, I had the good fortune to become friends with his son, Paul, Jr.

The Bryants lived just north of the A&M campus in Bryan and just down the street on Greenway Drive from my great-aunt and -uncle, Bess and "Doc" Sprague. My great-uncle had been an athletic trainer at A&M, thus earning his moniker.

Tim and I spent a lot of time with the Spragues. It was their idea that I go over and meet their neighbors, the Bryants.

"They have a boy about your age," Aunt Bess told me. "He seems like a real nice young man."

Knocking on the Bryants' door, Bear's wife, Mary Harmon Bryant–she was commonly called "Mary Harmon"–answered. She welcomed me with a warm smile and invited me to come in to meet Paul, Jr. It turned out the cub Bear was two years older than I was, but despite our age difference, we hit it off as friends.

Paul, Jr. would have made a great member of the Bryan family. He grew up to be a banker and has reportedly given millions of dollars to the University of Alabama football program. With the

Tide's recent success under Coach Nick Saban, Paul must be happy with his return on investment.

Come to think of it, maybe he's not. Saban has won five national championships in Tuscaloosa, just one less than Bear's remarkable achievement at the school.

I met Coach Bryant only a couple times during his stay at A&M. He was a giant of a man, standing about six feet four inches tall, with a deep gravelly voice and a friendly nature, at least off the football field.

About his home, I distinctly remember two things:

The walls of Paul's room were covered in wool pennants, the kind depicting the name and mascot of college teams. These represented, I think, the road trips his father had made to out-of-town football games.

Meanwhile, the Bear kept his own memento of his coaching achievements in view of his family. Paul, Jr. called it his dad's "crying towel." The towel was draped over the door to the carport of the house and on it, according to Paul, was marked the opponent and score of every game Bryant had lost as a head coach.

I suppose the towel served as a reminder of Bear's failures as he headed to work each and every day.

On one of my visits to see Paul, Jr., his dad happened to be entertaining some of his players. Among the contingent at the Bryant home: John David Crow, Jack Pardee, and Charlie Krueger. All three were All-Americans under Bryant. All three are today enshrined into the College Football Hall of Fame.

And Crow is one of only two Aggies to have won the Heisman Trophy.

Needless to say, those guys were my heroes growing up.

Texas A&M's other Heisman winner is Johnny Manziel, who dazzled the nation with his playing exploits during the Aggies' storybook season of 2012, their first year in the SEC.

I met Johnny once, a year or so after his NFL career had come to a disappointing end. While he has struggled in his personal life, and those struggles have impacted his on-field performance, I still hold Johnny in high regard and will never forget the two seasons he put together as A&M quarterback.

On his way to the Heisman Trophy as a redshirt freshman, he beat Alabama in Tuscaloosa and knocked off Oklahoma in the Cotton Bowl.

Johnny gave up his last two years of college eligibility and entered the NFL draft.

Following his final game at Kyle Field in 2013, the stadium underwent a two-year, half-billion-dollar redevelopment. At the time, at least one member of the A&M System Board of Regents, Jim Schwertner, wanted to rename the place "The House That Johnny Built."

I would have been okay with that.

I have to admit, meeting Johnny "Football" in person was a pretty big deal, even for someone old enough to be his grandfather. I had my picture taken with him on the club level at Kyle Field.

That photo now sits framed on the credenza of my office at the Brazos County Courthouse.

I sure hope Johnny gets his act together.

As for Bear Bryant, I have to say I've had sort of a love-hate relationship with the man, dating back to my inaugural season of football in the seventh grade at Lamar Junior High School.

When Bear Bryant first took over the A&M football program, I was just seven years old. He inherited a pretty rag-tag bunch that was not only unaccustomed to winning, but also, at least in Bryant's mind, unacquainted with the price that had to be paid for success.

Prior to taking the job at Texas A&M, Bryant spent eight years at Kentucky, and during his time there, his teams never failed to have a winning record.

As Bryant prepared for his inaugural campaign in College Station, he decided to take his players away from the distractions of campus life, not only to get better acquainted with them, but also to see whom he could trust in the heat of battle.

The destination was Junction, a small Texas Hill Country town where A&M had set up a meager adjunct campus. Bryant's intentions, however, were anything but meager.

He proceeded to put his players through the worst kind of torture in the midst of a record-breaking Texas heat wave. So grueling and rigorous were the practice sessions in Junction, a large chunk of his A&M squad quit the team.

The "survivors" are today known, with the highest regard, as the "Junction Boys."

Bryant's training regimen at the time, and for many years to follow, was akin to taking his players to hell and back. By the time I reached seventh grade, the "Bear Bryant way" of coaching was all the rage in Aggieland. The success of Bryant's Aggie teams had ignited a special passion in football-minded people, and I was no exception. From an early age, my only real goal in life was to play football at Texas A&M.

Even though the beginning of football practice at Lamar was only a week or so removed from the hallway debacle on my first day of class, I was ready to put on the pads and toss around the pigskin on my way to football stardom.

Little did I know the price one had to pay to do it "the Bear's way."

From the first day of pre-season workouts, the Lamar coaches put us through the wringer. We practiced every day in full gear. We ran laps every day in full gear. We hit each other constantly, and our reward every day was not a single drop of water to drink until we were done.

That was a lot for a bunch of twelve- and thirteen-year-olds to deal with, both physically and psychologically.

By the end of the first week, I'd had enough.

When Daddy picked me up after practice on Friday, I had news for him, but not the kind of news he was hoping to hear.

"I've decided I don't want to play football," I said.

"But you've been looking forward to this experience since you could walk," Daddy responded. "Aren't you excited?"

"No, Daddy," I replied without emotion. "I don't want to play football.

"I want to quit."

And, just in case he hadn't heard me, I clarified, "I'm going to quit football."

"No, you're not going to quit," came the immediate response.

"You don't understand," I continued, "You have no idea what those coaches are doing to us."

"They're making you winners and better men," he informed me.

I gave my father a quizzical look. He obviously didn't understand what was going on.

"We can't have any water. We're hitting all the time. We run laps constantly. I'm exhausted. My mouth feels like cotton. I'm SO THIRSTY!"

I paused for dramatic effect, a tactic that later worked well in the courtroom.

"I want to quit."

"You're not quitting," Daddy said again.

"So, you're going to make me play football?" I asked, incredulously.

Still calm and collected, Daddy replied, "Yep. And here's why."

I was certain nothing he could say would change my mind about football.

"You're going back out there Monday because you're never in your life ever going to quit anything you start. You start something, you finish it.

"That's going to be who you are from this point forward." Daddy gave me a look that said he meant business.

Having inherited my father's stubborn streak, I was not yet finished with my opening argument.

"PLEASE let me quit. I just don't want to go back...SO BAD!"

"Nope, you're going back out there."

And just like that, my conviction that football had become a thing in my past wilted into sheer nothingness, as I sat beside my father in the front seat of his car.

By the next Monday, though, I sprinted out to the practice field after school. Over the preceding weekend, Daddy had continued to work on me and by the time he was done, he had convinced me that quitters were losers.

Second Chronicles puts it like this: *"Be strong and do not give up, for your work will be rewarded"* (2 Chronicles 15:7).

I quickly adjusted to the rigors of seventh-grade football. As the years passed, the Bear's ways troubled me less, at least until I ran into Coach Bryant's most ardent coaching disciple as a freshman walk-on player at Texas A&M.

I absolutely loved my high school years in the sport. As for Daddy, he never missed a single one of my games. In fact, after his return from the Second World War until he died in 2009, Daddy missed a grand total of only five of his hometown's high school football team's contests, both before and long after my own playing days.

Eventually, my father served as president of the Bryan school board for nearly twenty years. Shortly after he died, the Bryan Independent School District renamed the city's high school in his honor: Travis B. Bryan High School. Of course, in doing so, the school remained "Bryan High."

Daddy certainly loved that school, and he loved their football teams.

So much so, that his unending quest for football excellence wound up derailing my senior year on the Bronco baseball team.

A fellow my dad knew came into Daddy's bank one day, entered his office, and closed the door.

"Travis, I know a guy that gathers eggs at the chicken hatchery in Hearne," Daddy's friend said, "and he's got a boy that can really play football. He tells me he wants to move his son to Bryan so he can play here."

After a short period of silence, the man continued, "Do you think you might be able to help arrange a job for his dad here?"

Not one to pass up news of a great prospect, Daddy was soon on his way to Hearne to watch the boy play. Although just a ninth grader, the youngster, named Pete Martin, was obviously an outstanding future talent on the gridiron.

Daddy pulled a few strings and got Pete's father a job offer in Bryan. But in the end, Pete's family stayed in Hearne. News of my father's attempt to "recruit" him did not. A grain dealer in Hearne by the name of Sam Degelia blew the whistle on the whole affair. Degelia reported the activity to the Texas University Interscholastic League, which then investigated the claim.

Daddy led the contingent from Bryan to answer to the accusations at UIL headquarters in Austin.

By the time of the meeting, our football season was over. We finished a disappointing 3-7, but I was named most valuable player of the team, still my greatest accomplishment in sports.

My father somehow convinced the UIL investigating board that he had recruited the young Martin to play baseball. His prospective participation in football would have been merely an "afterthought."

Somehow, the UIL bought the story and, rather than punishing the Bronco football team, they cancelled our entire season of baseball games.

I would have been the starting catcher on that squad.

In a "true-crime" aside to that story, Degelia, the Hearne whistle-blower, was later murdered in a contract killing orchestrated by his business partner and carried out by Charles Voyde Harrelson, the father of actor Woody Harrelson. Charles later went on to assassinate Federal District Judge John Woods in San Antonio.

By 1971, the Bryan Independent School District had opened a new high school and taken advantage of the move to fully integrate its schools. This was some seventeen years after the U.S. Supreme Court ruling *Brown v. Topeka Board of Education* constitutionally mandated the abolishment of "separate but equal" public-school facilities.

The new high school also adopted a new mascot. Gone were my Stephen F. Austin Broncos and in their place, local townsfolk rooted for the Bryan Vikings.

Bryan High School's football fortunes soon faltered, in large part because of "white flight," the relocation of affluent and middle-class white families to the newer neighborhoods which had been built in College Station. To try to restore gridiron success to the school, Daddy went in search of a new football coach, someone whose presence could keep the best players in the Bryan school district.

His top target was the coach of the über-successful Abilene Cooper High School program, a gentleman by the name of Merrill Green.

Green and the Cougars had come up just inches short of winning a state championship in 1967. The quarterback of that Cooper team was Jack Mildren, who went on to become a standout signal caller at the University of Oklahoma, where Green himself had played under the legendary head coach Bud Wilkinson.

Because of his success in Abilene, Green was one of the most well-known and highly regarded high school coaches in the Lone Star State.

With nothing to lose, Daddy gave Green a call. After a few minutes exchanging pleasantries, Daddy cut straight to the chase, offering Green the Bryan High School job.

"Mr. Bryan, I'm very happy in Abilene," Green said.

Daddy responded, "What kind of salary are you making there now?"

Green threw out a number. Daddy laughed.

"Well, it would appear to me," Daddy said, "that you're going to be the next head football coach at Bryan High."

With that, Daddy threw out a bigger number for Green to consider, bigger than the Abilene coach might ever have imagined.

In his twenty years as head coach at Bryan High School, Green won 197 games, nearly ten victories a season.

Today, the Bryan High School football stadium–next to Travis B. Bryan High School–is named, and deservedly so, for Coach Merrill Green.

And someplace in our fair community, there needs to be a marker or memorial or even a statue dedicated to my great uncle, Carl "Doc" Sprague.

In his youth, Doc–although everyone called him by his last name–played baseball at Texas A&M. There's a picture of him and his Aggie teammates on a table at the Longhorn Tavern Steak House, an eating establishment in downtown Bryan popular with the courthouse crowd. My great-uncle taught me a lot growing up: the finer points of baseball, how to pick out a tasty watermelon, how to hunt and fish, and how to maintain a purposeful and organized lifestyle.

He was also the consummate Christian. He read the Bible, offered beautiful prayers over meals at his home, and sang in the church choir.

Doc loved to sing.

For most of his adult life, Doc sold life insurance. Occasionally, he would take my brother and me on business trips to places like Houston and Dallas. On those trips, he would regale us with song. On fishing or camping trips, Doc would pull out his guitar and sing about a cowboy life. We sang along with him on the songs that we knew, not because we had heard them on the radio, but because he had sung them to us so many times.

Little did we know that our uncle had been, in his youth, "the Original Singing Cowboy."

Here's an excerpt from his remarkable story pulled from the *Encyclopedia of Country Music:*

> *Carl Sprague, the "Original Singing Cowboy," had the pedigree to prove it. Texas born, a veteran of World War I and graduate of Texas A&M, Sprague learned his songs while working on a cattle ranch. Inspired by fellow Texan Vernon Dalhart, whose "Wreck of the Old 97" took the nation by storm in 1924, Sprague proved that cowboy songs had commercial potential when his version of "When the Work's All Done This Fall" sold 900,000 copies for Victor. Sprague would make a total of 33 recordings for Victor before the Depression ended his musical career.*

And then there's this from the Texas State Historical Society's *Handbook of Texas Music:*

> *Carl Sprague lived in Bryan, Texas, from 1920 until his death. He married Lura Bess Mayo in 1926. They had no children. His wife, a pianist and music teacher, assisted Sprague in arranging music for his recording sessions and was an important musical influence. In later years, they led singing at the Bryan Lions Club and Businessmen's Bible Class of the First Baptist Church of Bryan. Carl Sprague died on February 21, 1979, in Bryan. In 2003 a collection of his twenty-four songs, including "When the Work's All Done This Fall," "Rounded Up in Glory," "Last Great Round Up," and "Utah Carol," was released in an anthology titled* Cowtrails, Longhorns, and Tight Saddles: Cowboy Songs 1925–1929.

That album, renamed *Cowboy Classics*, can be found on iTunes today.

Carl T. Sprague was an absolute sparkling gem among all the people I have ever known. Whatever redeeming qualities I may possess, many came from him.

9

Walk-On

Although he never said so to me, I suspect my father held hope that one day he might see his elder son play football at Texas A&M. I certainly felt that way about my younger son.

Daddy's "don't be a quitter" lecture to me in the seventh grade offered a valuable life lesson, but his love of football was such that seeing me advance in the sport as far as possible was important to him.

And on that deal, I was with him every step of the way. Or so I thought.

Daddy did not play football at A&M, but he was a member of the Aggie golf team. In fact, he was their top player, and for decades after he graduated, he could hold his own on the golf course against the best young players A&M had to offer.

Again, just so you golfers will keep reading, I'm devoting a whole chapter to golf later in this book. What you'll find there may not cure the ills of your golf swing, but it could help steer you down the fairway of life toward Eternal Salvation.

I was by no means a "big man on campus" when I arrived at Texas A&M. Despite my grandfather's and father's influence in the local community, I entered A&M just like every other first-year student in the Corps of Cadets, a lowly "fish," that belittling term–then, more than now–for incoming Aggie freshmen.

Even though I was most valuable player of my high school football team as a senior, I knew I wasn't scholarship material at a school like Texas A&M. So, like many other young men harboring dreams of suiting up in the maroon and white, I honored the Aggies' "12th Man" tradition and walked onto the team.

"Home of the 12th Man" is the sign adorning the east grandstands at Kyle Field. That's the side where students watch

Aggie home football games, standing the entire time in support of their team.

The original 12th Man of Texas A&M was a student by the name of E. King Gill.

Gill had been a substitute running back on the 1921 Aggie squad which won the Southwest Conference championship. After the season, Gill left the football team to concentrate on basketball, a sport in which he ultimately would be an all-conference performer.

Thus, when the Aggies met top-ranked Centre College in the Dixie Classic football game played on January 2, 1922, in Dallas, Gill was a spectator and not on the sidelines with his former teammates.

Centre College dominated the game early, and several Aggie players were injured in the process. When two key running backs left the game, Aggie coach Dana X. Bible called for Gill to come down to the field.

He needed another able-bodied player.

Gill borrowed a uniform from one of his injured former teammates and took a spot on the sideline. He never entered the game, and the Aggies stormed back to post a 22-14 victory over the Praying Colonels.

That story resurfaced during A&M's 1939 national championship season. Only then was it tagged with the "12th Man" label.

So vital to the legacy of Texas A&M is the 12th Man tradition that there are *two* statues of E. King Gill on the school's campus. One, the original version donated by the Class of 1980 was located at the north end of Kyle Field for many years. When the stadium was renovated, beginning in 2013, the statue was moved to a plaza outside nearby Rudder Hall.

With the completion of the Kyle Field redevelopment, a new statue of Gill, sculpted by Dallas artist Robert Hogan, was placed at the northeast corner of the stadium complex.

Today, A&M coaches designate a "12th Man" from the ranks of the team's walk-ons each year. That individual wears jersey number 12 and is said to represent the school's entire student body.

While I wasn't officially a "12th Man," my presence on the A&M freshman team did provide me relief from the Corps' traditional hazing of first-year cadets. Instead of taking residence within the quad of military-style barracks on campus housing the Corps, I lived in a dorm next to Henderson Hall, where A&M's scholarship athletes resided at the time.

While the hazing practices back then could get pretty intense–each year for many years numerous students left school because of the rigors of their "orientation"–I'm guessing that probably paled compared to the physical punishment associated with playing for the Aggie's new head football coach in 1965.

Gene Stallings is a native of Paris, Texas. Stallings was a Junction Boy under Bear Bryant as a sophomore on the A&M football team. After graduation, Stallings joined the Bear's new coaching staff when Bryant took over the football program at Alabama.

Thus, Stallings was deeply rooted in the Bear's "take no prisoners" coaching philosophy when he became the head man at A&M.

Back in my college playing days, freshmen football players, even those on scholarship, were ineligible to participate in games with the varsity squad. Relegated to a freshman schedule of "junior varsity" contests against other Southwest Conference schools, walks-ons like me were merely "fresh meat" for the Aggie varsity during each week of game preparation.

It turned out, though, that the unit delivering the biggest blows on the practice field was Stallings' coaching staff.

Up to that point of my life, my most serious football injury had come when I was a kid playing a pickup game with my friends in the side yard of our house. I got clobbered in the face one time, and within minutes I felt like my eye was going to pop out of my head.

Mama was our unofficial trainer for those matchups, and when I ran inside the house to show her my injury, she simply gave me a hug and told me everything was going to be okay.

"You're going to have quite the shiner," she reassured me.

Whenever I think of my mother today, that's always one of the first memories that comes to my mind.

Mamas, though, didn't hang around the A&M practice field.

During my freshman year, I played mostly defensive back on what today you'd call the scout team. In that role, I frequently had the assignment of defending Tommy Maxwell, a starter on the Aggie varsity who spent some time playing pro ball after college. A superior athlete, Maxwell often beat me on pass routes. One day in practice, I made it look too easy for him, slipping and falling while trying to tackle him on his way to the end zone.

Just as I got to my feet—and as if I wasn't already embarrassed enough—I got blindsided like I'd never been hit before. With the play ended, the collision came as a complete surprise, and for a good while, I lay prostrate on the field in utter shock. When I finally rolled over onto my back, I looked up to see my position coach, Lyde Huggins, standing over me, his face flushed in anger over my having blown coverage on the play.

He had sprinted at least forty yards from the sidelines and clocked me at full speed to express his displeasure.

After Junction, Bear Bryant's 1954 A&M squad, his first at the school, went on to post a 1-9 record.

Gene Stallings, in his first year as head coach, finished with a not-much-improved 3-7 varsity mark.

Two years later, however, both men took their Aggie teams to conference championships, so something has to be said, I suppose, for their "disciplined" approach.

Both Bryant and Stallings called their coaching philosophy "hit 'em harder" football. Looking back on that, at least as I experienced it under Stallings, my opinion is that the abuse we endured then would constitute criminal assault today. Nobody gets away with coaching like that anymore.

By trying to put some "fight" into us, Stallings and his staff eventually managed to take all the fight right out of me. But I refused to quit and survived to season's end.

Just twenty-nine years old and the youngest head coach in college football at the time, Gene Stallings appeared to do his best to channel both his inner and outer Bear Bryant.

Stallings prowled the practice field, as did the Bear. He growled at his players, as Bryant did. And, just as his mentor was known to do, Stallings was not averse to putting his hands on players to drive home a point.

One time after a freshmen game, I saw Stallings grab a player in the locker room and, gripping him by the front of his shoulder pads while seated, he shook the tar out of him in front of his teammates. In doing so, he repeatedly banged the kid's head against the metal eraser tray at the bottom of the chalkboard behind him.

That player was Javier Vela. He stuck around and eventually saw playing time for Stallings as a reserve running back his senior year. Javier was not a quitter.

Another time at a freshmen practice, two of our players, my friend Rolf Krueger and another local boy named Carl Gough, were taken to the hospital suffering from heat stroke. Denying players water breaks during practice was the "Bryant way" and much the norm at the time; few people–neither trainers, nor coaches–gave that any thought.

I have to say I'm proud that I was able to take the best those coaches had to give and make it to season's end.

In fact, by the time spring practice was over that school year, I had risen to second team on the varsity depth chart. My teammates, I think, respected my hard work, and many of the top stars on the roster had become friends of mine.

Of course, the brand-new yellow Corvette which Daddy had purchased for me before I left home for college may have factored into the formation of a few of those friendships.

Frequently during my freshman year at A&M, members of the Aggie varsity could be seen driving around town in a shiny, new yellow Corvette. Eyebrows must have been raised as onlookers speculated how Aggie football players could afford such a slick ride.

Fortunately, the car was merely a loaner from me.

As a lowly non-scholarship freshman walk-on, I would have been barely an afterthought to most of my teammates on the varsity, if not for that car.

Occasionally the car got trashed when a teammate borrowed it for "date night." Once, it was returned to me with a small dent in the front bumper. Mostly though, the guys got it back in reasonably good shape.

That year, 1965, was the first year women were openly admitted as full-time students on the A&M campus. Prior to that, the college had been a male-only educational enclave with only a few females–wives or daughters of faculty members–allowed to take classes.

During my freshman year, the coed enrollment at A&M stood at about seventy-five, compared to the nearly 9,500 male students on campus at the time. The gender disparity made recruiting more than a little difficult for Stallings, but football players, particularly the stars, were never short on female companionship.

At the conclusion of spring practice, Coach Stallings did his best to meet individually with each of his players. Given my perceived status as a second-teamer, I looked forward to a discussion about my football-playing future. I felt good about the possibility I would be placed on scholarship.

Not surprisingly, I was one of the last players scheduled to meet with Stallings. But when I got to his office, his secretary told me he had already left for the day. I never got a call to reschedule the meeting, which left me more than a little heartbroken and my status for the future left very much up in the air.

Meanwhile, A&M's golf coach, Henry Ransom, a fine tour player who had taught my dad how to play the game, had arranged for me to take a summer job at a golfing resort in Wisconsin. With no idea where my future football fortunes might be headed, I accepted Henry's offer, and after final exams my yellow Corvette and I headed north to Lake Geneva, Wisconsin, and the Big Foot Country Club there.

Man, I had a good time that summer.

And I made an important decision.

I was going to quit football. This time, Daddy didn't say no.

I wish he would have, because that was one of the worst decisions of my life.

Two years later, I made it to the Cotton Bowl in Dallas. And just like E. King Gill, I was sitting in the stands watching my former teammates take part in the matchup. A&M's opponent that day wasn't the Praying Colonels, but rather Bear Bryant's Alabama Crimson Tide.

And once again, the Aggies pulled the upset, knocking off Alabama 20-16.

Coach Stallings, however, never called me down to the field to suit up for the game.

Still, as part of the figurative 12th Man, I cheered my head off for the Aggies that day.

After the game when the two coaches met at midfield, Bryant–keeper of the "crying towel" during his time as A&M head coach–unexpectedly gave his protege a big embrace, lifting Stallings high into the air.

I guess you could call that a "Bear" hug, and the celebratory gesture was well deserved. As it turned out, that victory marked the end of Gene Stallings' only winning season in his seven years as head coach of the Aggies.

However, a quarter-century after that game and as head coach of the Crimson Tide himself, Gene Stallings won his own national championship at Alabama.

What I did not know about Coach Stallings the man, during my too-brief time playing for him at Texas A&M, was that he was also a father. He and his wife, Ruth Ann, had a trio of young healthy daughters and a son named John Mark, called "Johnny," who suffered from Down Syndrome.

In his book about Johnny, entitled *Another Season*, Gene Stallings wrote of his first year coaching at A&M:

> *As a young football coach there were plenty of times when I didn't have the best judgement. Sometimes I was just plain too tough on my players. I'd work them harder than I needed to or I'd discipline them a little too harshly if they broke training rules....*
>
> *[F]rom watching the girls work with Johnny, I was becoming more tolerant, more compassionate, and it was carrying over into my work. If a player needed a little extra help or time to learn something, I would give it to him. If a guy was having a problem at home, with his girlfriend or with his parents, I found myself listening a little longer, wanting to help.*

Any hard feelings I had for Gene Stallings long ago have vanished. After his retirement from coaching, he became a member of the Texas A&M University System Board of Regents, and in that capacity, he provided an influential voice which ultimately led to Texas A&M becoming a member of the Southeastern Conference in 2011.

He's also, as I've been told by many, a true gentleman and a devout Christian man.

Gene Stallings got his national championship coaching at Alabama, and while Texas A&M has not won a national championship since 1939, I'm certain we will reach those lofty ranks again someday.

And when we do, I'll be in the stands, as always, cheering my head off.

10

The Best We Had to Give

There was another side to my college experience.

In the late 1960s, protest marches were a common occurrence on college campuses across the land, as students voiced their disapproval of an escalating war in the southeastern Asian country of Vietnam.

On the Texas A&M campus, we marched, too, in drill formation, because that's what you do when you're a member of the Corps of Cadets.

The Corps and A&M have gone hand in hand, virtually since the school first opened its doors in 1876. One of the missions of the original Morrill Act, which established land-grant colleges like A&M, was to provide military training for young men as a part of their advanced education.

That was a natural at A&M, since a preponderance of former officers of the Army of the Confederate States of America played key roles in establishing the school.

In fact, Jefferson Davis, the former president of the Confederacy, was asked to lead the new Agricultural & Mechanical College of Texas, but he declined. In turn, he recommended the superintendent of public instruction for the State of Mississippi, and Thomas Gathright was given the job.

Gathright and those leading the military instruction at the school never saw eye to eye. After just three years as A&M president, Gathright was dismissed. Unfortunately, he never really grasped the intent of the Morrill Act.

What became the Corps of Cadets took hold at A&M and lives on. Its numbers have diminished since President Earl Rudder made membership in the unit non-compulsory back in 1965. My class, the Class of '69, was the first in which incoming students were not obligated to join the Corps.

Rudder, a military hero himself, made the move to try to bolster the sagging fortunes of his school. Then-vice-president Lyndon Johnson had encouraged Rudder to "adapt to the times."

In addition to shaking up the Corps, Rudder also opened enrollment to women, and oversaw a name change for the school. His foresight has helped Texas A&M University become a leader in public education.

I didn't give much thought to not joining the Corps. As a diehard Aggie growing up, I had no intention of bucking that tradition.

While membership in the Corps has never obligated a student to military service, many are the Aggies who have served their country with honor and distinction. It is said that A&M produced a larger contingent of American officers during World War II than any other school, including the combined total of the U.S. service academies at West Point and Annapolis.

What it means to be an A&M student, or "former student," as alumni are known, is a rewarding and yet complicated experience. We like to say that being an Aggie "is hard to describe from the inside and impossible to comprehend from the outside."

However, Texas A&M's conservative culture remains deeply rooted in the Corps. Today, cadets number about 2,500–for many years now, both men and women–on a campus with a total enrollment of more than 60,000.

After I left the Aggie football team, I remained in the Corps with my athletic outfit. As a sophomore, I was an infrequent target for "instruction" by upperclassmen. My course load included military science classes, and on most days I moved around on campus clad in my "pinks" and "greens," pink being military code for the khaki shirt and pants I wore, and green symbolic of the green jacket which completed the cadet uniform of my day.

During my final year of school, I proudly added senior boots to my ensemble, and welcomed a "whip out" salute from "fish" who were passing by.

Giving the orders in that equation was a much less stressful experience than being on the receiving end.

"Fish Bryan is my name, sir!" I would address an upperclassman when called upon to do so during my first year. The "whip-out" had to be done in a very precise manner, and after making my introduction, the ensuing dialogue could go in all sorts of different directions.

On campus, away from the darkened corridors where much of the extreme hazing took place, interactions between fish and upperclassmen were fairly straightforward and respectful. As president of the school, Earl Rudder was not a fan of the Corps' hazing tradition. Still, it was said President Rudder could dress down a cadet of any rank when the need arose and leave him shaking in his shoes.

Daddy was good friends with President Rudder. My father worked on Rudder's campaign when he was elected Texas Land Commissioner before taking the A&M job.

As a kid, I went door to door handing out campaign fliers for Rudder. While Daddy's relationship with the general was lasting, I also got to meet the man a time or two during my years as a student. I continue to have the utmost respect for how he turned around the fortunes of my alma mater.

The Corps and Texas A&M athletics overlapped then, as they do now, in dramatic ways. When I was in school, the Corps would do "march-ins" at Kyle Field prior to home football games. At the time, a track encircled the playing field and the entire Corps would march into the stadium and around the track before taking our seats, although as a part of the 12th Man, we never sat in those seats.

At halftime of home games, the "Fightin' Texas Aggie Band" performed. I still get goosebumps watching their military-style precision marching routines.

Of course, the very *best* tradition associated with the Corps and Texas A&M football was the obligatory kiss that cadets received from their dates when the Aggies scored. I was a recipient of a few of those during my time in the Corps, and to a small degree those moments soothed my disappointment at not being down on the field.

My second biggest regret during college was failing to actually learn much in class.

Foolishly, I did not work hard in my studies, and I really didn't get much of an education. That lack of discipline came back to haunt me during law school, but like most of my fellow cadets, we had other matters on our minds in the late 1960s.

Seeking to follow in the footsteps of my grandfather's military service during World War I and my daddy's service in World War II, I fully expected to be called to active duty for my country as well.

As prospective military men, we in the Corps did not live in fear of the war in Vietnam. Because of A&M's pro-military construct, we existed in somewhat of a vacuum, far removed from the counterculture which existed on many other college campuses.

In many of the military science classes offered at Texas A&M, cadets were exposed to the precepts of hostility and conflict in a disciplined and pragmatic fashion, apart from how the war was being showcased on network news. We all knew the potential stakes of combat, but we were instilled with a true sense of duty, honor, and country.

I was very proud the day I graduated from Texas A&M. Everyone in my family was there for the commencement ceremonies held at G. Rollie White Coliseum, which also doubled as the home of Texas A&M basketball back then.

In the days which followed, I donned my uniform and was commissioned as a second lieutenant in the United States Army. I was destined for field artillery school and eventually, I thought, the war in Vietnam.

While I had come to grips with a future that would take me halfway around the world, I also had become enthusiastic about the possibility of going to law school. After I was accepted into Baylor Law School, I was given a deferment from active duty.

Several of my friends who graduated from A&M with me were soon "in country" fighting the war.

And some of them never returned.

Steve Mullen was my suitemate in college. He was a tall, friendly guy from the Rio Grande Valley area of Texas. He was on a football scholarship, but the program had handed out so many scholarships Steve wound up living with me across from the "jock dorm," Henderson Hall.

After graduation, Steve also took his commission, joined the army, and was sent to Southeast Asia. There, his jeep ran over a landmine, and he was killed.

I was deeply saddened by news of Steve's death. In looking back through the years now, I can't imagine having your life cut short at such a young age.

Steve was brave. I'd like to think most all of us in the Corps would have been brave, too, faced with circumstances similar to Steve's. When our country told us to go fight, we did as we were ordered. In our preparation, we learned always to "give it the best we had to give."

Back then, immersed in the Corps' culture, I didn't pay much attention to the "whys and wherefores" of our country's strategic military and political vision. Like Steve, I was ready to serve. Law school offered me only a deferment.

After I finished law school and returned to Bryan, I spent a summer at Fort Sill in Lawton, Oklahoma, receiving training in the Field Artillery School located there. Exposure to the actual weapons and munitions used in combat brought the war much closer to home. What I experienced at Fort Sill was much different than what I had been taught in the classroom at A&M. Not only was it more *real*, but also it was more *earth-shattering*, in both a literal and figurative sense.

I paid close attention, not only to what I was being taught, but how the war was going. I remember feeling that my life would soon be on the line.

However, after my summer in Oklahoma, the war began to wind down, and there was no real need for second lieutenants like me. I was assigned to the Army Reserve, and had I been called to active service from there, I would have dutifully gone.

But in hindsight, I now know Vietnam was an immoral war. To my friends and colleagues who fought there, I offer my deepest appreciation for your service.

I remember watching on television–admittedly from the safety of my own home–the helicopter evacuations from the rooftop of the U.S. embassy in Saigon, dramatic images symbolizing the war's end. It was a humbling and disconcerting sight, akin to tucking tail and running.

America wasn't supposed to lose wars, and yet we did not win in Vietnam.

In fact, it was a war in which we should never have been involved. I think of Steve and the thousands of others who died with him and the wall in Washington, D.C. which bears so many of their names.

What was it all for?

As I've already shared, I'm a serious and committed "pro-lifer." Sometimes the horrors of war are inevitable, but when they become a necessity, it's critical that the cause be just, noble, and righteous.

About twenty years ago, I came to the conclusion that Vietnam was not such a war, at least not for America.

As you're aware now, my take on life is also viewed through the prism of Embracing The Cross and its "death and resurrection" tenets. Was the Vietnam War a death-and-resurrection experience for our country?

Did anything good come from the experience?

The answers to both questions, in my mind, are "no."

I feel the same way about the aftermath of the events which occurred on American soil September 11, 2001.

For a brief time after those attacks, our country and its people rallied and unified and seemed ready to answer both the patriotic and spiritual wakeup call we had received.

People here, for the first time in a long time, were talking about things that mattered, contemplating why these unimaginable atrocities had taken place so close to home.

And Americans all across our land were talking about God.

Within a few short months, however, everybody went back to living their old lives. We ultimately entered another war of suspect origin, and the lives of many more American men and women were lost.

That day, 9/11, was all about death, for sure. But from my point of view, there was little in the way of "resurrection" which followed.

Before I continue with my story, let me pause and take some time to explain to you what it is I mean by the term, "Embracing The Cross."

11

Embracing The Cross

"Then Jesus said to His disciples, 'If anyone wishes to come after Me, he must deny himself and take up his cross and follow Me. For whoever wishes to save his life will lose it, but whoever loses his life for My sake will find it'" (Matthew 16:24-25).

The Bible makes clear that it's our sufferings that bring us into Enlightenment and onto new paths.

What may sometimes seem like a failure, what may feel to us like a fall, many times is God creating space in our lives for us to go in a different direction or to really mature.

In other words, to experience Transformation.

By "Embracing The Cross," we take hold of the real meaning of the death, burial, and resurrection of Jesus Christ. The way to God, I believe the Bible tells us, is not by climbing up to Him, but by "falling" into our Heavenly Father.

Opportunities to do this take place every day.

Let's say you've been passed up for a promotion, or your spouse has misinterpreted your mood after a particularly rough day at the office. When we are wounded, either in mind or in body, whether by accident or purposeful action taken against us, or whether through a devastating event or the smallest of setbacks, life is knocking us down into God.

For many of us, including myself, more than I still would like to admit, our fleshly reaction to this part of the "death and resurrection" process is to look somewhere to cast blame. Blame your boss. Blame your wife. Blame yourself.

Even blame God.

Too often, and I see this frequently when individuals land in the criminal justice system, we channel our blame through a process psychologists call "self-medication" by using drugs or alcohol to mask the pain of our hurts.

Or by following the earthly "wisdom" of some false prophet.

As we face "death," we seek a quick and easy change to our circumstances, rather than just holding onto the pain and accepting it for what it is.

"What you sow does not come to life unless it dies" (1 Corinthians 15:36).

When we Embrace The Cross and take personal ownership of our sorrows and setbacks, our failures and pain, real Transformation begins.

Think of it as "marinating" our souls.

Here in Texas, barbecue is as popular a pastime as football. Cook-offs are attended by thousands of people, and participants spend thousands of dollars on state-of-the-art mobile outdoor kitchens.

Every chef has his secret ingredients, but every one of them understands the importance of the slow marinade, usually a combination of salt, spice, sauce, sugar, and seasoning.

Good things on the barbecue grill take time. A flavorful outcome cannot be rushed.

In the Bible, Paul said, "[I] delight in weaknesses, in insults, in hardships, in persecutions, in difficulties. For when I am weak, then I am strong" (2 Corinthians 12:10).

Paul understood his personal suffering as a catalyst for growth and wisdom.

And, just like Paul, we oftentimes hurt, too. With that pain can come confusion in our attempts to find an answer to the simple question, "Why me?"

The answer is also simple: It is in our darkest moments where real Transformation occurs. Through our personal suffering, we can present our bodies as living sacrifices to our Creator. Like Paul, we can rejoice in our persecution because God has allowed it to come our way for an important reason.

These are the moments in which God provides us His greatest Wisdom, gives us His most abundant Grace, and most of all, LOVES us unconditionally as His children.

Think about the last time life brought you to your knees. Chances are, when you reached the other side, when you experienced your own resurrection, you felt a sense of peace and understanding beyond "earthly reason."

Where did that "Miracle" come from? How did such sorrow turn into Joy?

That's what happens when you're "Embracing The Cross."

In many of the world's religions, God is portrayed as a judge, sitting on a heavenly throne, casting His righteous authority on mankind.

That's more in line with someone like me, an "earthly" judge.

In a courtroom, there's accusation, there's blame, there's condemnation, there's incarceration, and sometimes there's even death. As a district judge for the state of Texas, I have pronounced the death penalty on two individuals in response to the lawful will of the people.

As I've already written, I no longer believe in capital punishment, just as I do not believe in abortion. But in both cases, death remains the law of our land, and I am sworn to uphold that earthly law.

I know this as much as I know my own self: God does not kill people. He dies for people.

He doesn't accuse but takes the accusation. That's what Jesus did at the cross upon which He died.

This sort of thinking is foreign to a lot of contemporary Christians. We've lost sight of a critical element of Biblical teaching and that is the nature of what the Bible calls "*agape* love."

"*Agape*"—pronounced ah-gahp'-ay—means one-way. Simply put, if I have *agape* love for you, it means I love you unconditionally–regardless of whether the feeling is mutual–and I expect nothing in return.

That's how God loves. That is His essence.

God cannot do anything that goes against His nature. God's Love is both unconditional and unending. It's there for us constantly.

As a judge, I see examples all the time of how people accept this concept and how they also fail to do so.

There are two kinds of defendants in my courtroom. One constantly seeks to shift the blame to others.

"I didn't do it!" they will say, even after both the evidence and a jury have found them guilty.

"The jury was wrong. They're wrong about me! The system has screwed me over!"

I hear that in my courtroom a lot.

Every now and then, though, an accused individual will stand up and own their crime.

"I was wrong," they'll say, "I did it, and I'm here to face the consequences."

Most importantly to me, they'll also sometimes add, "I'm sorry. I don't ever want to do this again."

That person has already been spiritually received by God. They've begun the process of both earthly rehabilitation and heavenly restoration, through both death and resurrection.

When I pass sentence on a convicted criminal, I try to look past the details of the case or what prosecuting attorneys may have said. Instead, I try to peer into that individual's heart. How has he or she responded to their experience before me?

For the many that wish to cast blame elsewhere and refuse to take responsibility for their own actions, my sentence will usually be severe and, hopefully, just. For the individuals who admit to their wrongdoing and are sincere and contrite in accepting the consequences for their crime, my punishment will be more moderate.

Those individuals have already moved toward their own Resurrection.

> "Therefore, confess your sins to one another and pray for one another, that you may be healed. The prayer of a righteous person has great power as it is working" (James 5:16).

Of course, a lot of defense attorneys, knowing I'm a Christian, will try to persuade their clients to offer me what amounts to a tale of "jailhouse conversion."

I see through that most of the time. Having represented hundreds of clients as a defense attorney myself, I know when someone is sincere and when they're trying to pull the wool over my eyes.

I've spent my life seeking to find the truth. I've spent years in study of the law and years more in intense Biblical inquiry looking to find God's truth. The theology that I've derived from that analysis could be called orthodox, and I'm okay with that.

In the last hundred years or so, many Christians have lost their way. Some churches, particularly in recent times, have softened their message to attract larger congregations. Some prominent ministers put forth before their flocks a concept some call "the Prosperity Gospel."

"If you have enough Faith," Prosperity proponents preach, "you won't suffer, you'll have plenty of money, and you'll live in a big house."

Not many Christians today have ever heard of the Keswick Convention. It started in the late 1800s in Keswick, England, and continues sporadically even today.

In my search to find God's truth–as a result of personal heartache and misfortune of which I'll write about later–I began with a Biblical immersion and from there expanded my studies to books written about the interpretation of God's Holy Word.

That's how I first learned about the Keswick movement.

The fundamental Keswick precept involved what they called the "exchanged life." By laying down our figurative lives and seeking death for our egos, mankind receives–in exchange–the Life of God.

Christian life, so the Keswick followers believed, is not of the natural world, but of a "supernatural" existence that comes to you through death and resurrection.

In the Bible, Paul calls embracing the cross a "mystery." What he describes sounds a lot like undergoing a heart transplant. The Great Surgeon, Jesus Christ, removes our old, hardened, and infected heart and exchanges it for a new one.

This is nothing you can do yourself, no matter how hard you try.

When you Embrace The Cross, you must give of yourself completely and entrust yourself completely to the Lord.

As egocentric beings, we mostly rage against that notion. We refuse to yield control. But that's the key element in this Transformation. When we spiritually die, we allow our egos to die. We are then willing to give up control of our being.

And from there, good things happen.

In our world, Satan has an order, and God has an order. God's order is called the Kingdom of God, or God's Reign, or the "New Creation." Through the Cross, God is ending the creation that began in the Book of Genesis and bringing about the New Creation.

To be a part of that New Creation, we must welcome death, burial, and resurrection.

When that New Creation is complete, "the earth shall be filled with the knowledge of the glory of the Lord as the waters cover the sea" (Habakkuk 2:14).

The Cross is the fulcrum event of the universe. People are not just individually going to be saved, the entirety of all Creation will be saved and transformed.

The fallen world lifted up through the Cross.

Through my own eyes and in my own experience, I have come to believe that the only force that will conquer evil in this world is the power of unconditional Love.

In our courts, in our prisons, in every aspect of the American judicial system, I've seen that power. Guns won't do it. Threats won't do it. Clout won't do it. Not even education will do it, not even what we call "street smarts" achieves the objective.

Love is the only thing that will conquer evil.

And yes, many times that Heavenly Law of Love will motivate you to turn the other cheek. Yes, you will have to absorb some blows. Vulnerability must become our hallmark. And more often than you will like, you'll have to get comfortable with being Vanquished.

But God will protect you if you have Faith. Just love people and open yourself to receiving in return their hatred–or their love–without passing judgment. God will work through that. Maybe not immediately, but He'll plant a seed of love in the hearts of others, thanks to you.

My brother Tim and I share a house in Carmel, California, and our families visit there frequently.

One morning during a recent trip, Becky and I went for a walk along the cliffs bordering the golf links at Pebble Beach. Not a lot of people do that, but as an avid golfer myself, I know how to stay out of the way.

As we were walking, a golfer and his caddy came over a hill. The caddy veered off in our direction, obviously in search of a lost ball. He put forth a minimal effort, and when he spotted us he yelled out "Hey, you picked up my player's ball!"

While my daddy wasn't above the recruitment of high school athletes and leveraging himself for the best outcome on a business deal, he never cheated anyone, and he never infringed upon the sacred constructs of the game.

And in that respect, he taught me well.

The caddy's unfounded accusation infuriated me, and from a good bit away, I let him have it verbally. I did not swear, but otherwise I read him the riot act. I was livid in the moment and walked away fuming for some time.

Becky, who is familiar with my teachings on The Cross, and also acquainted with my occasional bouts of egotistical weakness, spoke to me calmly as she said, "You didn't really 'embrace the cross' there, did you?"

Her words cut me to the quick, and in her truth I experienced my death.

Shortly before lunch the next day, I headed over to Poppy Hills for a tee time there. Before I hit the course, I decided to grab a bite to eat. I walked up to a hamburger stand close to the first tee and asked, "What's for lunch?"

The proprietor, busy at his grill, turned and scowled at me. "Can't you see the sign on the wall?"

I looked up and saw his menu.

"Okay, I'll take a hamburger," I said.

He jerked open his icebox, hastily unwrapped a patty, and slapped it onto the grill. As he did so, without even looking my way, he snarled, "Get back away from my counter so somebody else can order!"

Usually, every day is a good day on the Monterey Peninsula, but this week was not heading in that direction.

As I stepped back, I again felt anger boiling in my gut, the same anger I had felt when the caddy had barked at me that morning.

Then, I remembered my wife's words.

The better course of action at the hamburger stand was to take a Christ-like approach to the situation.

I fought off the urge to tell the guy off and walk away. Instead, I paid heed to the "other" voice in my head.

"Give him a big tip," God told me.

When my order was done and I had paid my bill, I handed over an extra $10.

"Keep the change," I said, mustering up a smile.

The guy was stunned. And in the next instant, he, too, was resurrected.

"Can I put some cheese on your burger?"

"For sure!" I replied.

Once I got my cheeseburger back, he reached out and grabbed five different kinds of chips from his chip rack. "Take your pick," he offered. "No extra charge!

"Do you want a drink? No charge for that, either!"

With no one else around, the burger man and I carried on a ten-minute conversation about everything: our lives, our families, our troubles, and our hopes. I got to know that guy simply because I died to myself, and God moved into the situation and created a connection between the two of us.

It was a small event, but a major miracle as far as I was concerned.

To me, that episode is the perfect example of how, when you're willing to die to self and just Love someone in the moment, Good Things will happen in the Lord.

12

"Mad Dog"

My first time in a court of law was when I was about eight years old watching my father's cousin, Bill Davis, defend an accused man in a murder trial.

I don't remember too many details from the experience. I do recall my parents and I visited the courtroom several times. The proceedings attracted such a large audience that I had to stand on a cigarette butt can in the back of the courtroom to see over the throng.

There is no smoking in the courthouse today.

The "star" of that trial wasn't Bill, nor the accused. It was the lead attorney for the defense, Percy Foreman.

Texas is home to the "larger-than-life" criminal defense attorney. Dick DeGuerin and Richard "Racehorse" Haynes became rich–and famous–as defense attorneys. More recently, Rusty Hardin has gained national notoriety for his legal representation.

But the name that trumps them all is that of Percy Foreman.

Foreman's appearance in the Brazos County courthouse was major news in Bryan and the reason my parents wanted to watch the trial. For many, it was like getting to see Mickey Mantle play baseball or Arnold Palmer tee it up on the golf course.

Foreman's list of clients is a "who's who" of the dastardly and nefarious, people like James Earl Ray, Jack Ruby, and Charles Harrelson. Foreman defended the former General Edwin Walker when he was accused of lewd and malicious behavior in Dallas.

It is said that Foreman handled more than 1,500 capital murder cases during his career—many of which, I assume, never went to trial because 1,500 is an awfully big number—with only one of his clients being put to death. In his defense of Charles Harrelson in the murder case of Alan Harry Berg, Foreman won an acquittal for his client.

Both Haynes and DeGuerin worked for Foreman in their formative years as defense attorneys. The Texas Criminal Defense Lawyer's Association annually hands out a "Percy Foreman Lawyer of the Year Award."

Although I don't exactly remember the outcome of the trial I witnessed as a kid, I'm fairly certain the defense prevailed.

When Daddy helped me decide to become a lawyer, I didn't really have visions of being another Percy Foreman. I was just hoping I could get into law school somewhere and take it from there.

Truth be told, had it not been for the fact that one of my daddy's high school classmates, Angus McSwain, was dean of Baylor Law School, I might never have had the chance to become an attorney.

As I've told you, I didn't learn much in college, through no fault of my beloved Texas A&M. My "study habits," if you could even call them that, boiled down to cramming for exams and keeping my fingers crossed.

In hindsight, I really didn't go to college to learn, and I regret that to this day. Honestly, I don't think I possessed much of a desire in my youth to learn. I was just kind of a "get by" guy and averaged a low B at A&M.

That all changed in Waco.

Day One at Baylor Law School, I ran into a buzz saw.

My first law professor was an old railroad attorney by the name of William Boswell. He had to be at least eighty years old by the time I took his class.

Serious "as a heart attack," Boswell made no effort to get acquainted with his students that first day and did not bother to introduce himself. Instead, he immediately got down to the business of teaching us the law. For our first assignment, Boswell presented us a case scenario. It was our job to interpret the case and glean from it pertinent details.

The next class, Boswell called on me first.

"Young man," he said, "I need a lawyer to advise me on the following fact situation."

A "fact situation" is legal-speak describing a summary of the details of a case for which relief is sought.

Boswell presented me with a few of the facts. After he concluded, he told me, "Now that you know what happened, please stand up and give me and your classmates your legal opinion on the matter.

"By the way," he added, "you'll be representing the injured party in this exercise."

I sat there stunned. Just like Lyde Huggins, Boswell had blindsided me from out of nowhere. I hadn't touched my homework assignment. I didn't read a single one of the cases. I was under the assumption I could "get by" in law school as I had my four years at A&M.

After rising slowly from my seat and turning to face the class, I put forth a rambling and incoherent response that had a few in the room snickering. I felt pathetic.

When I sat down, Boswell looked at me silently for a few moments.

"Sir," he finally said, addressing me, "I'm going to have to get me another lawyer because you obviously don't know a damn thing about the law."

My entire first year of law school went pretty much that same way. I put in too little effort and felt completely out of my element the entire time.

But I wasn't going to quit. Daddy had spent a lot of money to put me in this position, and I didn't want to fail him.

What I had to do went well beyond just "buckling down." I knew I had to transform my whole approach to learning. There was no way I was going to skate by in this competitive environment.

My study habits dramatically improved the following year, in part due to a Baylor coed I had started dating, my future wife Becky. She made me feel good about myself, and with that boost in personal confidence, my grades picked up dramatically. I still wasn't an "A" student, but in making Bs, B-minuses, and C-pluses, I was at least on the road to successfully completing law school.

As I neared the finish line, I had one final challenge before receiving my degree. That last hurdle between me and becoming a real attorney was a former personal-injury lawyer by the name of Matt "Mad Dog" Dawson and his two-quarter Practice Court class.

Dawson was a Waco native, a Baylor graduate, and a highly respected trial attorney. He was the son of the Reverend J. M. Dawson, a distinguished Baylor alum and highly-regarded local Baptist minister.

Physically, Mad Dog was a pretty unassuming character: bald-headed and bespectacled. As an instructor, he was tenacious.

Dawson was new to the Baylor law-school faculty, and it was my good fortune–as it had been with Gene Stallings at A&M–to be enrolled in his first Practice Court class.

Like Stallings, Dawson had little patience for screw-ups, which is why we began calling him "Mad Dog." He was a fanatic about the correct and ardent interpretation of the law.

Despite my improved study habits and my desire to get law school behind me, I really struggled in Dawson's classes. He humiliated me on several occasions, and when he called on me that first quarter–even though I thought I was prepared for his class–I invariably gave him the wrong answer.

Or, at least answers he didn't want to hear.

In no time at all, Mad Dog had my stomach tied up in knots. His classroom was a frightening experience for me.

By the end of that first quarter, I was a wreck. I studied for his final exam like I'd never studied before. Still, when I took the test, I only managed to finish about forty percent of my work.

Leaving his classroom that day, I felt an overwhelming sense of impending doom.

I was certain I had failed the class. I was positive I wouldn't be getting out of law school.

And for sure, I wasn't going to become an attorney.

By then, Becky and I were married. Even though we were newlyweds, she had already seen me hit rock bottom on more than one occasion. She always tried to put a positive spin on things, but I was firmly established in my habit of taking a sordid comfort from my gloom.

This was long before I found my Salvation in Embracing The Cross. While in law school, I had great difficulty even seeing the "sunny side of the street." Personal remorse and despair were my too-constant companions.

With Mad Dog having gotten the best of me, Becky did what any good Baptist girl with a teaching degree from Baylor would have done for the despondent and forlorn man she had married: She got me drunk.

Both Becky and I grew up in the Baptist church, but neither of us were brought up in strict Baptist homes. There was a time when we Baptists were thought to be "teetotalers" and pursuers of the straight-and-narrow highway.

Neither my wife nor I have ever thought of a drink or two as any kind of sin.

As Becky sought to comfort my Mad Dog sorrows with a little "Mad Dog 20/20," there was definitely no consumption of alcohol in moderation. After she was through with me, I passed out.

(Point of clarification here: Becky and I would never have had any Mogen David street wine in our Waco apartment. I'm not sure what elixir she used on me, but my co-author couldn't resist linking the notorious inebriant with the law-school instructor of the same sobriquet. So, I've gone along with that, succumbing to his "literary license" and alliterative spin at the end of that last sentence.)

The next morning, I woke up feeling miserable. But with the hangover came, surprisingly, a newfound sense of optimism. Rather than clinging to my hopelessness, I realized that with Becky by my side I'd make something out of my life one way or the other.

It turned out Professor Dawson gave me a D on the test. I hadn't failed. Yet.

With hope somewhat restored, I moved into my final quarter of law school, which included Mad Dog's "practice court" mock-trial exercise.

For some young lawyers-to-be, practice court is as close to courtroom proceedings as they'll ever get. I figured to fall into that group. My plans, if I could successfully navigate the law-school experience at Baylor, was to move back to Bryan with Becky and take up a job at Daddy's bank.

I had not yet discovered my passion for litigation.

In a mock trial, students try a hypothetical case before their fellow classmates. Mad Dog presented each team a fact summary, and it was our job to look up the law and defend or prosecute our position.

In Mad Dog's class, the mock trial included actual opening statements, cross examinations, and testimony from witnesses. Ultimately, much hinged upon our summations and the closing arguments we presented. The class then voted on the outcome of the case.

Mad Dog assigned me a partner who was a worse student than I was.

Realizing our disadvantage, I decided to go talk to a real attorney and seek advice on how my partner and I might pull an upset and win our mock trial.

That attorney was, of course, Bill Davis.

Back in Bryan, Bill gave me good counsel: He told me to relax. Bill knew me well enough to understand I could be my own worst enemy. I suspect Daddy probably lamented to Bill from time to time about his "high-strung" older son. In addition, Bill provided tips on relevant procedural matters we were likely to face and techniques on how to sway the opinions of the classmates who would serve as the jurors in our case.

His final words were simple: "Enjoy the experience."

When it came time for my partner and me to take center stage, we had agreed that I would present the opening statement. In competition with another pair of students, I just tore them up with my remarks.

I'm sure it came as a surprise to the class, but what I had to say was well thought out. It was convincing. It was based on the facts. And as I progressed, I felt a surge of confidence that I had never felt before in *any* kind of academic pursuit.

As I sat down, I thought to myself, "Damn. I can do this!"

I'll never forget that feeling.

The rest of the mock trial went even better.

I suspect now that God had a hand in my endeavors in that course. While I may not have been "brilliant," like Percy Foreman or Bill Davis, I was good, better than I ever imagined. I set witnesses up perfectly, closed the doors down paths I did not want them to go, and took control, as a good attorney is supposed to do.

After it was over and the class voted on the outcome, my partner and I won our mock trial. The margin of victory wasn't even close.

Before leaving class that day, Mad Dog told me he wanted to see me in his office later that afternoon.

Dawson hadn't said much to me during my time with him, and when he did, his words were less than encouraging. Yet, in his office after the mock-trial victory, he was no longer a mad dog.

"Did you tell me you came to law school to be a banker?" he asked.

"Yes, sir."

Without pause, he continued, "You don't need to be a banker, you need to be a trial lawyer because you have what it takes."

Talk about a resurrection!

Dawson's "endorsement" was a tremendous turning point for me. If I could convince Mad Dog that I was capable of successfully trying a case, then I was confident I could actually do so because he had such high standards for excellence.

Professor Dawson died in 2015 at the age of ninety-eight. Each spring, the winner of the Baylor Law School's mock-trial competition receives the "Mad Dog" Award. I am proud today to have been one of his first students.

In preparing to take my bar exam, which was held in Austin on the University of Texas campus, I enrolled in a two-week-long review course. We had some great instructors, and in those two weeks they covered pretty much the entire law-school experience. I took the course seriously and worked hard to ready myself for the task at hand.

In the week preceding the scheduled test date, a couple of my law-school friends and I rented a motel room in Austin and sequestered ourselves morning, noon, and night to prepare for the exam. By the time we were done, I knew more about the law than I had before or, quite frankly, have since.

I was primed.

When I entered the room in the "tu" Student Center (I still can't capitalize those two letters when they stand symbolically alone) where the test would take place, I was surprised by the number of attendees. There had to be at least 400 people there.

The bar exam is a timed event. After issuing preliminary instructions and words of encouragement, proctors handed the test out. As it was placed on my desk, I sat there staring at the cover sheet.

This was my ticket.

A bell rang which indicated we could begin.

I opened the exam booklet and read the first question. In a matter of moments, a familiar sinking spell came over me, and I totally froze.

I looked again at the question, and it was as if it was written in a foreign language. Nothing about it made sense to me. Not a single neural transmitter clicked in my brain, and nothing came out of the pen that was poised above the page.

I moved on to the next question. "What does *that* mean?" I asked myself.

For twenty minutes, as everyone around me wrote frantically, I sat in a semi-comatose state certain of just one thing.

"There is no way I can do this."

After another five or ten minutes of mining the black hole of my legal knowledge—where everything went in but nothing came out—I began to consider just getting up and leaving. I looked over at the friends with whom I had studied so diligently in that Austin hotel room. They, seemingly, had all the answers.

I had none.

At first, I was too embarrassed to give up, remembering my father's insistence that I was not going to be a quitter.

But eventually I did.

I walked out of the room. A proctor eyed me but paid little attention and said nothing. I strolled aimlessly through the hallways of the student center before finding a door and making my exit.

All around me, students went about their daily lives: walking, talking, laughing, with nary a care in the world, each of them oblivious to my humiliation.

Drifting for a time, I felt completely and utterly alone. I didn't know what to make of my circumstance.

And then it hit me. There was someone I could talk to.

"Okay, God," I whispered to myself, walking downtrodden across campus, "What am I going to do now? What do I do with my life?

"I've wasted all my daddy's money on law school, and here I am. I can't pass the bar. I won't become a lawyer. What do I do?"

I nearly walked into the path of a pretty coed pedaling her bicycle from the opposite direction. She swerved to avoid me. I paid the near collision little attention.

"What do I do, what do I do, what do *we* do, God?" I had gotten Becky mixed up in my failures.

I kept walking and began to notice something about the people around me. They all seemed really happy. "How could that be?" I thought to myself, "How can anyone be happy when the world is such a miserable place?"

I thought about that for a while and then came to an important realization: Everyone goes through bad things every once in a while.

I suddenly didn't feel quite so alone.

"How do people get through it when they're down on their luck?" I asked God.

Continuing my quiet conversation, I mumbled, "God, I believe there *are* other things I can do. I don't have to be a lawyer to make a living, right?"

But before this encouraging new line of discussion with my Maker could get started, the familiar sinking feeling returned. The devil had now entered into the dialogue.

Satan was insistent that my plight was hopeless. As the clock was ticking back in the exam room, Satan demanded that I keep heading in the opposite direction.

The devil wanted me to get into my car and go somewhere, anywhere but where I really needed to be.

I rationalized that I couldn't leave just yet. My buddies would need a lift later after they had passed the bar.

Suddenly, God's voice became clear.

"Maybe you can take the exam again. People do that, you know."

A flicker of optimism sparked my imagination.

"If you do take the test again, it might be good to know what to expect. You oughta go back into that room and look through the exam booklet; see what's there. Get an edge on the next time you take it."

God's wisdom made perfect sense to me, although I was a little surprised by the informal manner in which he offered His good advice. I never imagined God using the word "oughta."

Without giving it another thought, I stopped in my tracks, turned around, and trotted back to the student center.

When I got there, I walked back into the room. The proctor who watched me leave probably figured I had been dealing with some intestinal issues in the bathroom and again paid me no mind.

I sat back at my desk. As they later told me, my buddies never noticed my absence, so immersed were they in the work. I picked up my pen, opened my booklet, and turned past the first couple of pages I had seen before.

On page three, a miracle occurred. I found a question I was certain I knew how to answer. I began writing, slowly at first, but the tempo soon quickened.

Before I knew it, I'd finished with that question. Upon turning the page, I found another subject for which I was eminently prepared.

And the hits just kept on coming.

As time expired, I had not only finished the exam–including the first two questions that initially had proven to be stumpers–but as it turned out, I made a damned good grade and became a real attorney.

So, what happened? What made the difference at that crossroads of my life?

As I've said, God spoke to me. It wasn't a "divine intervention" or anything like that. I just let Him come into my presence and have a talk with me. He spoke to me in words that resembled my own thoughts and sent me back into that room to get the job done.

In as emphatic a manner as I've ever experienced, I died there in Austin that day. But, in as dramatic a Resurrection as I've ever had–and far more quickly than is usually God's will–I was Raised and Transformed.

Think about your own life. Aren't there moments and events where you've felt lost and become hopeless? Aren't there times where you have completely given up?

But, look at where you are now. Right now, as you read this book. How did you get here? What has been your journey?

Now think about those times in terms of Death and Resurrection. Consider that Jesus came back from death after His time on the Cross.

My friend, you've come back from the dead, too, and that's the essence of Embracing The Cross. Behind the Cross of Jesus Christ, we can always have Faith that a Resurrection is coming.

13

The Tyler, Texas Wedding Brawl

This is the chapter where I talk about meeting my wife of almost fifty years, so let me clarify the title I have chosen for it.

Becky and I have had a long, loving, and nurturing matrimonial relationship.

Yeah, I can still be a stinker on occasion. There are times, despite my theological wisdom, that I succumb to the imperfect nature of my earthly existence and lose my patience or say something I really shouldn't have said.

But, most of the time Becky takes those things in stride. She's my counsel and my confidante. That's why I call her "Coach." I may be the breadwinner of the family and the spiritual head of our household, but she's the real deal…and the "brawl" referenced in the title to this chapter had nothing to do with us.

It did occur at a wedding, but it wasn't *our* wedding.

Let me explain.

I met Becky Wood from Longview, Texas, in the cafeteria of Penland Residential Hall on the campus of Baylor University in Waco. As an out-of-town law-school student, I lived at Penland, and Becky, an undergraduate coed majoring in education, lived in Russell Hall next door.

The women of Russell took their meals at Penland.

Sitting at a table with friends at lunch one day, I happened to notice Becky sitting with her friends across the room. In that first glimpse, I thought she was the most beautiful woman I'd ever seen.

I still feel that way.

Given that Becky and I took our lunches "together," I saw an opportunity to make her acquaintance without putting myself too much on the line. Like a lot of guys, I was terrified of being rejected by a member of the opposite sex.

Throughout much of my time in high school, I had a terrible problem with acne. My already shaky confidence was further eroded by the fact that with my horrible complexion I bore a striking resemblance to a swamp monster.

By the time I got to college, my zits had cleared, and my social life was improved. Maybe it was also the yellow Corvette I drove, but I did have a girlfriend at A&M.

Nothing too serious, though, as it turned out.

When I finally introduced myself to Becky–and her friends–I was relieved she did not bite. Soon, my friends and her friends started to mingle at lunch.

Even though I was still a little awkward around the ladies, I had a fool-proof tactic to get and keep their attention.

Somehow, someway–probably in the Sbisa Dining Hall on the Texas A&M campus with a few hundred of my closest cadet friends–I perfected the art of flipping a cube of Jell-O off my plate and into my mouth.

Something possessed me to show Becky and her friends that talent, and when I did, they giggled. Later, they even brought over more friends to watch me do it.

I was proud of that skill back then, and while you may chuckle, the fact of the matter is Becky Wood wound up marrying me.

I will say we got off to somewhat of a slow start dating-wise.

The first time I worked up the nerve to ask Becky out, she told me, "I have other plans."

I interpreted her remark to mean she had plans with another fellow. I refused to consider the possibility she wasn't interested in going out with me at all. So, I asked her, "Who do you have plans with?"

Of course, that was none of my business, and she refused to tell me. Later, I found out she had been occasionally dating a guy by the name of Tom Friedman.

"Tom Friedman!" I proclaimed aloud upon learning this key bit of information about Becky.

I knew that son of a gun!

Tom Friedman played basketball for the Baylor Bears.

During my senior year at A&M, I relished time spent at G. Rollie White Coliseum cheering on the Aggie basketball team.

Under head coach Shelby Metcalf, the Aggies were a force that '68-'69 season. The Southwest Conference race that year ultimately came down to two teams: Texas A&M and Baylor.

On a chilly Tuesday night in February, Baylor came to town to meet the Ags. The Bears had edged us 66-65 two weeks before in Waco. Tom Friedman had scored nineteen points in the game, sparking a Baylor comeback from a thirteen-point deficit. Earlier in the season, the Bears had also beaten the likes of both Virginia and Virginia Tech, suggesting they would be a force with which to be reckoned in Southwest Conference play.

In fact, the only thing standing between Baylor and the league title was Texas A&M.

During Aggie home games at Rollie White, members of the Corps stood courtside opposite the team benches. A&M football players, a notoriously rowdy bunch at basketball games, stood behind one of the baskets.

In the second half against Baylor that night, 6'9" Aggie center Ronnie Peret, later to become a member of the Texas A&M Athletic Hall of Fame, stole the ball and on a fast break seemed a shoe-in for an easy layup. Dunks were not allowed in the college game back then.

But as Peret made his move to the bucket, he got clothes-lined—hard—by none other than Tom Friedman.

Friedman's biggest mistake wasn't committing a foul on the play but doing so in front of the A&M football team. Friedman's flagrancy brought the wrath of the 12th Man down on him—hard—from all corners of Rollie White.

A wild brawl quickly ensued—not the one, though, mentioned in this chapter's title—and it involved not only players from both basketball teams, but a contingent of the A&M football players in attendance. Order was finally restored when the Fightin' Texas Aggie Band began playing the "Star Spangled Banner."

Friedman took a beating in that skirmish and was ejected from the game. He had to be helped off the court, and as he limped past, the Corps and I were still screaming for his blood. In reply, Friedman raised his arm and flipped us the bird.

The ensuing cacophony was unlike any other I'd ever heard at Rollie White.

So, yeah, I knew Tom Friedman.

He wasn't nearly good enough to date Becky Wood.

I guess I finally convinced her of that because soon after she initially rejected me, Becky asked me to be her date to a "Sadie Hawkins" event on the Baylor campus. We had a great time, and there has not been another woman in my life since then.

People ask me the secret to being married twenty, thirty, forty— and for Becky and me soon—fifty years.

There is no "secret," really.

When you take your marriage vows, you make a marriage commitment, both to each other and to God. My commitment to Becky was simple: "I'm going to stay with you for the rest of my life. Divorce is not an option. Through 'better or worse,' I'm intending that we will make this work."

In marriage you learn, if you're lucky, that two people can truly become one spirit. Becky is a part of me in the very best sense of the term.

And the biggest thing, of course, is that our marriage gains impenetrable strength by the fact that God reigns at the center of our union

> *"Be completely humble and gentle; be patient, bearing with one another in love. Make every effort to keep the unity of the Spirit through the bond of peace" (Ephesians 4:2-3).*

Becky and I have our moments, our little arguments and disagreements, but in those tiny deaths come the rebirth associated with Forgiveness and Fulfillment. It is from those things that a lasting Love springs forth.

I married Becky in her hometown of Longview, Texas, before I graduated from Baylor Law School. Upon receiving her Baylor degree in education, Becky taught at a Catholic school in Waco until I finished up.

Once I had law school behind me and my presence in Southeast Asia was not required by the United States Army, Becky and I moved to Bryan, where we have lived ever since.

About a year into our marriage, we received a wedding invitation from a friend of mine–who shall remain nameless to protect the innocent. He was getting married in Tyler, which is not far from Longview in East Texas.

My friend's best man and groomsmen, a group in which I was included, were all products of Stephen F. Austin High School. His wife-to-be was from Tyler and came from a big family. I think she had eight brothers, if I remember right.

Upon meeting her for the first time, I was a little taken aback by her demeanor. But my friend seemed happy, and that was all that really mattered.

The wedding went off without a hitch, but the blissful state of affairs surrounding the event did not last long.

As the reception drew to a close, the groomsmen and I busied ourselves decorating our friend's car. You know the routine: a somewhat suggestive shoe-polished message smeared on the back window and tin cans tied to the rear bumper, the whole "just married" thing.

As we were doing that, we heard a commotion coming from near the church. We looked around and saw that the two mothers had come out onto the balcony at the back of the church and were arguing in full view of those of us standing below.

We knew things were getting intense when the mother of the bride, when asking the whereabouts of her daughter's new husband, called him a "son…"

Her exact words were not "son…in law."

Obviously, something untoward had happened at the reception. Our curiosity was piqued.

As the mothers continued to quarrel, the bride's brothers suddenly made an appearance. And they weren't happy, either. Their source of concern seemed to be the decorating job we were completing on the car.

"That's disrespectful," one of them said to us.

"Not your business," I offered.

The meanest looking one in the bunch, who turned out to be a brother-in-law, slowly made his way toward me, stopping inches from my face. The brother-in-law proceeded to give me an earful regarding our handiwork, calling it "disrespectful to the bride." I kept my cool until he uttered what any decent, self-respecting man would consider fighting words:

"You must be a damned Aggie," he hissed right before slugging me in the face.

The donnybrook that ensued was a lively happening. I was immediately pounced upon by several of the bride's brothers. I got in a number of good licks before my chums joined me in the fray. By the time order was restored—local law-enforcement authorities were never called or ignored this kind of thing as a common occurrence in Tyler town—I had a few scrapes, a fat lip, and my rented tuxedo was very much the worse for wear.

You'll be interested to know my friend's marriage did not last long. It was annulled about a year later.

As it turned out, Becky had been a witness to the whole affair. As I dusted myself off, she came up to me and said, "Are you okay?" I feared that she would take exception to my actions, but she seemed to be supportive of my role in the fracas. She was mostly concerned with my well-being.

"Let's go home," she said. Home, in this case, was her parents' house in nearby Longview.

I adored Becky's parents, Ed and Laura Wood. Ed was an Aggie, too, with a degree in engineering. He was a beautiful person, just the kindest and gentlest man. Not once did I ever have a cross word with either one of my in-laws.

When we arrived at their house, it was late. Ed must have heard us drive up because the front porch light came on. I opened the door for Becky and followed her in. Ed was there in the living room, clad in his pajamas and robe.

As he looked curiously at me, he asked, "So, how was the wedding?"

I hemmed and hawed, but Becky cut me off. "It was fine, Daddy. Just fine."

"Looks like you had….a…good…time," he said nodding his head.

I was ready to come clean with him regarding the sordid events of the day, but as soon as I began, Ed cut me off.

"Glad you two made it home safely." He looked at me with a knowing smile. Ed reached out and grabbed my shoulder. He patted me on the back and said simply, "Get some rest, son."

14

Attorney for the Defense

By the time I said my piece about Sandra Day O'Connor, I was two and a half years into my term as Brazos County DA. Not long after that, I told Becky I wouldn't be running for re-election.

As you know about me now, I can have a pretty hard time letting go of things, and such was the case with the O'Connor controversy. I took what others were saying about me at the time pretty hard, and I didn't spend a lot of time in prayer about it.

I guess I had "convicted" myself, rather than seeking the Lord's instruction. This was still a while before I launched into the journey of Biblical enlightenment which led to my spiritual redemption.

Even though I only did it for five years, I believe I turned out to be a pretty good district attorney. In fact, I never lost a case. I got twenty-five convictions and three hung juries which resulted in mistrials.

A jury never acquitted a defendant in a case which I prosecuted.

I knew I had become a good lawyer. But in choosing to give up my role as district attorney, I was sparing myself and my family, or so I thought, the embarrassment of being voted out of office.

So, I decided to do what a lot of former prosecutors do. I went out on my own as a criminal defense attorney. There was a very practical reason I chose that course.

I needed the money I thought I could earn running my own practice.

As a prosecutor, I was a state employee, restricted in my earnings to a specific salary scale. As an in-demand defense counselor, which I was mostly certain I could be, I could make a lot more money.

By this time, Becky and I had three children: Austin, Joel, and Becca. My brother, Tim, with two daughters of his own, was succeeding in the banking business in Houston and was doing a lot better financially than I was.

When it comes to making and managing money, I am not my brother. I am fortunate, however, that my brother is my "keeper" in that regard. Wealth seems to trickle through my hands, but Tim has helped me get a handle on financial responsibility through the years.

For about five months after leaving the DA's office, I practiced on my own. There's good and bad in that. On the one hand, you don't have to share space with anyone else. On the other hand, you don't get to share expenses, either.

As DA, I knew a lot of the attorneys in town. Ultimately, I fell in with a group of men, and we formed the law firm of Youngkin, Catlin, Bryan, and Stacy.

Each of us practiced a different facet of the law. That made us "noncompetitive" with each other. At the same time, each of us regularly met prospective clients with needs outside our own areas of expertise. Thus, we had our own little referral network.

That worked pretty well for the next twenty-five years.

Bill Youngkin and I were classmates at Texas A&M and fellow members in the Corps. His senior year, Bill was "head yell leader" for the university, something he enjoyed discussing with clients and co-workers.

Unlike other colleges, A&M has no cheerleaders or pom-pom girls, dating back to the days when the college was an all-male military school.

The group of five male yell leaders—a highly distinguished and coveted position on campus—are elected each year by the entire student body and serve as the "official spirit organization" for the university.

Former Texas governor and Secretary of Energy Rick Perry was a Texas A&M yell leader.

Bill and I came through A&M, as I have mentioned, at a time of great change.

Enrollment at the school started to plateau around 1960, and then went into a state of gradual decline. President Earl Rudder determined that one of the big issues A&M faced in the sixties was a lack of coeds to attract male students.

Plus, as the Vietnam War escalated, the patriotic notion of service to country became less important to some.

The whole idea of what Texas A&M College had historically represented became a little "outdated."

Plus, being a "college" wasn't helping things, as Rudder learned. Many other institutions of higher learning had started calling themselves "universities." The term purportedly created an impression of something larger and more inviting than a mere "college." Rudder eventually convinced the Texas State Legislature to allow him to make the change. "Texas A&M University" was born in 1963.

Also that year, a year before the Civil Rights Act and at the urging of the vice president–and fellow Texan–Lyndon Johnson, Rudder welcomed the first black students onto the A&M campus.

Two years later, in 1965, my freshman year, Rudder made membership in the Corps optional for incoming male students and, as I've already mentioned, welcomed women to pursue degrees as full-time students on the Texas A&M campus.

Bill was head yell leader during the 1968-69 school year. Elected with him that year was the first "NC" to serve on the yell squad. "NC" stood for "non-Corps." That young man's name was Garry Mauro.

Mauro went on to become Commissioner of the Texas General Land Office under four different governors. He also ran for governor himself, unsuccessfully, against George W. Bush in 1998.

While many of us changed our party affiliations, Garry remained a Democrat in his statewide political pursuits.

Bill always enjoyed telling the story that President Rudder–also a general during his distinguished army career–made him personally responsible for Mauro's wellbeing as a yell leader. Rudder had run into considerable opposition in his quest for open ethnic and gender enrollment at A&M. Even the name change bothered some "Old Ags."

He had learned that traditions died hard at his school.

Rudder wanted to avoid any bad publicity which could come if Mauro wasn't given a fair chance to fulfill his duties as A&M's first "civilian" yell leader.

As you might imagine, it was inevitable that Mauro would somehow "screw up" in the eyes of the Corps. When he did, there was hell to pay for it, not only for Gary, but also for Bill Youngkin.

The fateful day came when Mauro made the mistake of borrowing a belt from one of his friends in the Corps. When other cadets found out about it, Gary received a pretty severe beating for his unintended transgression

If you're not in the Corps, you're not allowed to wear any part of the cadet uniform.

Mauro had just needed something to hold up his pants for yell practice. He was unaware of the strict code of the Corps of Cadets.

The several times that Bill shared this story around the office, he made it clear that the pummeling Mauro endured was nothing compared to the world-class dressing down he was given by General Rudder himself, as well as the commandant of the Corps and a few other adult administrative officers.

"Dereliction of duty," Bill said Rudder called his offense.

Another of my partners in the law firm was Larry Catlin.

People always used to ask me if I really knew the country singer. I would explain my partner's last name is "Catlin," not "Gatlin."

Larry grew up in Mobile, Alabama, and earned his undergraduate degree from Birmingham-Southern College. He went to law school at Southern Methodist University in Dallas and then became an assistant district attorney in both Bexar and Brazos counties. He also became a local city attorney and was a member of the Bryan City Council.

Larry and I attended the First Baptist Church of Bryan together. As a part of our firm, he mostly practiced family law.

Pierce Stacy III, my other former partner, was an outstanding real estate attorney in Brazos County for many years.

I left the partnership when I became a district judge in 2008.

Leaving the DA's office and becoming a defense attorney, even with a trio of partners alongside, created more than a little anxiety in my life in those first years out on my own.

That "fear of failure" thing again reared its ugly head.

As a schoolboy, I was afraid of bringing home poor grades. In high school and college, I feared tarnishing my family's good name. In law school, I was afraid of flunking out. As a DA, I was deathly afraid of losing a criminal case, which is why I never did.

Fear has plagued me all my life, and with that comes residual heartache manifesting itself as anxiety and depression.

Ultimately, the physical and emotional fatigue from those burdens brought me closer to God.

For years I sought solace from other sources. I can tell you now that when you're looking to address real problems in life, every answer is hollow except those that come from the Lord.

On many of the cases I prosecuted, the mental stability of defendants would become a point for debate in the courtroom. In preparing for trial, I frequently would meet with psychiatrists and psychologists, "expert witnesses" hired to help me win.

On occasion, if I was down about something personally, I'd ask a doctor "hypothetical" questions about matters pertaining to my own life. In hindsight, I probably should have sought out my own professional counselor, but pride prevented me from doing that.

A medical doctor once prescribed Prozac for me, and I tried that for two or three years. I put on a considerable amount of weight as a result of the medication, and I don't think it ever really tempered my anxiety.

I know mood suppressant medications like Prozac have done wonders for other people, but it didn't do much for me.

Instead, God had a plan.

Alcohol was a magic potion that one time back in law school. But I've never really looked for answers from a bottle. I've been a social drinker my whole life, but nothing more than that.

I have seen, time and again, what alcohol and drugs can do to a person's well-being and decision-making ability. The majority of accused criminals I've represented–or stood in judgment of– suffered from addiction issues of some kind. When substance abuse is not harnessed and winds up hardening the heart, the final outcome is almost always destructive behavior and the collapse of relationships with family and friends.

The solitary heart becomes a hardened heart. By the Grace of God, my life did not go down that path…but it could have.

As I entered into my late thirties, I had grown weary of my emotional struggles. To put it honestly, I was falling apart.

It wasn't just the demands of my job. My obligations as a husband and father were often overwhelming to me as well. For years I worried about keeping all the balls in my life up in the air.

As young parents, Becky and I dutifully attended church with our children. But as the pressures on me mounted, our attendance became sporadic. Becky went along with that, but she felt strongly that our sons and daughter should be rooted in the Word as much as possible.

She found a woman, Janet Loveless, who held a Bible study for mothers one day a week. Women were encouraged to bring their small children with them, and our kids loved the experience. Becky and our brood got a lot out of their time at the Loveless home, more, I began to think, than they were getting from attending regular church.

In my mid-thirties, after I'd left the DA's office, I became friends with Janet's son, Bill Loveless. At the time, Bill was a general construction contractor in the local area.

Over lunch one day, I shared with Bill a little about my personal and spiritual struggles.

"I know I can be a better Christian," I told Bill. "I wish I could be more patient, but my worries and woes sometimes get so big I can't wait for God to take charge of my life."

"So, you're kind of miserable?" Bill looked at me knowingly.

"Man, that's an understatement," I admitted.

It turned out Bill had been searching for God, too. At the time, he was a little further into his journey than I was in mine.

"Travis, do you know you're not under 'the law'?" Bill said.

"What do you mean?" I laughed. "Until recently, I *was* the law in this town!"

Bill chuckled, too.

"No, that's not what I mean. As a Christian, you don't live under the law. That's not God's way."

I was puzzled but interested and asked him to go on.

What Bill told me was that salvation wasn't a matter of "right and wrong." The path to Redemption–and the Peace that comes with that–wasn't found through acting in the role of a "good Christian."

ATTORNEY FOR THE DEFENSE

"You're under God's Grace," Bill continued. "And that's 'Grace' with a capital 'G.' It's a whole different way of relating to God.

I thought about this for a moment or two.

"You know in your heart that God loves you," Bill continued, "and that Love is what enables you to love others and bear Christian fruit in your life.

"You can't do that through your own human effort," he said.

Bill handed me a book he had brought with him.

"Here, read this."

I looked at the cover: *The Saving Life of Christ*, by W. Ian Thomas.

"Thomas writes about the 'exchanged life,'" Bill told me. "When Christ died, He took all of the trash that we need to get rid of with Him into His death. In exchange for that, His resurrection gave us His Life.

"That's how Christ saves us, by taking all of our fleshly weaknesses and giving us His perfection."

I took the book home and read it. A greater understanding of what Bill had told me at lunch that day soon began to surface in my thinking.

Bill Loveless and his mom are now living in Dallas. In 2001, he joined Exchanged Life Ministries Texas. After three years there, he went out on his own and launched Christ Is Life Ministries.

Let me share something with you from Bill's website at www.christislifeministries.com:

Bill's Personal Journey

Ian Thomas said, "God never intended for you to live the life that only Christ can live in and through you." When I first heard those words in the fall of 1998, I was stunned! Why? I had become a Christian at age 18, but in the ensuing years I believed that it was up to me to live the Christian life with God's help. As a result, I worked for God, trying to be worthy enough to earn His love and to be accepted by Him. It was a life of jumping through religious hoops and hoping to measure up to God's standards for living the Christian life. During that time I had tremendous struggles with inadequacy, fear, and anxiety. I would read the promises of freedom, victory, healing and transformation but none of them were becoming an experiential reality in my life. The abundant life promised by Jesus in John 10:10 seemed unreal and impossible to ever experience.

After 30 years of living this "performance-driven" life, I was exhausted, in despair, and ready to give up! It was at that point that God revealed to me the truth through Ian Thomas that it is not about me living the Christian life FOR God. Rather, it is about God living His life in and through me. As a result, at age 48 I began letting God do this, and He began to make radical changes in my life. The greatest transformation came in the form of freedom from my bondage to inadequacy, fear, and anxiety. As I began to experience His transforming power in transforming my life, my passion grew to share these truths to Christians. I closed my business, and in 2001 I went into full-time ministry to share with others these same life-transforming truths that are so radically impacting my life.

Bill's words of his personal plight in life are a nearly identical description of my own circumstances, both before and after Redemption.

From the Thomas book Bill let me borrow, I branched out, reading other works about the Bible and where the Important Truths reside there. In time, I discovered the theologians and philosophers of the Keswick Convention.

Bill and I attended several Christian conferences together, learning more about the "exchanged life" principle. I was hearing things that had never come up in any church that I had attended, and much of it was making sense to me. So, I kept digging.

I found that God had given me a real desire to learn. On weekends or during a holiday or whenever I had some free time—without shirking my duties to my family or my livelihood—I would pore through Biblical subject matter. I had books stacked upon books on tables all around our house.

Becky and the kids tolerated my new "addiction." The kids occasionally tugged me away from my studies, but sometimes, surprisingly, even they asked pertinent questions about God and His purpose in our lives.

My wife simply wanted me to get better.

That hunger for knowledge became insatiable. I was taken over by the Holy Spirit.

This went on for ten or twelve years.

Before, I had never been much of a reader. It was only in preparing for the bar exam that I ever really immersed myself in books. With this new fire, I recognized that God was instilling in me an awareness and a clarity about His Purpose.

I'm grateful for the Instruction which He provided.

What I've learned is this: Before being exposed to the "exchanged life" principle, I was trying to live under earthly law— self-reliance or "self-effort," as some Biblical scholars like to say— and not by Grace. There is an enormous chasm between those two ways of relating to God. When you're doing it by earthly law, *you* have to be in control of your life.

When you do it under Grace, God is the power. You simply yield and surrender and go with the flow.

Giving up control is one of the most difficult things I've ever done, and I can honestly tell you I'm still a "work in progress." Giving up control is a death to personal ego. A person under earthly law doesn't like giving up control.

How many times have I seen that in a courtroom?

Spiritually, people under earthly law try to please God through their actions: going to church every Sunday, witnessing to others, reading the Bible, and praying every day. I'll bet that's how a lot of you live your lives.

Sorry, Salvation doesn't come from those actions. You have to "die" and let God work His "mystery," as the Apostle Paul described it:

> *I tell you this, brothers: flesh and blood cannot inherit the kingdom of God, nor does the perishable inherit the imperishable. Behold! I tell you a mystery. We shall not all sleep, but we shall all be changed, in a moment, in the twinkling of an eye, at the last trumpet. For the trumpet will sound, and the dead will be raised imperishable, and we shall be changed. For this perishable body must put on*

*the imperishable, and this mortal body must put on
immortality* (1 Corinthians 15:50-53).

My first real breakthrough in understanding came about three
or four years after I met Bill Loveless. I like to think that's the real
starting point for my spiritual story.

Six or seven years later, I had another epiphany of sorts. I built
on that.

Then about twenty years ago I reached an even greater level of
understanding and adopted the principle that I call "Embracing
The Cross."

I don't mean to give the impression that I now know it all…or
that I have given up my day job to preach my beliefs. When I retire
from the bench, I'm planning to devote much more of my time to
doing God's work.

I have a great admiration for the direction Bill Loveless took
with his life. He *did* quit his job and went full-time into the ministry.

He had a very good teacher and role model in his mother.

What makes me a little different–perhaps somewhat unique–is
that I've been able to see the Exchanged Life in action from the
proving grounds of our legal system.

In my work, I know and practice a form of "earthly law." But
time and time and time again, I have been witness to the power of
Heavenly Law in the lives of distraught and defeated human
beings.

That is the law of "*Agape* Love."

Between earthly law and Heavenly Law, mankind wages a
fierce struggle.

I know, because I've gone through that struggle myself.

That's Stephen F. Austin pictured above and William Joel Bryan to the right. Austin led the first American settlement of what would become Texas and is considered the founder and father of the state. Bryan was among Austin's first settlers and, along with being my great-great-grandfather and Austin's nephew, is the namesake for my hometown of Bryan, Texas.

My grandfather, the original Travis B. Bryan, was a self-made success. With only a business college education, he rose through the ranks to become president of The First National Bank of Bryan, and one of the leading citizens in the community.

I may be biased, but my mother, Norma Norman Bryan, was a saint. She had to be to have dealt with her two sons, pictured here. That's my brother, Tim, on the left, and me on the right. With us are our two family dogs, Lupa and Lady.

Grown up and successfully making our way in the world, Tim and I are seen here again with our father, Travis B. Bryan, Jr. Like his father before him, my father also served for many years as the president of The First National Bank of Bryan. This picture was taken in the lobby of Daddy's bank, and the portrait hanging on the wall behind us is of William Joel Bryan.

Perhaps the highlight of my life's athletic endeavors occurred as a senior in high school when I received the "Most Valuable Player" trophy from my Stephen F. Austin High School head football coach, Doyle Weldon. Our team went 3-7 in 1964.

My parents join me as I graduate, both from Texas A&M University and its Corps of Cadets. Mama is pinning on my lieutenant's bar as Daddy looks on. That stern and serious look on my face came naturally and has proven a useful facade in my legal career, as you'll see later.

A statue of my favorite law-school instructor, Matt "Mad Dog" Dawson now stands sentry outside a practice court classroom at the Baylor School of Law in Waco, Texas.

Brazos County voters in large enough numbers favored me as their choice for local district attorney that I earned the office in 1978. As you can see in the photo below, I was a reasonably well organized DA who never lost a case during my four years in office.

BRIARCREST MEMBER GUEST
1983

My dad and I spent a good bit of time golfing together over the years. Briarcrest was the local country club in our hometown of Bryan.

Our children...then and now. That's me, Becky, Becca, Austin, and Joel in the top photo, perhaps commiserating after a Little League defeat. (Becca and Austin don't look very happy, do they?) At bottom is our family today. And yeah, that's a proud pair of grandparents in the mix of three generations of Bryans.

I met this young man when he was just a teenager and in trouble with the law. From that place, Shaun Carney has become a remarkable individual, a caring provider to his family, and a fervent believer in the redemption to be found by Embracing The Cross. He is like another son to me, and I'm proud that he calls me his "dad." That's his own son, Parker, with him in the photo.

With Texas A&M Heisman Trophy winner Johnny Manziel, top, and college football coaching great Mike Leach at bottom.

Seeking justice for all from the State of Texas' 272nd District Court.

Above, a recent photo of my good friend, Billy Carter, and me, sitting at the defense table inside the Grimes County Courthouse in Anderson, Texas, where twice we represented Donnie Sullivan, accused of killing a Walker County deputy sheriff. To the right, with another good friend and legal brother, David Barron, who prosecuted the Sullivan case three times.

My wife Becky and I enjoy our trips to
the Monterey Peninsula of California.
This picture was taken near the Pebble
Beach Golf Links. I can almost hear the
Pacific waves crashing on the rocks and the
seagulls crying overhead. Spend just a day
here, and you'll find yourself closer to God.

I look forward to my future and spending more time bringing others closer to God through the message of The Cross and the Faith in Resurrection Ministry.

15

"Donnie Did It," Part 1

Not long after I'd hung up a 1991 "World's Greatest Golf Courses" calendar in my downtown Bryan law office, I received a phone call.

"Travis, this is Billy Carter."

"Hey, Billy. What's shakin'?"

At the time, Billy Carter—not to be confused with the ex-president's sometimes "cheeky" younger brother—was a criminal defense attorney in Madisonville, a small town about a hundred miles north of Houston in Madison County. I knew Billy and liked him. We remain good friends to this day.

Billy is a native of Madisonville. He played basketball at Lon Morris Junior College in Jacksonville, Texas, before earning a scholarship to Rice University in Houston. As a Rice senior, Billy averaged 2.5 points and 2.6 rebounds a game for the Owls during the 1967-68 season. Always a team player, he mostly came off the bench in a reserve role. He saw enough playing time to earn his varsity letter that year, something a man can be proud of for the rest of his life.

I missed that opportunity myself when I decided to give up playing football at Texas A&M.

Billy received his law degree from the University of Houston.

"Travis, I've got a deal over here that I want to talk about with you, see if you might be interested in helping me."

"I'm listening."

He went on to tell me about his case.

"The guy's name is Donnie Sullivan. He's lived here for several years. He's originally from Mississippi. Pretty popular fellow around town. He's a friend of mine."

"What happened?" I asked.

"He was arrested about a year ago in connection with the shooting death of a Walker County sheriff's deputy. You probably read about it in the papers."

"Oh, yeah," I said, "'Cop killer.' That's never good."

"I'm not sure he did it, Travis."

"How long has he been your client?"

"Technically, he's not my client right now, but I might be put back on the case."

Billy reminded me the shooting had taken place on the night of January 26, 1990, at about 8:30 p.m.

"Early the next morning," Billy told me, "I got a call from Donnie's ex-brother-in-law. It was about 3 a.m. He told me about what had happened."

"How did he find out?" I asked.

Billy fell silent.

"Are you still there?" I asked.

"Yeah," Billy said.

"Here's the thing, Travis. The shooting took place at the home of Donnie's ex-wife."

"That's right. I remember."

Billy continued, "The shooting occurred in her kitchen. The victim was not only a deputy, he was also her boyfriend."

The fuzzy details of the crime were coming into focus for me.

"As I recall, she said she saw the shooter," I said, "and the shooter, she claimed, was her ex-husband?"

"No...and yes. Well, maybe," Billy said.

"She didn't see the shooter?" I asked, puzzled.

"No, the shooting occurred from outside the home. I don't think she could have seen who pulled the trigger."

"And it was a Walker County deputy that was shot, right?"

Billy told me the victim's name was David Stallings.

No relation to Gene Stallings.

"David was a good cop. People liked and respected him," Billy said.

"So, this Stallings guy was killed in the kitchen of Donnie Sullivan's ex-wife's home." As a defense attorney, I was glad Billy had called. From what he was telling me, this case could get very interesting.

"Her name is Becky," Billy told me. "Your wife's name is Becky, too, right?"

"Correct."

"Apparently this other Becky and Stallings had been dating for only a short time."

Suddenly, everything made perfect sense to me, or so I thought at the time.

"Donnie shot his ex-wife's new lover," I summarized on the spot. "Billy, how many times have we seen that happen?"

"Travis, I don't think Donnie is guilty."

"We've got a potential 'crime of passion' here, right?" I said. "What makes you think he didn't commit the crime?"

When he first visited Sullivan in the Madison County jail, Billy told me, Donnie Sullivan seemed like "a pretty cool customer." At least as calm as a suspected killer could be, particularly one believed to have gunned down a law-enforcement officer.

I figured Billy had the experience and innate legal ability, as I did, to quickly size up when a prospective client was and was not telling the truth. If you're in the business long enough of being a criminal defense attorney, you're usually able to get to the heart of a matter pretty quickly.

It turned out Billy previously had been Donnie's defense lawyer, but only for a short time.

Back in Mississippi, Billy said, Sullivan's mother had some surprisingly good contacts within the law-enforcement world. On the advice of someone within the Georgia Bureau of Investigation, she had dismissed Billy as Donnie's lawyer and hired an out-of-state attorney from Atlanta.

As Donnie Sullivan's trial neared, apparently both Billy and his mom were having second thoughts about that decision.

"So, if you don't think Donnie pulled the trigger," I asked, "why do the authorities think he did?"

"Because," Billy replied, "Donnie's ex says that Stallings told her he did it."

"And how would he have known?"

"Well, he was standing in front of the window above the kitchen sink. The shot was fired through that window. And in the moments afterward, he apparently told Becky, 'Donnie did it.'"

"Really," I said, at a complete loss for words.

By the time Billy Carter had called me, Donnie had returned home to Mississippi and was living with his mother while he awaited trial. Usually, when a suspect is charged with killing someone like a sheriff's deputy, the bond amount is beyond the reach of the accused.

Maybe the local judge had tried to do that in this case.

It turned out Donnie's mother had the financial means not only to free her son from jail, but to pay the fees of an expensive big-city defense attorney, although that person was apparently on the verge of being fired.

Billy said he was scheduled to meet Donnie's mother, Frances, in a few days.

"You going there?" I asked of an impending trip to Mississippi.

"No, she's coming here. We're set to meet in Huntsville."

Billy said Donnie's mother had been despondent when she had called him. The fact that her son's murder charge was still hanging over her son's head rankled her.

From what Billy told me, the current defense attorney wasn't doing a very good job.

"His first big mistake was to let Donnie go before the grand jury on his own," Billy said.

We both knew that wasn't a smart move, whether Donnie Sullivan was innocent or not.

"She's apologized for taking me off the case," Billy said of Sullivan's mother. "She's a really nice lady. I think she's divorced from Donnie's dad, and her current husband isn't doing too well health-wise.

"She and Donnie are close."

I told Billy, "If you think I could be of help, I'm glad to be at your disposal."

But first, I had one more question.

"So, you really believe he's innocent?"

Most of my clients through the years I practiced criminal defense law came to me with claims of innocence. A good attorney finds the truth up front and works from there. Many times, in matters where the evidence of guilt is overwhelming, a defense attorney's job is to get a reduced sentence, if possible and warranted.

But all my clients, under the Constitution of the United States and the laws of the state of Texas, deserved zealous representation and a fair trial.

I agreed to help Billy with the Sullivan case, and the two of us drove to Huntsville on the day Frances flew to Texas.

Huntsville is about halfway between Madisonville and Houston's Intercontinental Airport.

Huntsville is also home to seven separate facilities within the Texas Department of Criminal Justice prison system. The most well-known is the "Walls Unit," which welcomed its first inmates in 1849 and is located not far from downtown Huntsville.

The Walls Unit houses the state of Texas death chamber. It's where Curtis and Danny Harris were put to death. Back in the days before lethal injections, Texas executed criminals in an electric chair which was given the name "Old Sparky."

During the Civil War, prisoners fabricated tents and uniforms for Confederate soldiers within the walls of the Huntsville prison.

The lengthiest hostage crisis in American prison history took place at the site in 1974. A good friend of mine, Bob Wiatt, was shot while helping to bring the standoff to an end. Wiatt was a longtime FBI agent based in Bryan. He later worked for me as a DA's investigator before becoming police chief and head of security at Texas A&M.

A bullet-proof vest saved Bob's life in Huntsville. Bob also played a role in a kidnapping case that was turned into a movie, *The Sugarland Express*, directed by Steven Spielberg.

Bob Wiatt was a throwback to the good old days of law enforcement and law enforcement officers.

When Billy and I finally met Donnie's mother, she turned out to be even nicer than Billy had described. She hailed from Okolona, Mississippi, where Donnie had grown up and was now biding his time before trial.

Okolona was named for a local warrior of the Chickasaw tribe. The word means "peaceful blue water." Both Thomas Abernathy and William Raspberry were born there. Abernathy was a racist white Mississippi Congressman who famously opposed the Civil Rights Act. Raspberry was a noted black public affairs columnist and Pulitzer Prize winning journalist who frequently wrote and spoke against racial inequality.

Frances started our meeting by again apologizing to Billy for letting him go as her son's defense attorney.

"That was a mistake," she told Billy and me.

"Donnie's been home with me for several months," she continued. "I sit right across from him when we have our meals. We say our blessing, and then I look him straight in the eye.

"I've asked him repeatedly, 'Donnie, are you telling me the truth?'"

"He says he did not kill this man, and, gentlemen, I believe my son is not only a child of God, but also a man of his word."

Donnie's mother was ready to hire us to represent her son right there on the spot. Burned once, Billy asked a few questions before bringing out the appropriate paperwork from his leather satchel.

Billy later told me that Donnie's mother came up with the funds to pay us by "digging up a sack of money in her backyard."

"That's what she told me," Billy said. "Where do you think that money came from?"

"I don't want to know," I replied.

David Stallings was shot standing over the kitchen sink of a three-bedroom brick home just outside the Grimes County community of Bedias, west of Huntsville. He was gunned down by an assailant outside the house who fired just one shot through a window from nearly point-blank range.

Donnie was arrested in the pre-dawn hours the morning after the shooting occurred. After his divorce from Becky, Donnie had bounced around from job to job and place to place. He finally took up semi-permanent residence at the Madisonville home of a friend.

Donnie and Becky had been divorced for about two years, separating shortly after the birth of their son Beau, whose real name was Donald Wayne Sullivan, Jr.

The Madison County Sheriff's Office incarcerated Sullivan after his arrest and launched the initial inquiry into the crime. Ultimately, both the Grimes and Walker County Sheriff's Departments also got involved in investigating the murder, as did the Texas Rangers. Their unanimous opinion affirmed Deputy Stallings' alleged dying words.

"Donnie did it."

And while a grand jury levied murder charges against Sullivan, it still remained the duty of a jury of his peers in a court of law in the state of Texas to determine his guilt.

Or innocence.

Since no one actually witnessed the crime, except perhaps for the deceased victim, circumstantial evidence would be key in the Sullivan case.

That evidence was plentiful, but conflicting.

The nine-millimeter bullet removed from Stallings' body suggested a somewhat exotic—at least for that time—type of handgun had been used to commit the murder. An investigation of Becky's home, which had once belonged to both Donnie and her, revealed a stash of ammunition in the attic, but the bullets found there were not a match with the one which took Stallings' life.

That did bode well for Donnie's defense; he also had an alibi which made it difficult for him to have even been at the scene of the crime.

Difficult, but not impossible.

Sullivan, along with his son Beau, had made a trip to the Houston area the day of the shooting. Donnie and Becky had joint custody of Beau at the time, and Donnie and Beau were seen at his place of employment, an oilfield services company located in the Houston suburb of Katy. It was there that Donnie had engaged in conversation with a co-worker while fueling his pickup truck for the return drive to the Madisonville area.

That individual later testified that when Donnie and Beau left the grounds, "It was 'dusky dark' at the plant."

For Donnie to have departed there, fought his way through Friday evening rush-hour traffic, and arrived at Becky's house in time to kill David Stallings, it would have required him to have made the drive at a fairly high rate of speed once he cleared the Houston metro area.

In Billy's mind–and I agreed with him–the timing and the distance of that journey made Donnie a less-than-likely suspect…if not for Stalling's dying words.

Plus, there was another mitigating factor: Donnie would have had to bring his son to the scene of the crime.

After his divorce from Becky, Sullivan tried hard to rekindle his wife's affection. The couple had managed a small furniture store in Madisonville but quit their jobs soon after they split. It was common knowledge among their friends that Donnie was determined to win back his ex-wife.

In court, witnesses spoke of the love notes that Donnie would leave for Becky on her car and outside their house. It was determined that, on occasion, Donnie still spent nights with Becky.

David Stallings was an investigator for the Walker County Sheriff's Department, specializing in drug crimes. Huntsville is the county seat of Walker County, and drug trafficking, perhaps because of proximity to the prison units there, runs rampant in the area.

Years later when discussing the amazing twists and turns of the Donnie Sullivan case, Billy Carter and I agreed that we had put our best efforts into representing the defendant, in part because of our affection for his mother, and also because we firmly believed that Donnie was innocent of the crime.

Donnie's mother was a woman with deep spiritual convictions and a large support network of church-going friends. During the ensuing trials–all three of which resulted in hung juries–Frances drove regularly from her home in Mississippi to attend the proceedings, often with church friends along to support both her and her son.

Her pastor became a courtroom regular. His presence was an important factor on Donnie's side.

In meeting Donnie Sullivan for the first time, I was struck by just how outgoing an individual he was. Billy had told me that Donnie had friends all over Madison and Grimes Counties, and, I have to admit, Donnie and I hit it off in a big way right from the start.

I quickly sized up Donald Wayne Sullivan as someone unlikely to have killed a man or to have fabricated an intricate ruse to give the impression of innocence.

The bigger question was: Could Billy Carter and I convince a jury that Donnie was not guilty?

Would they believe the story we intended to tell or the dying words of a respected sheriff's deputy?

David Barron was the local Grimes County district attorney charged with prosecuting the case, set to be heard in the historic and picturesque courthouse located just off the town square in Anderson, Texas, less than thirty miles from my office in Bryan.

Barron believed he had a fairly open-and-shut case against our client, but as we all sorted through the details of the crime, inconsistencies began bubbling to the surface.

Little did any of us know what the next three years held in store.

16

Embracing the Cross...Examination

Let me tell you what makes a good criminal defense attorney.

Rule Number 1: Embrace the "cross."

The cross-*examination*, that is.

The ability to cross-examine a witness is something you must be born with. You can't learn to do it in a fashion that will consistently get results.

An attorney's skill in that regard can make or break her as a defense counsel.

I say "her" because the gender gap in the world of criminal defense attorneys has been closing...slowly.

According to a report sponsored by the American Bar Foundation and the Commission on Women in the Profession, thirty-one percent of lawyers appearing as lead defense counsel in criminal cases are women.

So, what I'm describing here is not the exclusive domain of men like me.

What is the purpose of cross-examination? To get to the truth, of course. But, for attorneys on both sides of a case, the aim is to cast doubt on a witness's veracity in the collective mind of a jury.

In a criminal trial, the prosecution *always* has the "home-court" advantage. Juries are predisposed to believing those accused of a crime are guilty of committing it. There's not a court in the land where this isn't the case. It's the prosecutor's job to maintain that mindset, while the task of the defense counsel is to create "reasonable doubt."

The Texas Penal Code states, "all persons are presumed to be innocent and no person may be convicted of an offense unless each element of the offense is proven beyond a reasonable doubt."

Jurors are people, and almost all people have biases.

A juror may try to do his or her best to maintain impartiality during a trial, but as soon as the accused and the attorney for the accused step into the courtroom for the first time, the needle on the "bias meter" begins to swing.

As a defense attorney, it was my job to get that needle to point in the other direction.

"Beyond a reasonable doubt." Those words separate America from much of the rest of the world.

I like to think that there is a difference between "innocence" and "not guilty."

Innocence, to me, is freedom from guilt. "Not guilty" refers to the presence of reasonable doubt.

When I was a practicing criminal defense attorney, cocktail party conversations would frequently turn to my line of work. "How do you represent those 'crooks'?" people would ask.

My response was usually something like this:

"What if you were arrested? Would you be okay if I took you by the hand and led you to the courthouse and told them, 'Here, this person is guilty. I know, because based on what he told me, he sounds guilty'?

"No, of course not."

My job was to defend the accused legally and righteously under the laws of our land because that's one of the things that makes America great.

It's called the Sixth Amendment to the United States Constitution.

I'd include the entire U.S. Constitution in this book if I could, but you can find it online.

Here's the key component of the Sixth Amendment, which was ratified in 1791 as part of the United States Bill of Rights:

In all criminal prosecutions, the accused shall enjoy the right to a speedy and public trial, by an impartial jury of the State and district wherein the crime shall have been committed, which district shall have been previously ascertained by law, and to be informed of the nature and cause of the accusation; to be confronted with the witnesses against him; to have compulsory process for obtaining witnesses in his favor, and to have the Assistance of Counsel for his defence.

The spelling of "defence," as shown above, dates back to the late 18th century. The meaning is as relevant today—perhaps even more so—as it was when created by our Founding Fathers.

I never had reservations about representing someone who was guilty, because everyone, each and every person who falls under the laws and jurisdictions of the United States of America, deserves a fair trial. I believe that if we compromise the Sixth Amendment—and I see and read evidence of that all the time—we risk the sanctity of the entire Constitution.

Any criminal defense attorney who won't represent someone they believe to be guilty should find another line of work.

So, what is the role of defense attorneys when they know their client is in the wrong?

For me, that is a legal question and not a moral one.

Remember, the benchmark is "innocent until proven guilty." I always believed my client deserved the right to be proven guilty beyond a reasonable doubt. In representing clients who told me they committed a crime, my job was to see that if a jury found them guilty beyond a reasonable doubt, they received a just sentence for their crime.

Sometimes, the best way to do that is to plead "not guilty" and put the burden of proof on the state.

As a former prosecutor, I understood it was my duty to prove my case, and in my attempts to do so I looked not only for proof of wrongdoing, but also flaws in the evidence and testimonies presented to the court by the defense.

As a defense attorney—and as someone who holds truth sacred—I never told a client to lie. For starters, lying under oath is called perjury, and it is against the law. I never told a client point-blank what to say, either, but sometimes I worked with them on *how* to say what was important in their case.

Foremost in my efforts, I used every legal avenue available to protect my clients. My principal duty as their attorney was to be their advocate through the entire legal journey, because if he or she did not have an advocate working on their behalf, in a system that's designed to be adversarial, then the Sixth Amendment becomes a meaningless construct.

Do we always get it right? No. Innocent people sometimes go to jail. I had one client who was accused of molesting his daughters, and I believe to this day, with all my heart, that he was not proven guilty of the charge. And yet I failed in his defense to convince his jury...that it was not beyond a reasonable doubt.

The keys to being a good defense attorney are not unlike what makes anyone a success doing anything. Work hard, know the facts, be creative, and present your side of the case with passion, conviction, and certainty. In addition, a well-prepared attorney needs to be ready with all the law that could come into play.

Most importantly: Find the flaws in the story the other side is trying to tell.

Being an effective defense attorney means long hours and a tireless pursuit of the facts in a case. You can never overwork in preparing for a trial. The more time you put in, the greater likelihood you will find a "theme" to your case, a way to present it that will best serve your client's interests.

Although I've never been on a theatrical stage, I'm told that an actor can't really "act" until he or she learns his or her lines. Good actors go beyond memorizing and develop a real understanding of their characters' motivations. The same holds true in a court of law.

To present a case effectively, a defense attorney can't be fumbling for facts or shuffling through notes. The jury will never buy that performance. A good lawyer will not only know the facts, but also understand completely how those facts play into the storyline he or she is attempting to create.

In essence, you must "become" your case, and a good defense attorney will strive hard to outwork the opposition.

I was always willing to do that. Maybe it's because I played football for Gene Stallings for one year. Or went through Practice Court with Mad Dog Dawson.

Before I share with you the techniques I used for "embracing the cross-examination," let me tell you about another important facet of a trial: the selection of a jury.

During a trial, everything that is said and done is directed toward the twelve men and women sitting in the jury box.

How those jurors think during a trial is influenced, at least somewhat, by what goes on during the process of selecting the jury panel.

A lot of lawyers, both prosecutors and defenders, try to impress prospective jurors during jury selection. For me, that was the wrong approach. Given my cockiness as a young attorney, I tried that ploy early on with very poor results.

In time, I learned to make myself vulnerable during *voir dire*, or jury selection. The literal translation of that French phrase is "to see, to say."

The truth which attorneys are seeking during jury selection relates to bias, past experiences, present knowledge, and anything else which might prevent a prospective juror from sitting in judgment of another human being in as neutral a manner as possible.

In addition, I also sought to gauge the personality of prospective jurors and determine, as best I could, if I could bring them around to our side of the case.

Each side in a felony case can strike up to ten jury prospects. The process is less about finding the jurors you want and more about finding those individuals you don't think can be fair to you.

Courtroom movies rarely spend much time on the presentation of evidence, although that part of a trial is important. When I pounded the floor with the tire jack used in the killing of Tim Merka, I was attempting to create an emotional reaction in the hearts of the jurors. I wanted to put them at the scene so they could see and feel the horror.

Rarely in real life do attorneys do such "theatrical" things during a trial.

In my mind, Johnny Cochran did a helluva job with his famous plea to the jury in the O.J. Simpson trial.

"If it doesn't fit, you must acquit."

This is a great theme: short, succinct, rhyming, memorable, and repeatable. Shame on the prosecutors in that case for letting that glove make its way into the proceedings.

Much of the drama of what goes on in the courtroom during a criminal trial, both on the screen and in real life, comes from the opening and closing statements and the cross-examination of witness testimony.

The opening statement provides attorneys a chance to preview the story they intend to tell. In the last Sullivan trial, my opening statement lasted ninety minutes. The closing summation seeks to recap that story, oftentimes revised and made more complicated, given the many twists and turns a trial usually takes.

Easily the most famous movie line from a cross-examination scene is that of actor Jack Nicholson in the film, *A Few Good Men*.

"You can't handle the truth!" Nicholson bellows on the silver screen.

And Jack was right.

Many state's witnesses have a hard time handling the truth.

One thing that I've learned in my years of courtroom experience is that there are very few rigorous "truth-tellers" in this world. Despite swearing on the Bible to speak "nothing but the truth," most people on the witness stand will exaggerate or lie when forced into a tight corner, or when trying to give *their* version of the truth.

And that's okay, because it's the job of the criminal defense attorney, not only to seek the truth, but also to find the lies told in a courtroom, whether large or small.

The duty of a prosecutor, on the other hand, is slightly different. When a grand jury finds sufficient evidence to bring up criminal charges against an individual, the prosecutor's job is not to win the case, but to seek a just outcome. And just like a football or basketball coach, if a prosecutor loses too much of the time, he or she will be looking elsewhere for work.

The most damning testimony in most cases is that of witnesses called by the prosecution. Usually, these are people who either saw the purported crime, or whose experiences with the accused reinforce past behaviors somehow related to the likelihood of committing the crime. Sometimes, witnesses called by the defense speak to the character of the accused in the hope their testimony will lead to exoneration, or in the worst-case scenario, positively impact the punishment stage of a trial.

The thing I enjoyed most as a defense attorney was cross-examining the state's witnesses. I learned not to spend a lot of time on the "truth-tellers," but since they are such a rare breed, I got to spend a lot of my time playing "cat and mouse" with everyone else.

With the truth-tellers, the best course is sometimes, "No questions, Your Honor."

One key to cross-examination is listening—*carefully*. To be a good defense attorney you must be a good listener. Some attorneys are too busy thinking of their next question to actually pay attention to the answer to the one they just asked.

On the other hand, my favorite witnesses were the people who spend all their time trying to figure out where I was heading with my line of questioning. Almost always, they would jump to cut me off before I got to where they thought I was going. I learned to handle those individuals by sort of faking my intent. Their efforts to circumvent my line of questions usually put them right where I needed them to be—in the middle of a lie.

Occasionally during cross-examination, I would call into doubt the character of a witness. Witnesses hated that, and it would drive them into fudging on the truth. For whatever reason, most of us like to embellish our stories, and in the courtroom, a lot of witnesses actually make their testimony bigger than it needs to be. As an attorney, when you know your case well, you see those embellishments spring forth quite frequently. When you do, you pounce on them to gain an advantage.

As we say here in Texas: "If you can find one cockroach in a barrel, you can bet you're likely to find a lot more."

Same thing goes for lies in the courtroom.

Another way to get ahead in cross-examination is to play on the egos of witnesses. Big egos can also lead to blind spots. It's easy to spring a trap on a blind person.

The essence of cross-examination is to seek out a witness's lie and then use that lie to contaminate their entire testimony. Most people won't do business with a fellow who has a stain on his tie or isn't freshly shaved. That stain and those whiskers don't mean he's incapable of offering a good product at a fair price, but it does diminish his ability to convince his customers of the great deal he has for them.

People are funny that way.

Another element to success as a defense attorney is anticipating weaknesses in your case.

You can't cross-examine your own witnesses unless they become hostile to you while on the stand. I've called witnesses to testify with the intentional purpose of eliciting "hostility" so that I could, in turn, cross-examine them, enabling me to bring out the weak points in my case proactively, rather than having to backpedal when the other side made those discoveries.

We call taking the sting out of someone's version of the truth "inoculation," getting ahead of hurtful testimony that can be a distraction to your case.

For example, I had one client accused of sexual assault against a woman. That client was a good-looking college student, someone you wouldn't expect to see as a defendant in a criminal case.

Looks can be deceiving, but so too can the "facts" in a case such as this one.

Given my initial stance against Sandra Day O'Connor, I might seem an unlikely supporter of today's #MeToo movement. The fact is I'm a strong advocate for justice and a proponent for those who are truly victims of crimes to exercise the right to step forward and demand justice. Remember, I was a district attorney for five years representing victims, but I also believe in the rights of the accused as well.

In the case of this particular young man, I was hired by his parents to defend him. As I always did, I spent a great deal of time getting acquainted with him to determine the likelihood of innocence. Eventually, the story he told convinced me he was not guilty of the charges against him, but blameworthy of being something akin to a narcissist.

There's usually a degree of narcissism tied to those who pride themselves in being a "ladies' man," and in my view such was the case with this individual.

Ultimately, I decided my best defense would be to prove that my client was a "love 'em and leave 'em" kind of guy. That meant I needed to call some of his past girlfriends to testify to prove that point. And I did so, certain they would lash out at him and turn "hostile" toward my line of questioning. This would enable me to cross-examine them and get to the truth I wanted the jury to hear.

My understanding of the law includes the fact that it is not illegal to be a jerk. It's merely bad form and ungentlemanly behavior.

Neither my client nor his parents were keen about this approach at first, but when I convinced them that a conviction was a real possibility, punishable by an extended period in prison, they eventually agreed to my plan.

And sure enough, it didn't take long for the trio of ex-girlfriends who testified to express contempt toward my client for his past behavior. I was able to call each of them back to the stand later as hostile witnesses.

Each of their stories was the same: sex with my client was consensual, but he was sorely lacking in his ability to offer even the hint of a true commitment to them.

My client was eventually found innocent of his alleged crime.

I can't say whether or not he learned anything from his experience, but I do know that I hated to see the toll the trial took on his accuser.

I miss the thrill of being a trial lawyer. On the other hand, I do not miss the intense and never-ending preparation which each case required. I think being both a prosecutor and defense attorney have made me a better and more fair-minded judge.

Texans as a whole have always been known for their fondness of "hanging judges." My beloved home state has gained an international reputation for being tough on crime and particularly tough on killers.

"Try 'em and fry 'em," they used to say here. That was back when the Walls Unit in Huntsville put "Old Sparky"–the facility's electric chair–to frequent use.

As someone who morally opposes the death penalty, I am not to be confused with the hanging judge.

In fact, I gained a little more notoriety recently–to go along with the Sandra Day O'Connor thing–when I recommended reversal of a death-penalty verdict handed down by a jury in a murder case I heard in my own courtroom.

To my knowledge, this action may be unprecedented in the annals of appellate law.

The case involved a Marine Corps veteran who shot and killed his former girlfriend and her brother in their home here in the Bryan-College Station area in 2009. Both victims, as well as the vet, were students at Texas A&M University.

After committing the murders, the ex-soldier, who had seen combat duty in Iraq, immediately called authorities and confessed to the crime.

There was no question of guilt in the case. The only arguable matter was whether the defendant's post-traumatic stress disorder was a mitigating factor in the jury's rendering of the death penalty for the crime.

The effects of post-traumatic stress disorder, or PTSD, was briefly discussed during the trial, but as I watched and listened, I found that the matter was poorly presented, and little effort was made to show the significance the condition can have on the human psyche or its effects on the actions of the accused.

A judge can't call a "time out" during a trial, unless it's to discuss matters pertaining to procedural issues or interpretation of the law.

After the jury completed its deliberation in the punishment phase of the soldier's trial, I was handed a note. "The jury has reached a verdict," it read. Duty-bound, I read the verdict proclaiming the death sentence into the court record and gaveled the proceedings to a close.

That was the summer of 2010.

Death sentences in Texas are automatically appealed, and while the Sixth Amendment speaks to the accused's right to a speedy trial, the wheels of justice on appeal can grind much more slowly.

Four years later, in 2014 I took the unprecedented act of requesting that the defendant be given a new trial on punishment in the case, based on the ineffective representation of the client by his attorneys.

In my filing to the Texas Court of Criminal Appeals I stated:

> - *The defense did not start an investigation into the accused's Post Traumatic Stress (PTS) until a few months leading up to the trial, a year after the lawyers were retained as counsel.*
> - *The accused's counsel did not get the assistance of an expert witness or witnesses qualified to explain mitigating impacts of PTS.*
> - *The defense's ultimate presentation of information on PTS, including specific information on how it may have affected the accused, was "significantly incomplete."*
> - *The investigation and presentation of evidence that the Department of Veterans Affairs failed to properly*

diagnose and treat the accused for PTS "fell below the norms of professional standards for capital counsel."

- Defense counsel did not present sufficient evidence that accused would not pose a future danger to others, one of the three questions the jury is asked to answer in choosing life in prison or death as a penalty.

- The defense did not speak to witnesses of an incident the accused was involved in during his high school years that would have disputed a prosecution witness' account, nor did they cross examine the witness. The incident was used by the prosecution to convince the jury that the accused had violent tendencies before his war service.

- The accused's attorneys were ineffective during the jury selection process in fighting for and against potential jurors who could have helped or hurt the defense in the deliberations.

- The defense didn't present enough evidence concerning the accuser's family's history of mental illness.

- Defense counsel didn't raise the issue of mental illness in its opening argument in the punishment phase.

- The defense attorneys didn't object to a prosecutor's comment about the accused's stepfather's World War II service and PTS during closing arguments in the punishment phase.

My request to the Texas Court of Criminal Appeals ultimately was denied, and when the appeals hearing in the actual case finally took place in December of 2018, I was no longer involved. I had recused myself from the proceedings, having contributed to the political campaign of one of the original defense attorneys in the case, Michelle Esparza, who was campaigning to become a judge herself. While I thought the defense counsellors could have done more in exploring the PTSD aspect of the case, I still held—and continue to hold—both of them in high personal esteem.

In fact, the lead defense attorney in that trial was Billy Carter, my partner in the defense of Donnie Sullivan.

As a judge, I am not allowed to offer advice or "coach from the sidelines." I kept silent as long as I could regarding my concern about the sentence handed the murderous ex-Marine. Then, finally, my conscience got the best of me.

I remember squirming a lot during the trial of that ex-soldier, thinking what I would have done to ensure the Marine veteran did not receive the death penalty.

I guess a little of the defense attorney lives in me still.

And my desire for justice, for both victims and persons accused, remains as strong as ever.

While it took several years after the original trial, the panel of judges which heard the appeal in the case upheld the death-penalty verdict, and that young Marine now sits on Death Row awaiting execution.

17

"Donnie Did It," Part 2

Writing this book has given Billy Carter and me a chance to look back on the Donnie Sullivan case and reflect in both amazement and wonder.

Honestly though, we've been doing that on and off for the better part of the last thirty years. The case was unlike anything either of us had ever experienced, before or since.

Regarding the Sullivan case, Billy and I are both a little vague about some of the details of the series of trials which sought Donnie's conviction. As the lead defense attorney in the case, Billy kept all the records, which, I think were eventually relegated to his garage or a storage unit somewhere. He now practices criminal defense law in Bryan, so we bump into each other at the courthouse frequently.

Billy remains a great friend.

In offering his help with this book, Billy found the transcripts from the first two trials among the records he's preserved on the case. What he doesn't have and has been unable to locate at the Grimes County courthouse are the transcript records of the third and final trial.

Billy is a great friend and a fine defense lawyer. He's tall with longish gray hair and he keeps a smile on his face pretty much all the time when he's outside the courtroom. Like so many from Madisonville, where he grew up, Billy possesses a real Texas charm, and people seem to gravitate toward him. So much so, in fact, that when we teamed up on the Sullivan case, it quickly made sense for him to play the proverbial role of "good cop" in our collective efforts.

I agreed to be the bad guy, or "bulldog," as I preferred to be thought of. I'm sure that's why Billy asked me to work with him on the case. He knew my reputation as, if you'll pardon the expression, "a badass."

Heading toward the first trial in the late summer of 1991, Billy and I were hopeful we could find a way to counter what seemed to be the prosecution's ace in the hole: Donnie's ex-wife's account of the shooting.

"Donnie did it," were David Stallings' dying words, according to Becky Sullivan in her initial account of what transpired on that fateful final Friday in January of 1990.

Divorced from a husband accused of murder and mourning the death of a new suitor potentially gunned down by her ex, when it came time for Becky to testify in Donnie's first trial, she had a new name: Rebecca Broussard.

In the year and a half after the shooting, Becky had married a real-estate developer from nearby Willis, Texas. Rebecca, her legal name, and Rob Broussard have been married ever since, nearly thirty years.

After his divorce from Becky, Donnie was given visitation rights to spend time with his son, Beau. And Beau was with his father the night the shooting occurred. Our contention as the defense team was that Donnie might have had motive to shoot Stallings, perturbed as he was likely to be that his ex-wife had a new boyfriend, but he wasn't the kind of person who would have brought his three-year-old boy with him to kill another man.

After Donnie was arrested, Beau was taken to one of Becky's relatives to spend the next few days. His mother was, needless to say, distraught not only about what she had seen, but also the ramifications of her accusation.

The testimony of young children in a court of law was then and remains now a slippery legal slope. What kids have to say–if they say anything–is easily influenced by others and, thus, is sometimes considered unreliable. In fact, scientific studies have determined that most children can be made to believe–and say– almost anything.

Authorities did talk with Beau after his father's arrest, and the only information of interest which came from that conversation were these words: "Daddy drive fast down dirt road."

That led to other obvious questions which Beau could not answer: Did Daddy drive fast that night or simply in general? On what dirt road did Daddy drive?

Beau, of course, couldn't clarify. Still, his words sent a chill down my spine, even if they would be easy to deflect if they came up during court proceedings, which they did not.

A shell casing believed to be from the murder weapon was found outside Becky's home. Ejection marks on the casing provided possible identification of the handgun used in the shooting. When Donnie had lived in the Bedias home with Becky, he had kept ammunition in the attic and had not removed it when he and Becky divorced. Investigators could not match that reserve with the fatal projectile.

Later, a bullet matching the one recovered from the deceased's body was discovered in a tray in the back seat of Donnie's truck. While damning at first glance, Billy and I learned the bullet didn't turn up until a *fourth* detailed search of the vehicle. That significantly impacted the credibility of the find.

In fact, we believed—and told the court—that the bullet had been planted in Donnie's pickup, which of course suggested the possibility of a conspiracy against the accused killer.

There were several other puzzling attributes to the case.

One of the biggest mysteries had to do with an "off-duty" firearm present in crime scene photos on the floor near where Stallings collapsed after the shooting. While Stallings may have pulled the weapon in an attempt to defend himself and Becky from the gunman, his weapon ultimately disappeared.

What was even more troubling was the missing page from the Walker County Sheriff's dispatch log documenting seizure and storage of that weapon.

Was the missing page an honest mistake? Did someone else investigating the crime borrow the logbook and fail to return it intact? Were the missing page and the missing gun somehow connected?

Most critically to our defense: Was someone somewhere hiding something?

Those questions puzzle me more now than they did during the time we were defending Donnie.

In speaking with members of both the Walker and Madison County Sheriff's offices, we learned of yet another curious facet to the case.

While the crime was committed in Grimes County, Sullivan was arrested at his residence in nearby Madison County and taken to the Madison County jail.

Stallings was a sheriff's deputy in Walker County. Geographically, Grimes is west of Walker County, and Madison County is north of Walker County.

After Donnie was arrested, it is customary for law-enforcement officers to do gunpowder residue tests when the individual is believed to have discharged a firearm. As the Madison County deputies were performing their test on Donnie, Walker County Sheriff Dale Myers called to get an update on the case. When he learned that only one of Donnie's hands had been processed and had come up negative, he insisted the other hand not be tested.

Which begs the question: Why?

We presented these findings at Donnie's first trial, which got underway on July 24, 1991. That trial was delayed when, during the process of jury selection, one of the prospective jurors informed the entire jury pool, "We discussed this case at the feed store and pretty much decided the ol' boy did it."

Judge William McAdams was forced to dismiss that panel, which delayed proceedings a week or two.

By the time Donnie's first trial got underway in Anderson, Texas, it had been nearly eighteen months since the shooting. In that period, Donnie was released on bond, after which he moved back home to Mississippi. Becky remarried, and she and Beau moved in with their new family. Residents throughout Central Texas remained eager for the trial to begin, hoping justice could be done for the deceased law-enforcement officer.

During all three trials, many of our defense witnesses spoke of Donnie's character and easy-going manner. The prosecution's witnesses, meanwhile, painted a slightly different picture of the man. While everyone agreed Donnie didn't seem like a cold-blooded cop-killer, a strong difference of opinion arose as to whether or not Stallings could have actually seen his assailant through a double-paned glass window in the dark of night.

And, if he could, would he know what Donnie Sullivan actually looked like?

Based on what Donnie had told everyone, he had never met Stallings. The prosecution found a witness, the wife of a Walker County deputy, who claimed she had seen the two men together in a parking lot near the school in Anderson where Becky had taught.

Donnie denied that meeting took place. Early on in preparation for the first trial, Billy and I had agreed that we would not put Donnie on the witness stand to offer his side of any part of the story. His denials in front of a grand jury had proven ineffective. Donnie's cause would not be aided by allowing him to testify

And through the three trials of Donald Wayne Sullivan, he did not do so.

We've already discussed the Sixth Amendment to the Bill of Rights. Let me remind you of what the Fifth Amendment says:

> *No person shall be held to answer for a capital, or otherwise infamous crime, unless on a presentment or indictment of a Grand Jury...; nor shall any person be subject for the same offence to be twice put in jeopardy of life or limb; nor shall be compelled in any criminal case to be a witness against himself, nor be deprived of life, liberty, or property, without due process of law; nor shall private property be taken for public use, without just compensation.*

While employing Fifth Amendment privilege is every citizen's right, the act of "pleading the Fifth" is not really a good idea, because in uttering the words, "on the ground it may tend to incriminate me," it sure seems like that individual might have something to hide.

Keep in mind, too, what the Fifth Amendment says about "double jeopardy." Remember, Donnie was tried *three* times on the same murder indictment.

One of the key issues in the first trial was whether or not Stallings could have seen his assailant at night outside the home. Billy and I claimed, after visiting the scene of the crime ourselves, he could not have. Standing in the kitchen after dark, the only things visible through the kitchen window were reflections from inside the house.

Becky moved out of the house shortly after the murder. She then met her husband-to-be and got married.

By the time Billy and I revisited the home to conduct our "inside" investigation before the first trial, another woman had moved in. She was hesitant about letting us look around her property and was particularly resistant to allowing us to conduct our investigation inside her home at night, but eventually she agreed.

On our first visit, we didn't take up much of the woman's time. I stood inside the kitchen; Billy walked outside and assumed a position near where investigators believe the killer fired the fatal shot.

I could not see Billy in the dark outside that window.

Of course, no prosecutor would be willing to allow a jury to take our word for what we saw, so we made a second trip to the home with a videographer in tow.

Again, same results...or so we thought.

In the days leading up to the trial, the videographer sent Billy a note. Billy relayed the contents of the message to me at lunch.

"The camera guy says he *could* see out the window," Billy told me. "I'm not sure why he's bringing this up now." We had reviewed the content with the videographer weeks before.

"He says he thinks he could see a figure outside the window," Billy said. "He says the human eye can see better in high-contrast lighting conditions than a video camera."

"What the heck does that mean?" I asked.

"I think it means that, given the difference between the illuminated kitchen and the darkness outside, people can see into the darkness better than a camera."

Billy and I sat there for a moment pondering this new development. Both of us were perplexed and frustrated at this turn of events.

We had hoped the video footage would give us a definitive edge in proving that Stallings could not have identified his killer.

"We can't bring up the video in court," Billy said. "When they cross-examine the camera guy and he tells them he could see out the window, that's not going to play well with the jury. We're going to have to let that go."

"I don't think we should," I calmly replied.

"What do you mean?" Billy asked.

"They'll never cross-examine him," I said.

Billy looked at me curiously. "What makes you say that?"

"Because they'll be too scared to." I said.

Billy shook his head and pondered the position I was putting forth. He remained steadfast in his desire to keep the videographer out of the equation. In order to show the video in court, we would have to call the individual who shot the footage to testify.

For the one and only time during our years representing Donnie Sullivan, I stood firm against Billy in my opinion. I was usually afraid to argue with Billy because he was a great strategist.

"The video paints a pretty clear picture that looking out the window reveals nothing. When we play that video in court, there's nothing the prosecutor's going to do. He won't want to cross-examine the cameraman because he'll think the guy will corroborate what the jury will have already seen.

"Never in a million years would Barron think the videographer we hired as the defense team would refute his own video."

In court, we presented the video and questioned the videographer, being careful not to give him an opportunity to bring up his own personal viewpoint from the night he shot the footage.

When the judge offered District Attorney Barron the opportunity to cross-examine, he replied simply, "No questions, Your Honor."

Instead, Barron brought the new homeowner to the stand. Billy and I did not expect that, and when she was asked about our visit to the house, her response stunned us.

"I can see out that window at night," she told the court. She went on to explain how long she had lived in the house and how much time she spent in her kitchen. She told Barron a variety of other things designed to make her testimony convincing.

In my cross examination, I nearly brought her to tears. I regretted doing so, but much was on the line in her testimony.

So "rigorous" was my line of questioning, Judge McAdams ordered a recess. During the break and outside the presence of the jury, I overheard him try to console the witness. "You've done nothing wrong," he told her.

"Nothin' except lie," I added, making sure both the judge and the witness could hear me. I did not want her to feel comforted by the judge's words.

Back at our counsel table before the proceedings resumed, I looked over at Billy. He had a mischievous look in his eye.

"What's up with you?" I chuckled. "What devious thoughts are you thinking now?"

Billy is not normally a devious person.

"Travis," he whispered to me, "let's ask the judge to take the jury out there and let them have a jury view through that window at night."

A jury view is a "field trip" on which the entire jury panel is taken to the scene of a crime. In Texas, it's been disallowed in a court of law since the late 1800s.

"The judge will deny that motion in a heartbeat," I said, stating the obvious.

Billy said nothing. The grin on his face seemed to encourage me to think outside the box.

Suddenly, it hit me. "What a great idea!" I said.

"Let me handle this," I added. Billy nodded in agreement.

We both knew what would happen next, and it did.

Once Judge McAdams gaveled court to order, I stood and, as Billy had suggested, asked for a jury view "so they can see with their own eyes what we've seen in the video presented here today."

In leaping to his feet to object, Barron nearly toppled over his chair.

"Sustained." McAdams then explained to the jurors that jury views were not admissible evidence in Texas.

But a point in our favor had been succinctly and effectively made. So certain were Billy and I that Stallings could not have identified the shooter in the dark of night, that we had invited the jury to see that fact for themselves. Even though the judge would not allow it, we felt the jury had to be convinced that our conviction was strong.

Following deliberations in Donnie Sullivan's first trial, the jury could do no better than nine votes for conviction and three votes against. A guilty verdict requires unanimity among the jurors.

With the jury hung, a mistrial was declared.

Although Donnie wasn't acquitted, we had won the first round for our client.

Sullivan's second murder trial began six months later on January 15, 1992. The result was identical to the first trial: nine of the new jurors were convinced of Donnie's guilt while three were not. The prosecution had laid out basically the same case with the same evidence and witnesses. They brought in their own video expert, but to no real avail. On our side, we followed pretty much the same game plan as before, and we got the same result.

No less an expert than Albert Einstein once said the definition of insanity was doing the same thing over and over again and expecting different results. But there was one noticeable difference between Donnie's first and second trials: the testimony of Rebecca Broussard.

In the first trial she had been emphatic in recounting Stallings' dying words: "Donnie did it."

Testifying in the second trial, she offered a slightly different take on what she heard her boyfriend say that night.

"What were Deputy Stallings' exact words after he was shot?" Prosecutor David Barron asked Becky on the stand.

She paused and gave Barron a somewhat odd look before answering the question.

"I'm not real sure," she said, "I think he *might* have said, 'Donnie did it.'"

18

The Spiritual Nature of Golf

The Bryan family's love for golf goes back generations. Not quite as far back as Stephen F. Austin; he died in 1836, and the first golf course in America didn't come along until 1893 in Chicago.

The first country club in Texas was established in Galveston in 1898, but two years later, the Great Hurricane of 1900 destroyed both the golf course and the clubhouse, and devastated the rest of the island as well. The death toll from that storm is estimated to be between 6,000 and 12,000 people, making it far and away the worst natural disaster in U.S. history.

The first eighteen-hole public golf course in Texas, Brackenridge Park, is located in San Antonio. It opened for play in 1918 and is still going strong.

My grandfather, father, and I all learned the game at the old Bryan Municipal Golf Course, which got its start as Bryan Country Club in the 1920s. For many years, the only other golfing option in the area was the course on the campus of Texas A&M. Golfers still play that track today, and the Bryan-College Station area now has a total of five courses on which one can chase around a dimpled ball.

I do that myself on a regular basis. I'm not going to brag about my game because at this point in my life there's nothing much to brag about. I did play on my high school golf team, and for a time in my young life I was a pretty fierce competitor.

Unfortunately, the course I grew up on has since been closed. That closure, which occurred at the end of 2017, hit our family hard, as the site had been renamed Travis B. Bryan Municipal Golf Course in 2009, honoring my grandfather. Announcement of that compliment came in the days just before my daddy's death. We brought the news to his hospital room, and he was pleased with the tribute to his father.

A lot of people who knew Daddy and his love for the game assumed the course had been named for him. Our family got sort of a two-for-one deal out of that.

Plans are for the Travis B. Bryan Municipal Golf Course to be repurposed as a "super park," with baseball and softball fields, trails, lakes, and a variety of other outdoor amenities. Our family fully supports the City of Bryan's vision for the future of the location.

For many years, a trip to the old muni was, for me, a walk down memory lane. There were so many places on that course that brought back memories of my granddad, my father, friends with whom they played, and friends with whom I've played. If I looked close enough, ghosts of the many colorful characters I'd met there would pop out from behind one of the hundreds of oak trees which gave the course its physical beauty.

My grandfather was on that Bryan Country Club course when President Truman called him to share the news that his beloved Bryan Air Force Base was reopening. Daddy spent much of his free time at the site, too, winning almost all of the side bets he wagered.

He was that good.

I started playing there when I was seven. Daddy taught me the basics of the game and then let Henry Ransom refine my skills.

Those of you who are golfers know perfection on the golf course is an impossibility, but for a time in my youth, I sure thought I should make every shot I hit.

At the time, Ransom was the long-time golf coach at Texas A&M. His teams won six Southwest Conference championships, including four straight from 1960 to 1963. As a part-time touring pro and teaching professional at Bryan Country Club, Ransom had also taught Daddy the finer points of the game when he was young.

Ransom won five PGA tour events during his pro career and was a member of the 1951 U.S. Ryder Cup team. Like me, he was a fierce competitor, once getting into an on-course fist fight with one of his playing partners.

Henry was forced to retire from the tour in the late 1950s because he had developed an allergy…to grass.

Daddy played golf at A&M when he returned to college after World War II. And, as I've mentioned, he was a phenomenal player, both as a young man and throughout most of his life. I never came close to beating my father on the golf course.

Tim and I now share ownership of a home in Carmel, California, and the reason we picked that location was in large part because of our father. Our first cross-country family vacation came when I was about sixteen years old, and the ultimate destination was the historic Pebble Beach Golf Links on the Monterey Peninsula.

Pebble Beach has been a storied stop on the professional tour for many years. Actor and singer Bing Crosby hosted a pro-am at Pebble Beach for thirty years. It's now called the AT&T Pro-Am, and it's one of the most popular and successful tournaments on the PGA TOUR®.

When Daddy first introduced Tim and me to Pebble Beach, golfers could play the course as guests for about $12. Today, green fees there run about $500 per round, but a tee time isn't guaranteed. To gain access to playing the course as a non-member–locals can walk it if they're careful to avoid temperamental caddies–you have to be a two-night guest at one of the Pebble Beach Golf resorts on the peninsula, and that can easily set you back as much as $2,000.

After playing Pebble Beach for the first time in the mid-sixties, Daddy was determined we would also play at the nearby Cypress Point course.

My father fancied himself as a guy who could talk his way onto any golf course. His ruse, as I heard it at the Cypress Point golf shop on a breathtakingly beautiful California morning, went something like this: "I can call a man I know in Dallas who will call the bankers in New York. They, in turn, will call their people here, and then they'll call you. You're eventually going to have to let me on anyway, so why don't you save yourself the time and headache of getting that call and just let me pay the green fees for me and my two sons to play."

The answer he got was a firm and unequivocal "No." I think that might have been the only time that ever happened to my father. Daddy eventually befriended a wealthy local and got to play Cypress Point several times. I've had that same privilege myself, and every time I've played the course, I've given thanks to the golfing gods, who are not to be confused with my Loving Heavenly Father, although He gets some of the credit, too.

The Bryan family home in Carmel sits near the village's downtown area. Tim and I each have a golf bag at the ready there, always eager to experience one of life's great spiritual quests at one of the world's most inviting golfing destinations. Carmel is a "golfing Mecca."

I now subscribe to a concept held by many: the experience of playing a round of golf is a microcosm of a Believer's walk through life. There are book titles galore on the subject: *Golfing with God, Faith in the Fairway*, and *Golf for Enlightenment: The Seven Lessons for the Game of Life*.

The latter work is by Deepak Chopra.

Famed psychiatrist-turned-author M. Scott Peck–most well-known for his book, *The Road Less Traveled*–was an avid golfer in his lifetime. His book, *Golf and The Spirit: Lessons for the Journey*, uses a figurative round of golf on a fictional course and a series of golfing metaphors to describe many of life's obstacles, and how Faith plays a vital role in overcoming human frailty and the spiritual hurdles associated with that condition. The concept of "Embracing The Cross" is also contained within the pages of that book, as well.

As any golfer can tell you, there's "death and resurrection" waiting at almost every turn on what Mark Twain–and others–have described as a "good walk spoiled."

For a vivid account of the spiritual nature of golf, I highly recommend *The Legend of Bagger Vance* and the 2000 movie version of the book starring Matt Damon and Will Smith.

I ran across another little book a few years ago called *The Authentic Swing*, written by the author of *Bagger Vance*, Steven Pressfield. In the book's introduction, Pressfield says the work is "more for writers than for golfers" and explains how *Bagger Vance* came to be.

Little did I know at the time I first read *Authentic Swing* that I would become an author myself, although I must admit most of the heavy lifting in this book has been done by my collaborator, Tim Gregg, who himself is not a golfer.

I've explained he doesn't know what he's missing. He assures me he does.

When I find a book that speaks to me spiritually, I pull out a ball-point pen and highlight the heck out of its pages. Such was the case in Pressfield's account of how his *Bagger Vance* story came to be.

Let me share with you a few of the passages I underlined in my paperback copy of *The Authentic Swing*.

"The bond between a caddie and his golfer is a spiritual thing."

I carried a few bags in my youth but didn't see much spirituality in the effort. However, as a fan of the pro tour, I understand the importance of a caddie's role in his player's success. In some sense, I served as Billy Carter's "caddie" during certain stages in the Donnie Sullivan trials. He was the lead defense attorney in the case. Billy frequently asked my opinion on things, and I always gave it to him as honestly as possible. He called the shots in our defense of Sullivan and gets the lion's share of the credit for keeping Donnie out of jail.

Pressfield got a lot of creative mileage out of the "spiritual bond" he created between his two main characters, Bagger Vance, played by Smith, and Rannulph Junuh, the struggling local golfing prodigy played by Matt Damon.

According to Pressfield, the idea for *Bagger Vance* stemmed from a story in the *Bhagavad Gita*, which Pressfield calls the "Hindu Bible."

In the specific story from which Pressfield drew inspiration, a warrior by the name of Arjuna puts down his bow before a major conflict. He sees killing as senseless. His charioteer, who turns out to be Krishna in human form, "reads Arjuna the riot act," according to Pressfield, demanding Arjuna prepare himself properly for battle and his ultimate destiny.

If you've read the *Bagger Vance* book or seen the movie, you'll recognize that thematic concept.

Another passage I highlighted in *Authentic Swing*–including a big ol' asterisk in the margin–related to the poet John Keats' description of "negative capability."

Pressfield writes of the concept:

*"[Keats] means the ability to keep functioning with confidence
even when you don't know where you are or where you're going."*

That's writing or any creative enterprise…including trial
preparation, as I hope you're learning from the book.

I also recognize the concept of negative capability from my
own years spent practicing the law. The arc of my emotional swing
during the Good Samaritan case is a perfect example of that.

Below my asterisk I jotted down "Romans 12:1."

*"Therefore, I urge you, brothers, in view of God's
mercy, to offer your bodies as living sacrifices…"*

To that I added, "Selfish greed must be sacrificed in death, but
it is made possible by our faith that there will be a resurrection."

This, I believe, captures the essence of "The Cross."

One of my favorite chapters in Pressfield's *Authentic Swing* is
entitled "The Golfer's Greatest Enemy Is Himself."

Man, did I learn that a long time ago.

One time my daddy and I were playing in a tournament in
Calvert, Texas, which is about a half hour from Bryan. As I recall
I was about fourteen or fifteen at the time, so it would have been
before our historic first trip to California.

I had a pretty good round going that day, maybe one or two
under par. I then shanked a shot from the fairway and completely
lost my composure. Daddy had bought me a brand-new set of
clubs and a new golf bag, and I started pounding that bag with my
fairway iron.

Getting little satisfaction from that, I flung my club into the
rough and started kicking the crap out of the bag.

I just went completely berserk.

Finally, when there seemed to be no end to my tantrum, Daddy
came up and slugged me in the chest with his fist. That, finally, got
my attention.

Talk about "dying" on the golf course.

The rest of my round was pathetic, as I first contemplated then
obsessed about how much of an embarrassment I had been to both
my father and me.

Daddy and I talked about the incident on the drive home and through the experience I realized there might be a better way to channel my emotions on the golf course. I learned an important lesson that day, one which helped me begin to understand how I could be a better person in general.

When you screw up, just admit your mistake and let it go.

As for the notion of an "authentic swing," Pressfield writes:

> *What would be "authentic" to you would not be "authentic" to me. To say that there is such a thing as an "Authentic Swing" is to build upon the concept of not-learned-but-remembered.*

Scrolling down the side of the margin on that page, my words read, "Resurrection is remembering and rediscovery."

Toward the end of *The Authentic Swing*, Steven Pressfield summarizes the theme at the core of his most famous book:

> *The Legend of Bagger Vance is the story of a man, who after years of resisting, finally listens to his own inner voice.*
>
> *The mentor/guide/servant/savior character is that part of ourselves that has access to the Quantum Soup, the Divine Ground, the dimension of the eternal.*
>
> *That part of ourselves is the part that we write from, paint from, make movies from. It is the element from which all creativity derives.*

I would suggest it's always found at the foot of "The Cross." I scribbled 2 Corinthians 4:10 between Pressfield's words:

> *"Through suffering, our bodies continue to share in the death of Jesus so that the life of Jesus may also be seen in our bodies."*

What I know about golf now is that you don't go out to the course to fight par. You go out there to fight your own demons. The golf course is already a "battlefield" full of obstacles and enemies, even without the added pressure of self-doubt and the self-loathing that comes in the aftermath of a bad shot.

If you stay in that mindset and embrace the difficulties you encounter, taking them in stride, you'll learn how to better accept setbacks in your personal and professional life. Many times, the Christian Life leads us to taking three steps forward…and then two steps back. I call that "Embracing Your Setbacks."

When I try to be a little too "macho" on the golf course, hitting the ball too damn hard, or trying to play to the hole out of an impossible lie, I wind up elevating my score. In golf as in life, one shouldn't be afraid to take the occasional penalty stroke or to lay up so you can better address the next shot—or the next disagreement with your spouse or the next tough business decision.

I've played golf most of my life, but only in recent years have I learned the true spiritual beauty of the game. At about the age of sixty-five, I stopped losing my temper on the golf course and started Embracing The Cross.

19

"Donnie Did It," Part 3

Author's Note: Recounting the details of events that occurred more than a quarter century ago can be difficult. The Donnie Sullivan murder case is a memorable one, not only for the attorneys who defended him, but also everyone else involved in the series of courtroom proceedings which stretched out over a three-and-a-half-year period. Most of the individuals who played significant roles in the case are still alive as of this writing.

On the afternoon of Friday, June 28, 2019, former Grimes County district attorney, David Barron, who sought Sullivan's conviction in each of the trials, sat down with criminal defense attorney Billy Carter and District Judge Travis Bryan III to discuss the third and final mistrial in the case of Donnie Sullivan.

Tim Gregg: David, before we get started here, tell us a little about yourself.

David Barron: I was born and raised in Bryan. My family goes way back here. Barron Road on the south side of College Station was named for my great-great-uncle, Pickney Barron, who owned a good bit of property in that part of Brazos County. I went to college at Sam Houston State University and graduated from Baylor Law School. My father and grandfather were both attorneys and later district judges.

Tim Gregg: David, why do you think you were unable to get a conviction in the first two trials?

David Barron: There were three law enforcement agencies involved in the investigation of the case—four, if you include the Texas Rangers—and they all converged on the scene of the crime the night it happened. I think things got a little convoluted with so many different parties trying to figure out what happened. The crime took place in Grimes County, where I was DA at the time, and the Grimes County Sheriff's Department should have taken the lead. The Walker County Sheriff's Office in Huntsville really had no reason to be there, other than the fact that the victim was one of their "brothers in arms." Madison County became involved, both because Sullivan was arrested there and because the victim, David Stallings was taken to the hospital in Madisonville, where he died. But since the crime was committed in Grimes County, the investigation of the crime should have been the sole responsibility of the Grimes County sheriff. The problem was that for a good while after the murder occurred, the Grimes County sheriff was nowhere to be found.

Tim Gregg: What was your game plan as you sought conviction?

David Barron: It was a circumstantial-evidence case. Our main evidence came from Donnie Sullivan's ex-wife Becky, who was dating Stallings at the time. On the night of the incident, when Stallings was shot, she said that Stallings said, "Donnie did it," but throughout the three trials there was always a doubt as to whether someone could see out the kitchen window into the darkened night. A nine-millimeter shell casing was found outside that window, and I'm convinced that came from the murder weapon. There were several searches of Donnie's truck in which there were papers and clothes everywhere–almost as if he was living out of it– but they didn't find the bullet which matched the shell casing outside the house until, like, the fourth search of the truck. The defense said that was a conspiracy to set Sullivan up.

Tim Gregg: Billy, as co-defense council with Travis, you "won" the first two trials by getting hung-jury outcomes. What were your thoughts heading into the third trial?

Billy Carter: We were ready to go to war again. We had tried it twice, so we pretty well knew what the state was going to do and what the witnesses were going to say. That put us in a little better position than David was in, because we knew we could create reasonable doubt. Plus, the venue for the third trial was moved from Anderson in Grimes County to Livingston in Polk County. None of us objected to holding the third trial there.

David Barron: It was pretty much an agreement by all.

Billy Carter: Grimes County was a tough place to defend

somebody. Everybody knew David back in those days, and they liked him. That made it hard for us. And also, everybody had heard about the case and knew a lot about it. Judge McAdams knew it would be difficult to get an impartial jury in Grimes County, although we tried three times there.

Tim Gregg: That's right. Judge McAdams had to throw out the first jury panel because one of the summoned jurors spoke out and prejudiced the entire group against Donnie.

Billy Carter: Yeah. He said something like, "All of us at the feed store think he's guilty."

Travis Bryan: Once you get a hung jury, you start gaining some momentum on the defense side. From the outset, most of the momentum was with the state. That's the case almost everywhere, since the district attorney's office represents the citizens of a county. But history shows it's very difficult to get a conviction after a hung jury, and we had gotten two of them.

David Barron: Had the division not been for conviction in the first two trials, I probably would not have tried it again. I was getting a lot of flak from the taxpayers about the cost of the trials. But I was determined to get the conviction because I was convinced Sullivan was guilty, and I owed it to Dave Stallings' family to try it one more time. Looking back, it probably wasn't the best idea. I'm older and wiser now. I guess my ego as a younger man wouldn't let go of it.

Tim Gregg: What was it like calling the same witnesses and putting forth much of the same evidence a third time?

David Barron: It got to be a challenge. Each time testimony is given, it's a little bit different, although I gave my witnesses the opportunity to read the record from the previous trials. Some of them got frustrated about having to come back a third time. They were cooperative, but I think they also came across in their testimony as a little bit reluctant. I think that hurt my efforts a little.

Billy Carter: Mike Barber hurt your case a little, too. (All three men begin to laugh.)

David Barron: Yeah, just a little.

Tim Gregg: Mike Barber? The former football player?

David Barron, Billy Carter, Travis Bryan: Yes.

Author's note: Mike Barber was an NFL tight end who played six seasons with the Houston Oilers, five with the Los Angeles Rams, and a final year before retiring with the Denver Broncos. Barber was born in Marshall, Texas, and played high school football in White Oak. He played college football for Louisiana Tech. Barber has been head of Mike Barber Ministries, *a nationwide non-profit prison ministry program he started after concluding his professional football career in 1987.*

Tim Gregg: How did Mike Barber factor into the Donnie Sullivan case?

Travis Bryan: He was fraternizing with some of the jurors during that third trial. And that helped our cause.

David Barron: It was a brilliant move.

Billy Carter: As implausible as this may sound, in Mike Barber's prison ministry work, he became acquainted with Donnie Sullivan. Along with a couple of his friends, Donnie was active in prison ministry, too. Years before the crime Donnie was accused of, Barber had visited him in Okolona (Mississippi) and actually spent the night there at Donnie's house. Once Donnie told us that, I made a point to contact Mike and eventually did so by attending one of his events in Palestine, Texas. There, I introduced myself and told Barber about Donnie's situation.

Travis Bryan: Barber told Billy, "I don't think Donnie did this."

Billy Carter: Barber kept a really busy schedule back in those days. He may still do so today. At one point, he travelled all over the world doing prison ministry, and as I recall he was out of town for Donnie's first two trials. But when the third trial came around, Barber called me and told me he would come if we needed him.

Travis Bryan: And we did.

Billy Carter: When he got to Livingston, Barber told me again, "Donnie didn't do this." And I said, "How do you know?" He said, "I went up to him, I looked him right in the eye, and I said, 'Donnie, did you do this?'" He said that Donnie said, "No, I didn't do it." Sort of like what his mother told us and what everyone else told us who testified on Donnie's behalf.

Tim Gregg: Did Barber actually testify?

Billy Carter: We were ready to use him as a witness, which meant he couldn't come in the courtroom during the trial. So, he waited out in the hallway, and it didn't take long for word to get around that this famous football player was in the courthouse. During breaks in the proceedings, jurors would find him and ask for an autograph. And Barber was very happy to oblige. It was like, "Here you go, Mr. Jury Foreman." "What are you doing here, Mike?" "I'm good friends with Donnie Sullivan." I don't think David was very happy about all this.

David Barron: Like I said: brilliant move. But that was just one of many things that Billy and Travis did to protect their client. Even though it was a third trial and they seemed to know my every move, I was never sure what rabbit they were going to pull out of their hat. The Donnie Sullivan case caused me to start smoking, and I haven't stopped smoking since. Unfortunately, that case wasn't the only burden on my shoulders at the time.

Tim Gregg: Really? What else was going on in your life?

David Barron: Well, I was also going through a divorce from my first wife, and I was dealing with my own arrest for a DWI. So, I was under a lot of pressure. I'm not saying that took anything away from my advocacy ability on behalf of the state, but I had other distractions that were going on, too.

Tim Gregg: Not the least of which, from what I understand, was your deteriorating relationship with your star witness, Becky Sullivan.

David Barron: I don't know what went on in that woman's mind.

Billy Carter: David and Becky were really starting to get into it during her testimony in the third trial. I think David said something to her like, "I know you're under a lot of stress," to which she replied, "Yeah, and I've heard about the stress you're under, too, Mr. Barron," referring to his ongoing divorce proceedings and maybe even his DWI. She said that in front of all of us, including the jury, and I think Judge McAdams decided to shut things down for the rest of that day as a result of her comeback. There was some real tension between the two of them.

Travis Bryan: So much so that we decided not to even cross examine her the third time.

David Barron: I guess my biggest issue with her was that between the night of the crime and that third trial, she completely changed her testimony.

Tim Gregg: In what way?

Billy Carter: In the first trial, she was pretty adamant about what Stallings said as he lay bleeding to death on the floor of her kitchen. "Donnie did it!" she said Stallings told her. In the second trial, she made Stallings' words sound like a question. And in the third trial, I think she said, "Donnie *didn't* do it." I remember looking at Travis in the courtroom, and we both had the same thought: "What did she just say???"

David Barron: In the first trial she testified that Donnie did it, but then by the third trial she blamed me for coaching her into saying that.

Tim Gregg: She said that on the stand? In front of the jury?

David Barron: Yeah. She said that I had first led her into saying that in front of the grand jury, which was not at all the case. I wasn't out looking to convict an innocent guy. By the third trial, I think the antipathy between us was palpable in the courtroom and, from what I understand now, the jury felt sorry for her. So, maybe I overplayed my hand.

Tim Gregg: At what point of the third trial, David, did you feel like you weren't going to get a conviction?

David Barron: The judge had them take a vote during deliberations when they were out a day or two, and I think they were deadlocked 9-3 for not guilty, an exact reversal of where the juries wound up in the first two trials. It was at that point I knew my boat was sinking.

Tim Gregg: Not until then?

David Barron: I'd say not until then. I was probably self-delusional going into the third trial. I thought I had them on some tire tracks found near the scene of the crime. But they turned out not to come from Donnie's truck. There was also the matter of the missing dispatch log pages in the Walker County Sheriff's Office relating to the crime. I guess my competitive instincts took over and probably blinded me to the true facts of what was going on.

Tim Gregg: So, the jury comes back, and they're hung again. This time 10-2 for acquittal. What were your thoughts?

Travis Bryan: It's over.

David Barron: Initially, I think I said, "I'm going to try it again." Travis and I almost came to blows over that.

Tim Gregg: In the courtroom or afterward?
David Barron: In the courtroom. The jury was no longer there. We were both tired, but our passions for justice were still bubbling. I was frustrated at taking it on the chin yet again.
Billy Carter: I think Travis told him, "You try this case again, and I will oppose you with every fiber of my being when you run again for district attorney!" They both stood up and got into the familiar "fighting stance," and I truly thought they were going to start slugging it out right there in the courtroom. In fact, I remember Travis saying, "Just step outside, and I'll whip your ass!" As all this is going on, Judge McAdams is saying, "Boys, boys. Just relax!" And I'm not believing any of it, although knowing Travis and David like I do now, I can see that the heat of the moment simply got the best of them.
Travis Bryan: The idea that he would go back to trial in this case after four starts–remember, the jury pool was thrown out in the first go-round–was preposterous to me. It just angered me to the max. I couldn't handle it.
Tim Gregg: Technically, Donnie Sullivan has never been acquitted of the crime for which he was accused. Which begs a fair question: Twenty-five years later, who do you think murdered David Stallings?
David Barron: I will say I had a certain degree of sympathy for Donnie because I believed he was manipulated into doing it by Becky.
Tim Gregg: Where did *that* come from? You just blew my mind! Please, explain yourself.
David Barron: Before the night of the murder, Becky had been acting, according to witnesses, like she wanted to get back together with Donnie, while at the same time dating other men and bringing them into her house. Prior to the shooting, Donnie had spent a few nights at the house himself. Even during the trials, I could see what might have been going on in his mind, the jealousy factor.
Travis Bryan: You don't mean that she wanted him to kill Dave Stallings?
David Barron: No, no. Not wanted him killed…
Tim Gregg: Then, what do you mean?

Travis Bryan: Jerked him around to the point that he was irrational?

David Barron: She set the stage for it. I'm sure she never saw a murder coming, but the way she played her men off each other, I thought I could sense his mindset.

Tim Gregg: If Donnie "didn't do it," then who did?

Billy Carter: The only person I know that didn't do this was me.

Travis Bryan: I think it could very well have been some police officer or sheriff's deputy "gone bad." Stallings worked the drug beat, not only for the Walker County Sheriff's Office, but also with the City of Huntsville Police Department. He might have known something, and somebody might have been out to get him.

Tim Gregg: And, David, you've got the final word here. Who killed David Stallings?

David Barron: I still think Donnie did it. But there's something else I'd like to add here.

Tim Gregg: Go ahead.

David Barron: Not long after that final trial, I resigned as Grimes County District Attorney. I regretted my inability to see justice done for David Stallings and his family, but I was also facing a serious personal dilemma. I was an alcoholic. I became a defense attorney and moved my practice to Bryan. Billy and Travis remained good friends of mine. But it took me another fifteen years to get sober. Alcoholism runs in my family. My father, my mother, and my brother were all alcoholics. And so was I. Travis and Billy were kind enough to pull me aside one day and tell me they thought I needed to get some help. "You're going to La Hacienda," Travis said. That's a well-known and well-regarded treatment facility in Hunt, Texas. I told him, "Okay, but how do I pay for it?" I think it cost a minimum of $30,000 to get into the place back then. Travis said, "Don't worry about that. I've already taken care of it." And that got me on the right path, that and Travis's teachings about "Embracing The Cross." I'm happy to call Travis a good friend, and even happier to be a disciple of his Christian teachings. He's changed my life.

20

The Apples of My Eye

One of the things I remember most about my wedding day, January 1, 1971, was that Notre Dame beat Texas in the Cotton Bowl.

Actually, I'm kidding about that, although I vividly recall that game because the Fighting Irish foiled "tu's" quest for back-to-back national championships. (Again, "tu" is not a typo.)

In leading up to our big day, I told Becky that if the Aggies had played in the Cotton Bowl, we would have had to change our wedding date. Fortunately, there was little chance of that happening as the 1970 college football season played out.

While Coach Gene Stallings led the Aggies to a Cotton Bowl win at the end of the '67 season–marking Texas A&M's first Cotton Bowl triumph since 1941–the 1970 Ags weren't anywhere close to being postseason-worthy. After they upset twelfth-ranked LSU in the second game of the year, A&M lost its next nine outings to finish 2-9. For some reason, the Aggies' schedule that year took them not only to LSU, but also to Ohio State and Michigan…in consecutive weeks.

That has to be one of the toughest non-conference schedules in the history of college football.

So, with the Aggies football fortunes lagging, Becky and I were free to begin our new life together. Not only did I begin a new year by marrying the most wonderful and understanding woman in God's creation, I want to say again that Texas lost to Notre Dame in the Cotton Bowl, 24-11, snapping the Longhorns' thirty-game winning streak.

That news was definitely icing on the wedding cake, so to speak.

After the game, er, wedding, my new wife and I drove from Longview to Shreveport for our honeymoon. Before you begin to think poorly of me for taking my bride across state lines to a less-than-glamorous post-nuptial destination, let it be known that Shreveport was just a stopping point for the two of us.

We caught a flight from there to Miami, and then from Miami, we flew to Nassau and spent our honeymoon in the Bahamas. We had a great time getting nearly fifty years of marriage off to a fun and memorable start.

My biggest regret as a new husband, and in many of the years to follow, was that I wasn't nearly as attentive to my wife as I should have been. I've alluded to this in earlier pages, but I had a hard time shaking my self-centered nature. Fortunately, Becky knew this about me before we got married.

I realized that if I wanted to have a successful marriage and a chance at "happily ever after," I had to pay closer attention to my wife's wants and needs, and concern myself less with those of my own.

Eventually, I think I got the hang of that, but there was never any doubt about whether or not our marriage was going to last.

I went into marriage certain that my new wife was going to be the only woman for me. I believed strongly then that God never intended for divorce to be an option for married couples. Later, as both an attorney and a judge, I've become more understanding that sometimes divorce becomes an inevitable outcome within a deeply unhappy matrimonial union. Or in one that is fraught with physical or emotional harm.

Fellows, let me tell you: marriage is a work in progress. To make progress, you're going to have to work at it, particularly regarding the sin nature of your own selfish heart.

Don't ever forget that, because the rewards of a good and Christ-centered marriage are boundless.

One of the greatest riches of my life with Becky can be found in the three extraordinary children we raised together.

I take some credit but let me be clear: Becky did most of that work.

My wife poured her life into our kids. I've never seen a better mother. Our daughter, Becca, is a remarkable mother, too, but Becky was a fabulous mom from the beginning, and I'm proud to say our children all turned out to be exceptional adults, in large part because of the time, attention, and affection Becky gave to our children.

And now, two of our kids have "come home."

One of my life's greatest blessings occurred in 2018 when my two sons, Austin and Joel, moved back to Bryan.

At a time when many adult children are "boomeranging"—returning home to live with their parents for mostly financial reasons—my boys came back with good jobs, settling into homes they purchased on their own.

I hear a lot about the pitfalls of living with a grown child. But, to tell you the truth, if any of my children needed a roof over their head, they would be welcome in a heartbeat to come home and live with Becky and me.

Becca is the only one of our kids who has strayed away from the nest. She lives with her husband and children in Colorado.

My oldest child, Austin, has continued the family's banking tradition. After graduating from Texas A&M, Austin went to work with my dad and my brother Tim at the First National Bank & Trust of Bryan. In the mid-2000s, in a move I never thought I'd see my father agree to, my dad decided to sell the bank.

I'm a believer in the Biblical truth taken from the gospel of John that "a prophet has no honor" in his hometown. Tim left our daddy's bank when he was young and spent more than a decade making a mark of his own in Houston. He's been back in Bryan now for some time and, in my humble opinion, Tim is the best banker in Texas.

Austin left the First National Bank & Trust of Bryan—and the shadow of my father and brother—before Daddy sold the bank. Austin moved to Georgetown, Texas, where he continued working in the financial sector.

I told Austin at the time, "Get away from here. Nobody will know you there, so you're going to have to make it on your own. It will be hard, but you'll be a better man if you do."

Before he moved, Austin got married—in an ironic twist of family fate, to a woman whose name was Rebecca—and they conceived a son they named Milan. Technically, little Milan never made it into the world, as Rebecca miscarried near full term. That little grandson I never knew is buried here in Bryan City Cemetery, and I take comfort knowing that someday I'll get to meet him when we're reunited in Heaven.

Austin and his wife had another boy, my grandson, Will. What a godsend that young man has been for our entire family. Will is currently enrolled at Texas A&M, and he is majoring in psychology. What a joy it is to have both him and his dad in close proximity.

Austin is still in the banking business with my brother. After Daddy sold the First National Bank of Bryan, Tim and a few other officers from that bank launched The Bank & Trust here in the Bryan-College Station area. Then, in late 2019, Tim and his board sold The Bank & Trust. Both my brother and my son are still employed by what is now called First Financial Bank. I have no doubt my son will rise up the executive ranks of the bank. As for Tim, he's probably headed into retirement someday soon, enabling him to spend a lot more time on the golf course.

I'll be there right beside him when I step down from the bench.

Did I mention that Austin is also a heckuva golfer? He's proudly carried on another of the Bryan family's longstanding and important traditions.

At a course in Georgetown not all that long ago, Austin made his first hole-in-one…on a 360-yard par-four hole!

That doesn't happen every day.

While I wasn't there, Austin has shared the details of his accomplishment with me enough times I think I can describe the event to you in vivid detail.

It was a summer afternoon; Berry Creek Country Club was playing short with its hardened fairways and a noticeable southerly breeze.

At the tenth tee box, Austin and his playing partners waited as the foursome ahead of them made their way to the green. Given the distance on the hole, Austin felt there was little risk for him and his friends to tee off before the other group finished putting out. There wasn't any chance of anyone driving the green on the par-four hole.

Austin was and is a pretty big hitter. He's recorded two double eagles in his playing career. That's scoring a two on a par-five. So, with the weather conditions just right at Berry Creek that day,

Austin thought he had a small chance to reach the green with his tee shot.

Bucking golfing decorum, his friends suggested he go for it while the other golfers were putting out the hole.

One of Austin's playing partners ran ahead to keep an eye on the shot. As Austin swung, he intentionally hooked the ball over a creek to his right. He bent the shot back onto the fairway and with the extreme overspin of the hook, he got a fantastic roll.

Bouncing off the fairway once, twice, and three times, the ball rolled all the way onto the green. His buddy yelled "FORE!!!" to the group ahead.

The foursome putting out reacted first to the warning cry, then to Austin's ball rolling into their midst. As it rolled toward the hole, the group began screaming encouragement to the golfing gods, then raised their hands in celebration as Austin's ball dropped into the cup.

"I think you made the green!" Austin's pal shouted as he trotted back toward his group.

Every good golfer deserves the thrill of a hole-in-one at least once in their lifetime. I've come close—real close—but I'm still waiting for mine.

Our daughter, Becca, takes after her mother in the parenting of her four children. But in other ways, she's inherited some of my "idiosyncrasies." On the downside, she has occasional bouts with anxiety and depression, and she, like me, has an inherent fear of failure.

On the upside, she loves God passionately, and she immerses herself and her family in the Understanding to be found from study of the Bible.

And mark my words: Becca is going to be another Beth Moore someday. Becca has the wonderful ability to write and communicate clearly with others. She uses those talents regularly as the headmistress of a homeschool society where she lives in Eagle, Colorado.

Becca's husband Chad is from Breman, Indiana, which is close to South Bend where Notre Dame University is located. Chad grew up on a farm, and like his dad, he's a terrific handyman and a great husband to Becca and father to their children. Chad is "all man," a tremendous guy.

Chad got his college degree in data processing and had a good job in Dallas when he met Becca. Becca graduated from Baylor where she studied–much to her father's delight–religion.

The two met while both worked at a dude ranch in Colorado. Shortly after, they fell in love, got married, and Becca moved to Dallas. A bit later, Chad decided he wasn't cut out for a desk job. He asked Becca if she would be okay if the two of them moved to Colorado.

And, Becca, in full support of her husband, said yes.

They first moved to Bailey, Colorado, where they had their first child, Nathan.

Loving their new life in Colorado, Chad went back to school and got a master's degree in ranch management from Colorado State University. He was able to parlay that into a good position as a ranch director for a group of rich New Yorkers that owned a big spread in the foothills of the Rockies. Over time, though, the absentee-ownership group became a little too demanding, and he was forced to quit his job.

Being a capable hand, Chad's found enough freelance work to keep his home fires burning.

Just recently, Becky and I went up to Eagle to take care of our grandchildren while Becca and Chad went off on a second honeymoon.

Becky has an instinctive and maternal way with our grandkids that I lack. But on our trip, Becky wasn't feeling well, so I took on the duty of caring for the little ones.

Of course, that meant Becca's two boys and I hit the golf course, during which time the two girls stayed home and helped Becky convalesce. I also spent time with my granddaughters and enjoyed their company immensely.

Our eldest granddaughter, Lucy, is a fine dancer, and one evening while we were in Eagle, we got to attend one of her recitals.

All my kids were athletes growing up. Becca was a terrific softball player. Austin played baseball in junior college. Joel played football at Texas A&M and Kentucky. None of them, I will tell you now, had anything on little Lucy the dancer. Granddad, or "Bubba," as the grandkids call me, thinks Lucy may someday be a star!

My youngest grandchild is little three-year-old Margee B. The best word to describe her is "bold." I have no fear that anyone is ever going to intimidate her. She definitely didn't inherit any of my "worry" genes.

Becca and Chad's oldest son is Nathan, who is a little man at thirteen years of age. He's like a third parent in the family. He has a sweet-natured way of correcting his siblings without coming across as being bossy. He also has a tremendous golf swing.

The youngest of Becca's two boys is Travis, or "Trav," and, yes, he's named after me.

I chose not to name either of my sons Travis because, to be honest, the notion seemed a little pretentious to me. I sometimes struggled as my daddy and grandfather's namesake, so Becky and I made the decision we weren't going to bring "Travis Bryan IV" into the world.

Still, I have to say, I'm proud that Becca has chosen otherwise, and little eight-year-old Trav has a special place in his "Bubba's" heart.

As Becky and I were leaving Colorado to head back home, I gave all of my grandkids one final hug. As we got into the car, Trav came running out the front door calling my name.

He ran up to the driver's side of our rental car and held out his hand. "This is for you," he told me.

His parting gift was his favorite golf ball, one he had painted and repainted time and time again.

"Take this with you," he ordered. So I did and now have it on my nightstand, and I think about little Trav and the rest of our grandchildren and children every single day.

And just so you know, while my grandchildren call me "Bubba," or "Bub" for short, Becky is "Zsa Zsa" to them, as in the late Hungarian-born actress Zsa Zsa Gabor.

My brother and I used to call Daddy "Big 'Un." I think I picked that up from a football coach somewhere along the line. Our kids called him that, too.

Given our family's historical ancestry, we try to keep things informal in our day-to-day life. But if you got a peek at our birth certificates, particularly those of my grandchildren, you'd find a lot more formality, with names like: William Travis Bryan (Austin's son, Will), William Joel Bryan VII and Wyatt Jennings Bryan (Joel's twin boys), and Robert Henry Bryan (Joel's youngest, little Bobby).

And speaking of Bobby, I had the pleasure of coaching his Little League baseball team this past spring here in the Bryan/College Station area. His daddy was the head coach and it was an honor and privilege working on Joel's staff. Bobby may turn out to be the best Bryan athlete of all, which says a lot because his dad and uncle were keen competitors in their day.

Which seems like only yesterday.

Joel turned out to be a pretty good manager, too. The RiverDogs finished 12-1 and were crowned league champions. We accomplished that, thanks to Joel's wise decision to ratchet down the intensity from when I coached him as a kid.

Joel is our youngest and from the time he was a little boy he was just a real sweet kid. Even as a toddler, Joel was always concerned about the rest of his family, always trying to keep track of everyone's whereabouts.

"Where's Becca going?" he would ask. "When are Austin and Mom going to be home?" On a regular basis, Joel would approach me in the mornings before I left to go to work. "Dad, when will you get home so we can all be together?"

Joel never wanted any of us to stray too far away from his sphere. He's that kind of family man now with his lovely wife, Pam, and their three boys.

When I think of Joel as a child, I still see him at the bottom of the stairs in the house where Becky and I still live. In my mind's eye, he's looking up at me as if I have all the answers to life's questions.

I didn't have all the answers then, and I don't now, but I think I have a little clearer understanding of the big picture, thanks to what I've learned from my study of the Bible.

"Beloved, do not be surprised at the fiery ordeal among you, which comes upon you for your testing, as though some strange thing were happening to you"
(1 Peter 4:12).

21

"Mumme-fied"

While my wife Becky was doing a terrific job tending to our children in their day-to-day pursuits, I invested a good bit of my parental time coaching my kids in their organized sports.

Austin played both football and baseball through high school. He got a junior college scholarship to play baseball and was a fine infielder at that level.

Becca was a gifted young softball player whom I enjoyed coaching. In fact, I wanted her to play in college.

I may have overextended my parental authority when I wrote a glowing letter to the Baylor softball coach about her and her abilities. I did so with the full realization that Becca had no desire to play softball in college.

So, yes, I might have been one of those parents who was a little over-exuberant in support of my children in their sporting endeavors. I can assure you I was no Earl Woods nor Marv Marinovich, whose cautionary tales I encourage you to explore if you're not familiar with those names. I was simply intent on seeing my kids have every advantage in achieving success in their chosen athletic pursuits.

And for that matter, elsewhere in life, too.

Based on my experience as a parent, let me offer some of you parents reading this a piece of friendly advice: Please, if you're a pushy mom or dad when it comes to your child's extracurricular activities, take a step back, take a deep breath, exhale, and try to get over yourself.

If you're a grandparent, like I am, I'm assuming you don't have this kind of problem. If you do, see the paragraph above.

It's good to support your kids—or grandkids—but don't force them to live out your own forgotten dreams and never-realized fantasies. What's most important is that your son or daughter or grandchild has fun at what they do, learns to take instruction in those activities, and doesn't get too caught up in the winning thing, at least not when they're young.

And while I wasn't always a good loser myself, each of my three children turned out to accept setbacks in life with grace and humility. And that's made them healthier adults and probably better parents than their father.

It's not a matter of how much you love your kids. It's a matter of channeling that love in a positive and constructive way.

So, do what I say…not what I did.

I poured a lot of myself into my kids, in particular, my younger son, Joel. He got a lot more attention from me than he really needed.

Which led the two of us on a somewhat strange but intriguing journey.

From an early age, it was apparent that Joel had special athletic talents. With my own football dream never fully realized, I look back on Joel's young life and see that I attempted to live vicariously through his experiences. I think Joel may have overlooked a good bit of that, because he sure has his head screwed on right today.

Thank you, Jesus.

It was through my quest to give Joel every athletic advantage possible that I came to cross paths with Hal Mumme, one of the most enlightened coaching minds to dot the college football landscape in recent years.

I first met Mumme in my efforts to help hire a new football coach at Bryan High School.

If that sounds familiar, you'll remember that my father successfully recruited the great Merrill Green to coach at Bryan High in the early 1970s.

While my daddy, as head of the local school board, was operating in an official capacity in bringing Green to town, I was sort of an "interested outside party" when it came to Mumme. Some people–myself included–thought Joel might one day be a football star.

By the end of the 1991 calendar year, Joel was thirteen and still playing junior high school ball. Meanwhile, I had my sights set on the future, already thinking ahead to Joel's high school years. With Bryan High in need of a new coach, I wanted to lend a hand by finding the best passing-game coach around, one who would hopefully groom Joel through high school for the even bigger and better things I thought sure were his destiny.

I initiated my unsanctioned efforts by enlisting the scouting services of Bob McElroy, a long-time Texas high school coach and friend of mine. Bob had gone to A&M, and while a student there, he had coached my sixth-grade basketball team.

He would go on to become a successful Texas high school football coach.

In his search for a potential Bryan High football coach, Bob wound up putting together a list of ten names, none of which I intended to share with the school board's official search committee.

Okay, maybe I did share a few things in common with the likes of Earl Woods and Marv Marinovich. I don't think I realized that until just now.

> *"Be shepherds of God's flock that is under your care, watching over them—not because you must, but because you are willing, as God wants you to be; not pursuing dishonest gain, but eager to serve; not lording it over those entrusted to you, but being examples to the flock"*
> (1 Peter 5:2-3).

"The last name on the list is a small-college coach in Iowa," Bob told me as we reviewed his pick of prospective coaching candidates.

"Why did you include him?" I asked.

"He won at Copperas Cove as a Texas high school coach in the late '80s," Bob told me. "He beat the best there and has been setting all sorts of passing records at a small Christian school in Iowa.

"In fact, his team, Iowa Wesleyan College, made it to the national quarterfinals this past season."

"Why would he want to be a high school coach again?" I wondered aloud.

"As I understand it," Bob told me, "he's got a son who's entering high school next year, and I think he wants to coach him."

I nodded my head knowingly. That made perfect sense to me.

Bob introduced me to Hal Mumme by phone, and, based on my recommendation, the Bryan school board brought him to Texas for an interview. I hate to admit this now, but I wanted Mumme as our new football coach so bad that I spent way too much of my time lobbying for him to get the job.

Becky said the whole Mumme affair made me an insane person for about two months. My arm-twisting and cajoling may have cost me a friend or two.

Unfortunately, the Bryan school board didn't quite see things the way I did. In a closed-door meeting on the matter of Mumme, the board voted 4-3 against offering him the job. As you might expect, I did not take the outcome well.

With my plans for a pass-happy Bryan Vikings football team squelched, I began pondering legal action to see if I could reverse the decision.

Eventually, cooler heads than mine persuaded me to accept the defeat.

It was obvious to others that Mumme was not the long-term candidate the school board wished to hire. Had he taken the Bryan job, the board believed the chances were good he would have left with his son after Matt's graduation.

Still today, I wince with regret to think that Hal Mumme, given what he went on to accomplish, could have been head football coach at Bryan High. And even better, had he come, Mumme would have brought with him a young assistant coach by the name of Mike Leach.

For those of you not familiar with these names, let me go over a little recent college football history.

An offensive scheme called the "Air Raid" has become the rage throughout the game of football. Once thought to be a gimmick rather than a plausible way to put together a winning team, the Air Raid is the nearly unstoppable force today that the triple-option wishbone running attack—invented by former Texas A&M head coach Emory Bellard—was a couple generations ago.

While the foundation for the Air-Raid system was first conceived by long-time Brigham Young University coach LaVell Edwards, not until Hal Mumme—with the help of his offensive coordinator Mike Leach—did the concept blossom into its more robust and formidable form in the mid 1990s.

In assembling his coaching staff at Iowa Wesleyan, Mumme met and interviewed a Pepperdine law school graduate with no college football playing experience. Mumme was intrigued to learn that young Mike Leach shared his conviction that football's greatest minds had only scratched the surface of what a passing attack could really be.

Over the next decade, Hal Mumme and Mike Leach formed a "mad scientist" coaching partnership. After being turned down for the Bryan High School job, Mumme became head coach at Valdosta State University in Georgia. Then, in 1997, he became head football coach at the University of Kentucky.

Not only did Leach follow him from job to job, Hal's son Matt eventually joined his dad at Kentucky. Matt served as the backup quarterback to star Tim Couch, the number-one pick in the 1999 NFL Draft.

Couch arrived in Lexington before Mumme took the coaching job there. The youngster was an extraordinary talent, and his presence on the Kentucky campus was a big reason why Mumme was interested in the Kentucky job.

Mumme made Couch an All-American. The young quarterback finished as runner-up for the Heisman Trophy his senior year. Couch gave Mumme and Leach the kind of talent they'd long dreamed of incorporating into their offensive scheme.

Mike Leach eventually wound up as a head coach himself, first at Texas Tech. There, his quarterbacks, including current NFL coach Kliff Kingsbury–who coached Johnny Manziel at Texas A&M–and Graham Harrell, put up video game-like offensive numbers, far surpassing those of Couch at Kentucky.

Tim Couch and Matt Mumme finished out their eligibility at Kentucky at the same time. And one of the candidates who stepped forward in an attempt to fill their void was none other than a young standout from Bryan High School by the name of Joel Bryan.

My son was finally getting the opportunity to become "Mumme-fied."

The Lord indeed works in mysterious ways.

From early on, Joel was everything on a football field that I wish I could have been: faster, smarter, tougher, and more eager to learn.

About the time he turned eleven, I asked Joel, "Son, are you ready to play against the best?"

"Yes, Dad, I am."

"You know, the best aren't the kids you've been playing with. The best are kids of color."

Such was my abiding respect–then and now–for the African American athlete.

During my high school years, before racial integration in most parts of Texas, one of the most formidable opponents my teammates and I faced was a young African American running back by the name of Melba Cross.

Cross played football for Corpus Christi's Mary Carroll High School in the early 1960s and became a Texas schoolboy legend.

For what it's worth, NASCAR drivers Bobby and Terry Labonte also attended Carroll.

Hugh McElroy–no relation to Bob–helped integrate the Texas A&M football team under coach Gene Stallings in 1967 by becoming the first African American to start a varsity game and score a touchdown. That occurred five years before the Bryan school district achieved integration by combining the all-white Stephen F. Austin High School, which I attended, with the all-black Kemp High School, putting students from both schools into a new building which became Bryan High…named for the city and not yet for my father.

It was on the Kemp High School athletic grounds that Joel first learned to play quarterback. And as an eleven-year-old playing against superior talent, Joel did more than hold his own. By the time he reached high school, Joel was easily the best quarterback in the Brazos Valley. He started at Bryan High both his junior and senior years, playing for Marty Criswell, the coach who had been hired over Hal Mumme.

Hindsight reveals that the Bryan school district made a good choice. Criswell took the Vikings to the state quarterfinals in 1999, after Joel's time there. Upon his retirement from coaching, Criswell became a staff member of the Fellowship of Christian Athletes and continues that ministry today.

During his high school playing days under Criswell, Joel thought–and I was among a large contingent which agreed with him–that he stood a good chance of being able to play quarterback at the college level. As he and I began the process of assessing potential collegiate destinations, a friend of mine, Dr. Dick Harrison, proposed an alternative plan.

"With Joel's smarts and his good looks," Harrison told me, "he's destined to be a star one day…in Hollywood."

"You mean a movie star?" I had never considered that possibility.

"Yep," Dr. Harrison replied. "I bet he could become a multimillionaire."

It didn't take long before Doc Harrison convinced me that Joel had potential off the football field, too. When I brought this news home to Becky, she was much less enthusiastic about those prospects than I was.

"Absolutely not!" she proclaimed. "He's not going to Hollywood. That's ridiculous!

"Nooooo way!

"He can go to college, and he can be what he wants to be, but he isn't going to waste his time on trying to be a movie star. Are you out of your mind?"

Becky cleared up that matter in no time.

On the college football front, Joel considered a number of schools, but from the start, there was a clear frontrunner: Texas A&M.

My own A&M football experience had amounted to one season on the freshman team. As a walk-on, I was ridiculed and physically assaulted nearly every day. Given that Joel was coming out of high school as a star quarterback, I was certain he could do better than me. I had it from good authority–including Marty Criswell–that recruiters were excited about him.

To help "groom" my son for his inevitable future as a gridiron great, I started sending him to quarterback camps when he was eight. Among the camps Joel attended regularly was Hal Mumme's. Mumme left Iowa to take another small college coaching job in Valdosta, Georgia. It was there that he launched a kids' football camp. I made sure Joel attended every summer.

I also signed up Joel to attend camps put on by Steve Spurrier at Florida and Terry Bowden at Auburn University, big-name coaches with big-time programs. Thus, my own big-time dreams for both Joel and me were fulfilled in his youth.

R.C. Slocum was another well-regarded coach on the Joel Bryan bandwagon. What he thought counted for a lot since he was head football coach of the Texas A&M Aggies.

Richard Copeland Slocum is the winningest football coach in Texas A&M history. He led the Aggies from 1989 to 2002 and won four conference championships.

After he was fired, Slocum remained in College Station, and has been a leading citizen in the area ever since.

I'll never forget the day I got a call from Slocum asking if he could speak with me in person about Joel. He extended his invitation to include my father and the two of us paid him a visit at his coaching office on the A&M campus.

R.C. was a friend to the Bryan family. My daddy had been a staunch supporter of Slocum's program, and the Aggie coach and I mixed within the same social circles.

"I'd like to talk about your son's football future here at Texas A&M," Slocum said to Daddy and me as we settled around the conference table in his office, which was meager by today's standards. In his last year as head football coach at A&M, Slocum made $1 million, a pretty princely sum back in the early 2000s. His office at the time was located adjacent to the campus parking garage across the street from Kyle Field.

Jimbo Fisher, head coach of the Aggies today, earns $7.5 million to guide A&M's football program.

During his senior year at Bryan High in 1996, Joel had met frequently with recruiters from the A&M coaching staff. Joel told me he was reasonably confident there would be a spot on the Aggie roster for him, given what the recruiters had told him. The possibilities of a scholarship, according to Joel, had been mentioned.

I'm not sure my one year spent as an Aggie walk-on provided me much insight into my conversation with Coach Slocum about my son. After a few pleasantries and some glowing comments about Joel's abilities, Slocum got to the point of our meeting.

"We'd like for your son to play football here at Texas A&M University," the coach told Daddy and me, "and we have a full scholarship waiting for him."

With those words, my heart swelled with pride. I thanked Slocum.

"That's a great honor for Joel."

Slocum nodded his head. "Well, the Bryan family has meant a lot to our program through the years, and it will be great to have a Bryan on the team."

Slocum's words caught me a bit off guard. Was he suggesting that he was offering Joel a spot on the team because of our family's support of A&M football?

The notion gnawed at me a tad, but I held my tongue, not wanting to risk insulting a man I liked personally and admired professionally.

As we wrapped up the meeting, I thanked Slocum for his time and his confidence in my son's potential.

"This is not my decision to make," I told the coach. "Is it okay if I relay the news to Joel myself?"

"Absolutely, Travis," Slocum said. "He knows we're interested. If he has any questions, tell him he's welcome to come by and see me any time."

After I dropped Daddy off at the bank, I headed home to visit with Joel.

"You were right," I told my son. "Coach Slocum is ready to offer you a scholarship."

My son responded with humility and grace. "I was hoping that would be the case," he said.

"Give it your best shot," I told him, happy and proud for my son.

Joel took the scholarship and was redshirted his freshman year at A&M. As a redshirt, he could still practice with the team. But he saw no time at quarterback, and soon his season was ended.

This story appeared on the website 12thMan.com:

The No. 17-ranked Texas A&M Football team worked out for two hours in full pads Tuesday on the artificial turf practice field adjacent to Kyle Field.

No new injuries occurred during the workout, but one new injury was reported.

Freshman defensive back Joel Bryan, from Bryan, Texas, tore the anterior cruciate ligament in his right knee during the closing moments of Monday's workout. After further evaluation on Tuesday, it was determined that he

indeed had torn the ligament and will be out for the remainder of the season.
Bryan had not yet seen any game playing time.

During the '97 season, the Aggies had been unable to settle on a starting quarterback. Branndon Stewart had transferred to A&M from Tennessee, but when he struggled as the starter, Slocum turned to Randy McCown, a highly touted recruit from Jacksonville, Texas.

Those two remained at the top of the Aggie depth chart in 1998. Again, Stewart began the season as the starter, but was replaced after four games by McCown.

After recovering from his knee injury, Joel wasn't much more than a tackling dummy as he continued his duties on the scout team his second season in the program. As I remember, he suffered two and possibly three concussions that fall.

One night, a team doctor brought Joel to our house from practice. He was completely out of it, had no idea where he was, and this scared me. I remembered getting blindsided on the practice field myself, and this was not what I wanted for my youngest child.

It had become obvious to me that Joel didn't really figure into Coach Slocum's plans, at least at the quarterback position. Not only was the clock ticking on my son's football career, but also his physical well-being seemed to be at stake.

So, I gave Hal Mumme a call. His coaching talents had caught the attention of the major college football world, and in 1998 he was in his second year as head coach at the University of Kentucky.

Hal and I had become summer golfing buddies. We played whenever recruiting trips brought him to the Central Texas region. With him, I knew I didn't need to beat around the bush about my son.

"Do you think Joel could come to Kentucky and just be on the team?" I point-blank asked Mumme on the phone. After explaining my concerns about Joel's health, I added, "You don't need to give him a scholarship. I can pay his way to school there. But, given his talent and desire, I think he might be able to do something for you."

"Sure!" Mumme told me. "Send him up here. We'll take good care of him."

And just like that, Hal Mumme was finally going to coach my son...

...if Joel agreed.

I knew that stood to be a mighty big "if."

A few days later, I brought up the subject with Joel.

He took to the Kentucky idea about as well as I expected.

"No!" he said. "Dad, stop this!"

He continued.

"I'm on the team, I'm on scholarship, and I've got friends there now. The answer is no!"

Again, I found myself saying, "Okay. Alright."

A few days later I was back in his ear...and ready to make him an offer he couldn't refuse.

"Joel, I know how much you want a truck. So, here's what I'm going to do. I'll buy you a truck–any truck you want–but I'll only do so if you agree to transfer to Kentucky."

With my offer I was, in essence, illegally recruiting my own son. He called it "a bribe."

"Yeah, I'm bribing you, Joel," I replied. "I think it's in your best interest to get out of here and make a new start for yourself. You remember how disappointed you were when Coach Mumme didn't get the Bryan High School job. Well, now you can play for him at Kentucky.

"He's the talk of the college football world right now." I went on. "His quarterback, Tim Couch, may be the number-one pick in the NFL draft. Maybe someday that could be you."

Joel initially rejected my offer, but about a week later he changed his mind.

"Okay, I'll go to Kentucky."

A couple days later, he and I found the pickup truck of his dreams, and I paid for it on the spot, consummating our agreement.

When it came time to head off to his new school, Joel drove to Lexington in his new truck with his mother along for the ride. She was worried about her son being so far from home, and we both thought the drive up with Joel would help ease her concerns.

For his first few days at Kentucky, Joel stayed at Hal Mumme's home.

NCAA rules stipulated that as a transfer student, Joel had to sit out his first year at Kentucky, the 1999 season. That year the Wildcats made their second of back-to-back bowl game appearances, and the team's–and Mumme's–futures looked bright.

In fact, not since Bear Bryant had led Kentucky to the Orange, Sugar, and Cotton Bowls in consecutive seasons from 1949 to 1951 had Kentucky's football prospects seemed so promising.

But, by the time Joel's junior season rolled around and he was eligible again to play, the Kentucky football program found itself under the cloud of an NCAA investigation.

One day during the 1999 season, I got a call from Coach Mumme, a not uncommon nor unexpected experience.

But he didn't call to talk about Joel or his golf game.

"I need your help, Travis," Mumme said. "I'm going in front of the NCAA investigators in a few weeks, and I'd like you there to help me."

"I've heard about this," I said. "I'm sorry you're caught up in this mess. I'm happy to help however I can."

At the time–and unlike today–an NCAA investigation into recruiting violations had teeth. I'm sure Hal Mumme wasn't the first coach to ask for legal representation before an NCAA infractions committee. Although the potential accusations against him weren't "illegal" in the strictest sense, Mumme knew that if he was found to have violated NCAA rules, he could become a man without a football future.

At Mumme's request, I began putting together a dossier on the Kentucky recruiting scandal. At the heart of the matter, it seemed, was Kentucky's recruitment of Tim Couch and a few other players before Mumme arrived. I filed a brief and a statement of facts with the NCAA. Hal was slated to be interviewed in Indianapolis, near the NCAA's headquarters at the time.

When Mumme and I and walked into the hotel ballroom where his hearing would take place, we came upon a long row of tables in the center of the room. On one side sat NCAA officials. On the other were representatives from the University of Kentucky. It was one of the most intimidating settings I'd ever seen.

This wasn't a courtroom. The scene was more like an inquisition. Hal Mumme's career and professional reputation were indeed on the line.

Even though I was completely out of my element, I felt like I could get the job done for my friend.

God had given me that certainty. I would not let Hal Mumme die.

I proceeded to assume the role I was most comfortable with in proceedings of this kind: a bulldog criminal defense attorney. I was ready to take the fight to the other side in order to save my friend's reputation.

My principal argument on behalf of Hal was that Kentucky had managed its athletic department in a slipshod fashion. During much of Mumme's time with the school, Kentucky did not have a compliance officer in place.

That position normally monitors activities that run the greatest risk of violating NCAA rules, serving a watchdog role for the school's athletic programs.

I told those in attendance at the hearing that Mumme didn't have time to keep a close eye on all the activities surrounding his program. He was too busy managing the "X's and O's" critical to the task he was hired to perform: create and maintain a winning football program.

"Besides," I pointed out, "Coach Mumme wasn't around when a lot of these alleged violations took place."

The University of Kentucky as an institution could weather the shame of a football probation. The school's athletic reputation was already sound, thanks to the legendary basketball program that Adolph Rupp had built and others since then have maintained. For many years, football at Kentucky had been somewhat of an afterthought.

In fact, Rupp had been head coach of the Wildcats when a point-shaving scandal involving several of his players was brought to light in 1951. Those players had accepted money to alter the outcome of a number of games.

Anything Hal Mumme might have done, it seemed to me, paled in comparison to that.

After the hearings were over, Hal thanked me. I cautioned him that the investigation was likely to take several months, maybe into the next season, and that the outcome, as far as his future was concerned, was probably still hanging in the balance.

But, if he needed me again, all he had to do was pick up the phone.

Joel's only full season at Kentucky was the 2000 campaign. That year, the Wildcats went 2-9. Kentucky was eventually slapped with penalties stemming from major recruiting violations, and Mumme was fired from his job.

The only good news for Hal was that in the sanctions imposed by the NCAA, he was not among those blamed for playing a major role in the alleged violations. Had he been implicated more severely, he could have been saddled with a coach's worst nightmare: a show-cause penalty, in which sanctions against a coach at one school follow him to any future employment destinations, thus making that individual a coaching pariah and virtually un-hirable.

A show-cause penalty against Mumme also would have given Kentucky grounds to terminate his contract without any further compensation.

I'd like to think my efforts before the NCAA "inquisition" saved Hal from that fate.

When it came time for Mumme to settle with his Kentucky employers, Hal asked me to negotiate those terms. I flew back to Lexington and took care of that for him as well.

Still, I'm sad to say, Hal Mumme's coaching career has never been the same. He's still considered a coaching genius, and his latest job as of this writing had him in the role of offensive coordinator for the Dallas franchise of the reincarnated XFL.

As for Joel's own future at Kentucky, he returned for his senior year under new coach Guy Morris but gave up the sport in mid-season due to suffering several more concussions. I'm proud to say Joel channeled his passion for football into pursuit of a degree, and he graduated in 2002. He went into the marketing communications field and eventually started his own agency in The Woodlands, Texas.

In 2018, Joel moved his shop to Bryan, bringing his wife Pam—whom he met in eighth grade—and their three boys back home.

For the first time in a long time, I get to see Joel–and Austin, who also came home in 2018–pretty much whenever I want.

And for a father and grandfather, that's a very good thing.

22

Modern-Day Parables

I'm proud to be a Texan and proud of my ties to those who built this Lone Star State.

So, what does it mean to be a Texan? Let me offer one man's opinion.

A Texan is a southerner with a heavy dose of the western frontier at his or her core. Sprinkle in a little of the Hispanic culture of Mexico, and that's what a Texan is made of.

Texans believe everything is bigger here: the land, the people, and our ideas.

Football, as you now realize, is "king" in Texas. We take the game seriously and hold its heroes in reverence.

We're a "grandiose" people who live life large and offer no apologies for where we've been or where we're going. We're a tough, determined, and outspoken group. We hold our friends close, and we're not afraid of doing business with our enemies if we feel fairly certain a gusher or two might come in as a result of the partnership.

In Texas schools, our children stand each morning to recite both the Pledge of Allegiance and a pledge to the Texas state flag. It goes:

> *"Honor the Texas flag; I pledge allegiance to thee, Texas, one state under God, one and indivisible."*

"One and indivisible." How I wish that was the Texas of today.

Too many Americans have turned their eyes from God and have become ambivalent to the importance of His Word. As a result, too many people turn away from their fellow man, ignoring or condemning the plight of those who are downtrodden or outcast. Those lacking in righteousness do so saying that "God helps those who help themselves."

Nowhere in the Bible will you find that passage. Ben Franklin popularized the notion in his *Poor Richard's Almanack* series back in the eighteenth century.

What the Scriptures do say—repeatedly in both the Old and New Testaments—is that "God helps those who lack the ability to help themselves." And for the majority of my professional life, I have seen and worked with those people, men and women cast aside by the rest of society. Most often in criminal matters, the need for legal representation comes as a result of an individual's inability to address—or even recognize—personal, psychological, or moral shortcomings.

Blessed are the poor in spirit, for theirs is the kingdom of heaven.
Blessed are those who mourn, for they will be comforted.
Blessed are the meek, for they will inherit the earth.
Blessed are those who hunger and thirst for righteousness, for they will be filled.
Blessed are the merciful, for they will be shown mercy.
Blessed are the pure in heart, for they will see God.
Blessed are the peacemakers, for they will be called children of God.
Blessed are those who are persecuted because of righteousness, for theirs is the kingdom of heaven.
Blessed are you when people insult you, persecute you and falsely say all kinds of evil against you because of Me.
Rejoice and be glad, because great is your reward in heaven, for in the same way they persecuted the prophets who were before you (Matthew 5:3-12).

The job of a criminal defense attorney is to protect the rights of those whom too many of us would otherwise disregard if the opportunity presented itself. Flawed human nature easily condones incarceration with little thought given to the matter of due process of the law.

I've seen that with my own eyes.

Not every outcome in a court of law may be just, and in some cases, doubts may linger after a verdict is rendered. But every single American, regardless of gender, race, color, creed, political affiliation, or size of their bank account, deserves to be treated both fairly and constitutionally, and with respect as a child of God.

This holds true both inside and outside the courtroom and, I would argue, for every individual regardless of nationality or citizenship status.

Let me offer here a series of what I call "modern-day parables." These are stories from my own legal experiences that have helped bring me closer to God.

Jailhouse Conversion

We all know them: Those whose use their charm and personality to make their way through life. Their journey isn't always an easy one, and those individuals often go through relationships as if people were a disposable commodity.

Jimmy is sort of like that.

Both as an attorney and a judge, Jimmy was for many years a "repeat customer" of mine. He's a fellow close to my age who has hustled others most of his life. He's not a bad person, nor is he mean-spirited. He's just misguided and frequently seems to be in some sort of a financial predicament.

Too often, you could find Jimmy looking for comfort from the contents of a liquor bottle.

I became friends with Jimmy—which is not his real name—when I represented him in a DWI case years ago. That wasn't the first or last of Jimmy's drinking-related offenses. After I became a judge, he began showing up in my courtroom, facing the same charge time and time again.

Jimmy finally reached the legal end of his rope when he was arrested a few years ago on yet another DWI charge while on probation for a previous DWI offense. His case was assigned to another district judge, so I had a chance, as a friend, to counsel him on his plight.

At no charge.

My one condition for the advice I intended to give him was that he start coming to my Bible-study class. I've held those on weekends in and around the downtown Bryan area for years. It was in that setting that I began teaching Jimmy about "The Cross" and how he needed to die to his own "egocentricity."

Many of mankind's greatest problems stem from allowing our egos to control our behavior. The human ego is the devil's playground, and a key element of Embracing The Cross is accepting that our egos are oftentimes our biggest nemeses.

One must leave the "ego-life" in order to gain God's Life.

Bad things happen to everyone, whether through our own doing, the actions of others, or through "acts of God"–such as natural disasters, disease, or downturns in financial fortunes. Let me be clear: These come about as a result of God allowing the devil to bring us to our knees.

God wants us to understand—we must die to be resurrected in his Grace.

In my Bible-study classes, Jimmy was quick to take hold of these concepts. In fact, of all the people that I've encouraged to Embrace The Cross, Jimmy easily falls into the top ten percent of those who've grasped the concept and had their lives changed because of that.

I told Jimmy, "When bad things happen, we must 'Faith' our way through them. Only then will God bring Resurrection and Renewal back into our lives. We must never shake our fist at God."

Of course, in a legal jam, the timing for Jimmy to hear my message was perfect, but it was God's perfection, not man's.

Jimmy was facing the serious possibility of spending an extended period of time behind bars.

Back then, Jimmy was one of the people "least able to be incarcerated" I'd ever known. My fear for him was that if he spent any significant time in jail, he would either go crazy, become a menace to his jailers due to bad behavior, or wind up trying to kill himself.

I didn't want to see anything bad happen to Jimmy.

In the days leading up to his initial appearance in court, I told Jimmy, "When you go to the hearing, you need to humble yourself. Admit your wrongdoing. Don't try to fight it.

"Get honest before God and honest with the judge and, most importantly, do not fudge on one single thing. I want you to admit every bad thing you've done which has put you in this predicament."

Jimmy was scared. I could see that my words weren't providing him much comfort.

And I wasn't even finished.

"On the other hand," I urged him, "don't admit anything you *haven't* done. Just tell it like it is and tell them you're sorry.

"And be sure to tell the judge you'll take whatever punishment he finds just."

As he lingered after the final Bible-study session before he went to court, I looked at Jimmy and offered these words of "comfort": "Just go in there and fall on your sword."

Once I explained the meaning of that metaphor, Jimmy slowly nodded his head in understanding. My intended message was finally heard both loud and clear.

In court, Jimmy did exactly what I had suggested. The judge found him guilty and sentenced him to one hundred days in the Brazos County Jail. That was a heckuva better deal than being sent to prison for six or seven years, which is what I feared might happen.

Humility gets you a long way in a court of law. I know it does in mine.

Jimmy, it turned out, had a great attitude while he served his jail time. He understood why he was there. He was grateful for the opportunity to finally turn his life around. And, unexpectedly, during his time of incarceration, he began witnessing to other inmates about the importance of "Embracing The Cross."

He even read all the way through the Bible.

Have you?

In doing so, Jimmy became a disciple of the Lord.

After his release, Jimmy told me he thought God had used him to convert five or six people during his time in jail. I know for a fact he made one conversion.

Shortly after Jimmy's release, I got a letter from a young man who had met Jimmy in jail. He wrote of Jimmy's influence on him and how, while incarcerated with Jimmy, he had accepted Christ as his Lord and Savior.

All because of what Jimmy had shared with him.

Apparently, Jimmy told him about me, which was the reason the young man had sent me his letter. He wanted to thank me for helping him finally find the right path in life.

"Don't thank me," I said to myself, smiling. "Thank Jimmy.
"And thank God."

The Purple Camaro

One of my wife's friends in the Bryan-area antique business
was a kind and gentle woman by the name of Stella Brown.

Stella had a good-sized piece of property on South College
Avenue, not far from our house. On it were both her home and an
antique shop which she had been running for a number of years.

One day in the mid 1990s, Stella showed up at my office.
Without an appointment, she waited patiently to see me. When I
finally came out to greet her, I said, "Stella, I'm sorry you had to
wait. What a nice surprise to see you. What can I do for you?"

"I have a question," she said.

"Well, come on back and ask me that question."

It turned out Stella had been forced to close her business after
the Texas Air Quality Board had tested the soil on her land and the
furniture she was selling. Her property had been polluted by
arsenic from a nearby chemical plant.

Stella was heartbroken to lose her business. "This isn't right,"
she said. "But I don't know what to do."

Someone had suggested she talk to me.

"Can I sue someone?" she finally asked.

"I'm certain you have a strong case," I said.

"Would you represent me?" Stella looked hopeful for the first
time since we began talking.

I explained to her I wasn't "that kind" of an attorney. When
she asked if I knew someone who was, I told her I didn't, at least
not in the local area.

A sweet and refined woman, Stella knew little about her rights
under the law. What I knew, based on what she had told me, was
that she was nearing the end of the time she could legally file a
lawsuit for damages.

If I referred her case to one of the big environmental law firms
in Houston, I knew they would not be able to move quickly enough
to give her any chance at a fair settlement.

"Stella, you've got just a short time to do something here. I'll
try to find a lawyer who is an expert in this field and see if he or
she is willing to take your case."

Because Stella had waited so long, no one I contacted was interested in representing her.

So, I took the case.

The next day, I got out my law books, investigated the precedents, and drafted and filed a petition in federal court on her behalf. It was the least I could do for Stella.

As a small-town criminal defense attorney, I knew nothing about the federal courts. The best I thought I could do for Stella was to do more than just go through the motions. I wanted to follow the protocol for this sort of thing, hoping that I might get lucky and Stella would at least get something to restart her life.

But, after filing her suit, things moved at a snail's pace...until they didn't.

As time dragged on, all-too-familiar doubts began to plague me.

I convinced myself I couldn't go toe-to-toe against a team of corporate attorneys in an area of law that I knew little about. But because I had given Stella my word, I couldn't just throw in the towel. I was caught between the proverbial rock and hard place. Then, almost overnight, things started progressing very quickly.

When the company responsible for polluting an alarmingly large section of Bryan, a French firm called Elf Atochem, North America, finally responded to my petition, they did so in a very aggressive manner.

I had expected that. They would try to intimidate me in an effort to get the most meager settlement possible.

The judge in the case soon filed an order to hold a mediation on Stella's complaint. That would take place on the "home turf" of the firm representing the chemical company, the legal giant Fulbright and Jaworski in downtown Houston.

The thought of seeking justice for Stella against the likes of a law firm of that caliber sent my heart racing. My kindness had pushed me straight toward the lion's den.

One important aspect of my duties in the case was to oversee the discovery process in the case. What that meant was that our side would have to go through the boxes and boxes of documents relevant to the case which the defense was obligated to provide.

Unfortunately, Stella's side was just me. Just me, myself, and I.

I had a small staff, but this lawsuit was well beyond the pale of their experience.

It was also beyond mine.

I felt like a dog chasing a car, a scraggly mongrel which, in fact, catches the car and has no idea what to do with it.

When I began the physical process of going through box after box, I found myself battling the temptation to do what I was dead set against doing: merely go through the motions. There was no possible way I could get through all the discovery material, nor was I likely to find anything of use in what I did review, because I wasn't quite sure what I was looking for.

Still, I said my prayers and gave it the best I had to give.

The matter seemed hopeless, which meant Stella might lose everything.

On the day of the hearing, while driving from Bryan to Houston with one of my partners, Jack Dillard, who handled civil suits for our firm, I got a call from the office on my car phone. This was 1992, a long time before Steve Jobs put a smartphone in everyone's pocket.

"Pat Stacy needs to talk to you," I was told. Pat was another of the attorneys in our firm.

"Tell him I'm tied up today," I said. "I'm heading to Houston to meet my judge, jury, and executioner."

The blade of the guillotine was hanging perilously above my neck.

"Pat said it had something to do with that case."

"Okay," I said. "Tell him I'll give him a call."

I was about halfway down U.S. Highway 290 heading toward downtown Houston, when I reached Pat. He had some interesting news.

"Travis, I took a call from a guy late yesterday who said he had some important information about your lawsuit. I'm sorry, I didn't realize your mediation hearing was today."

"What kind of information?" I asked.

"I don't know. He wouldn't say, but he gave me his name and phone number."

Jack took down the information as I dictated it to him, I hung up on Pat and dialed the number he had provided. The phone rang once, twice, and then three times before someone picked up on the other end.

After we had introduced ourselves, I asked what information the man had for me. I didn't really care how he had found out I was handling the case for Stella.

He told me he had worked for Pennwalt, the company which Atochem had taken over, for about fifteen years.

"I know exactly how they polluted the area," he told me. "I've seen it with my own eyes."

He explained that arsenic was brought into the chemical plant by rail and then offloaded in what the man described as a "slipshod" manner.

"They just dump it out into piles and then scrape out the rail cars with shovels. They use backhoes and open bed trailers to move it around the plant. It's always been a mess.

"They're going to find out that all the water and much of the soil on that side of Bryan is polluted."

Which they ultimately did.

I'd had no success in finding what we now call a "whistleblower" to lend credence to my case. Now I had one on the line with me.

"Would you be willing to testify in a court of law about what you've just told me?" I asked.

"Yes sir, I would," he said.

All my failed efforts to help Stella had suddenly come to this.

In the weeks and months before that day, I had died the slowest and most agonizing of spiritual deaths. Numerous times.

It seemed my resurrection from death this time would be swift.

Early during the mediation hearing, attorneys representing Atochem offered Stella and me a $100,000 settlement. That might seem like a lot of money, but it was much less than Stella deserved. Little did the other side know that the "hick lawyer" they thought they were dealing with had an ace up his sleeve.

The back-and-forth between sides went on for at least two hours. At no time did I mention the conversation I had had earlier that morning in my car.

I guess you could say I was "priming the pump."

During a break, I told Jack, "Listen, I'm just going to give them the name that I have and see what happens. I won't tell them who the individual is. To be honest, I don't exactly know who he is or what role he might have played at the plant.

"Let's see how they respond to that."

Upon resumption of the hearing, I threw out the name of my caller.

It elicited no response.

But when I doubled down and shared what my "prospective witness" had told me, a noticeable chill came over the room. The expressions on the faces of the attorneys sitting across from me went noticeably slack.

They asked for another break.

Upon their return, I was offered the largest settlement I've ever seen. Attorneys typically get a third of a winning settlement, forty percent if the case is tried.

Stella's award was so large, I took only fifteen percent, which still easily cleared six figures.

Do the math.

Stella came out just fine.

So did my wife, Becky. She got a new purple Camaro convertible from the "resurrection" fee God had given me.

The Voice of God

College kids get into all sorts of mischief.

My office phone used to ring regularly with calls from parents wanting me to help get their kids out of trouble.

Not only is College Station home to Texas A&M University with an enrollment today of more than 60,000 students, but also Blinn College, a two-year school which educates about 19,000 students each term.

Not every kid who goes to college is bad–most aren't–but sometimes good kids wind up in the wrong place at the wrong time.

Randall Henry was just such a young man.

I met Randall–not his real name–in the early 2000s following an altercation in which he was involved outside a local college bar called Hurricane Harry's.

Randall was a student at Texas A&M, and, like many of his counterparts, he enjoyed ending a long day–or week–of school activities by sharing a few libations with his friends.

Hurricane Harry's is a popular hangout, mostly because it's located right across the street from the A&M campus. It's in close proximity to a wide array of student housing, from apartments within the Northgate District, which is adjacent to the campus and is the closest thing College Station has to a downtown area, to residence halls sitting on the campus itself.

In this matter, I didn't get a call from Randall's parents. He came by my office and hired me himself.

Randall made a good first impression, clean-cut and handsome. He was the kind of guy I would have loved to have seen my daughter date, save for one small detail.

"I've been accused of murder," he told me.

The rest of his story went something like this.

Randall had been drinking at Hurricane Harry's when a young coed sitting near the bar caught his eye. The two apparently chatted for a while, but when it came time to close down the bar, the girl told him good night and left with the friends with whom she had come to the bar.

Randall, a bit disappointed, accepted defeat and left by himself to head home for the night.

In the parking lot outside the bar, a guy tapped Randall on the shoulder and told him he didn't "appreciate you flirting with my girlfriend." Feeling he was falsely accused, Randall told me he fired back at the guy verbally, and what followed was fairly typical of how evenings can end in a college town: two intoxicated individuals mouthing off over something pretty inconsequential.

As Randall continued to tell me his story, he said that after he'd said his piece and reached his truck, he got inside, rolled down the driver's window, and put his key into the ignition. That's when, according to his side of the account, he got punched in the face.

"By the same guy that you'd been arguing with?" I asked.

"Yeah, same asshole. He came up to my truck, stepped on the running board and punched me through the open window. That really pissed me off."

People in a tough spot with the law frequently get emotional and in such a state often use vulgarities to describe their circumstances. Trust me, I've heard it all many, many times.

Randall went on to tell me that after being struck, he got out of his truck, grabbed a small pocket-knife he kept in the vehicle, and confronted his attacker.

He had grabbed the knife, he told me, "because I didn't know if the other guy had a gun."

It turned out he didn't, but before Randall could fully assess the situation, the new nemesis landed yet another blow with his fist. In retaliation, Randall lashed out with his knife and slashed his assailant in the chest.

"I thought I had just slit his shirt," Randall said. But it turned out to be much worse than that.

Instead, the blade of Randall's pocket-knife penetrated his attacker's chest and pierced the young man's heart. As a result of the injury, he died at the scene.

When the police arrived and listened to Randall's account of what happened, he was arrested for murder and then later released on bond.

Hearing what Randall had to say—he seemed truly remorseful and deeply regretted the incident—I took his case. My initial thought was an obvious one: to use a self-defense strategy. There seemed to be little doubt that Randall had not initiated the confrontation. But I also knew Texas law was clear about the use of "reasonable force" in confronting an attacker.

In Texas, you can't bring a knife to a fistfight, and Randall had.

In the Brazos County District Attorney's office, Shane Phelps was eventually selected to prosecute the case, which worried me.

In my thirty-one years of serving as a defense attorney, Shane was unquestionably the most powerful prosecutor I had ever faced. He was smart, a good forensic man, and carried with him an intimidating understanding of the law. I was a veteran, near the top of my trade, but in going against Phelps, at least with this case, I considered myself a sizable underdog.

As was my way when I lost or ignored my Faith in God, I begin imagining a worst-case outcome: life in prison seemed a distinct possibility for my client.

Before almost every criminal trial involving loss of life, the prosecution and defense attorneys seek to hammer out a reasonable plea agreement. Trying a case in court costs time and money, both for the taxpayers and the accused. If a deal can be struck that is satisfactory for both sides, everyone gets to go home feeling like justice has been done at a fair price.

In explaining this to Randall, I had told him that if we didn't seek to make a plea deal, there was a chance he could wind up being sentenced to a fifty- or sixty-year prison term. When Phelps and I met to discuss Randall's case, he offered fifteen years as punishment for the crime. If we accepted his proposal, Randall would most likely have to spend about seven or eight years behind bars.

I was in favor of a plea deal but was looking for a lighter sentence. While both Randall and his loved ones hoped for complete exoneration, I feared that might not be a possibility.

Eventually, I convinced Randall of that potential outcome. Just twenty-one years of age at the time of his crime, he could easily face imprisonment for that length of time or more.

We did not take the deal. Phelps said he would see me in court.

With the trial set to begin on a Monday, a pretrial hearing was scheduled for the preceding Friday. In it, we would argue my motion to have Randall's taped admission to having stabbed the victim disallowed as evidence in the case. That motion was denied.

After a restless night, I woke up at about 4 a.m. the day of the hearing in a state of complete and utter panic.

The grounds on which I wanted the recorded statement suppressed were fairly straightforward: Randall had volunteered to speak to authorities without legal representation. He had asked for an attorney but was forced to tape his version of the story without a lawyer being present.

Randall seemed to have understood his Miranda rights better than those who were investigating his alleged crime.

The young man's future was now firmly in my hands. I was uncertain I would be able to show reasonable doubt in the case and obtain a complete acquittal.

"Please, God," I prayed, having moved to the office in our home, "show me something that can give me strength to meet the challenge of this day."

I picked up the Bible that was always close at hand and sat down to peruse its pages. I eventually landed on a verse of scripture taken from Exodus 14:13. *"Stand still and see the salvation of the Lord,"* it read. I wrote down the verse on a notecard and placed it in my briefcase.

Despite getting an early start to the day, I was late for the hearing. After apologizing to the judge, we began the proceedings.

When it came time to play Randall's recorded statement, my mind drifted off to my impending failure and Randall's inevitable punishment. Yes, he had probably committed the crime, but it seemed obvious to me that he had not intended the dreadful consequences of his action.

At first, I paid little attention to the recording, having heard it several times before, but for some reason, I caught Randall's concluding words, "I guess I'll just sit still now and wait on my lawyer to save me."

Only the voice I heard wasn't that of Randall. It seemed to be the voice of God.

"Stand still and see the salvation of the Lord."

"Sit still and wait on my lawyer to save me."

Randall's remark resonated in perfect harmony with the passage I had found that morning. So close were the two lines in meaning that I saw the similarity as a sign from God. In that, it seemed as if He had answered my prayer, both strengthening my spirit and giving me greater legal resolve.

As I told Becky later, in that moment, I felt something warm come over the crown of my head. That warmth then descended into my ears, onto my cheeks and around to the back of my neck. It moved down the length of my body, and as it did, every part of me started to relax. By the time that sensation reached my toes, I was completely relaxed about my ability to match wits against Shane Phelps.

Randall was convicted and sentenced to ten years in prison. Phelps had offered a fifteen-year plea deal.

As a defense attorney, that's considered a win.

That may seem like a shallow triumph, but Randall was paroled after serving just five years of his sentence. After becoming a free man, he came back to Bryan to see me and thanked me for what I had tried to do for him.

He told me that he still thought of himself as a young man of promise and that he intended to make the most out of the rest of his life.

I wish I could say that's what happened, but I lost touch with Randall. I pray that he found peace and has been able to live a rewarding and contented life.

Killing a man can be a very heavy burden.

I continue to thank God for those times when I feel like He is speaking to me directly and lifting a burden from my heart.

I encourage you to listen for His voice, too.

23

Shaun Carney

Author's note: Shaun Carney is the father of four children, living and working in Louisiana. He's a college graduate and a veteran of the United States Army. As a fifteen-year-old gang member in Bryan, Texas, he was accused of murder. Travis Bryan was his court-appointed defense attorney. Carney shares here the story of how that relationship changed his life–saved his life–and brought him to the foot of The Cross.

I grew up in Ashtabula, Ohio, a small town about an hour east of Cleveland along the shore of Lake Erie. My mom was a drug addict. My dad was an alcoholic. He wasn't around much when I was young. Mom liked women.

Dad found a new start in Texas, and when I was nine years old, I moved to Bryan to live with him.

While he's my biological father, he's not the man I call "Dad" today.

There wasn't much structure in my real father's home. Most of his friends were bikers, and they were more into partying than taking life too seriously. From the time I started living with my father, it was my responsibility to get up in the morning and get ready for school. I always set an alarm and almost every morning fixed ramen noodles for breakfast. I had to walk to school every day, regardless of the weather, and when I got home in the afternoons, my father was usually drunk.

I can't say that I ever prayed for a better life when I was a kid because I didn't know anything about prayer or even about God. My mom and her friends were into witchcraft and satanic rituals, so that was the only "religion" I was exposed to as a child.

With no real structure or boundaries in my life, I joined a gang when I was eleven years old.

The Almighty Latin Kings are the largest and oldest Latino and Hispanic street gang in the world. Kings are everywhere: the U.S., Mexico, Puerto Rico; in big cities like Chicago–where the Kings got their start–to small Texas towns like Bryan. Despite my race– I'm white–and my age at the time, I moved up in rank with the Kings pretty quickly. I was a mean and angry kid, and that earned me respect from my fellow gang members.

For all practical purposes, the Latin Kings were the only family I had.

Most of what the Kings did around town was petty-crime stuff. We did get into some pretty serious brawls with other local gangs. One time about thirteen different guys jumped me and beat me up pretty bad. Even though I was in a gang, I was still going to school, so explaining what had happened to me, with all my cuts and bruises, took a little creative thinking on my part.

Unlike a lot of the Kings, I got myself to school almost every day. I guess I had an instinct that I wanted to try to find a better life.

When I was fifteen, a cousin of mine, Devlan, moved down from Ohio and moved in with my father and me. He brought with him a couple of his friends. They were all older than me, in their early twenties, and had been gang members themselves for a number of years.

Following the example they had set back home is probably the reason I joined a gang when I got to Texas.

My cousin and his friends called themselves Crips. The Crips are known mainly for being an African American street gang, but since I was a white kid who belonged to the Latin Kings, I guess Devlan and his friends could have been Crips. When Devlan found out I already belonged to a gang, he told me I would need to make a change real soon, or something bad would happen to me.

By the way, Devlan's legal middle name was "Lucifer."

Pretty soon after Devlan arrived in Texas, he and his friends began selling drugs on the street. Fearing for my life, I joined them. Over time, we started doing other things, too. One of Devlan's favorite activities involved a pretty, young girl he knew. Under Devlan's guidance, she'd go into one of the local college bars late at night and start flirting with some guy.

Eventually, she'd pretend to leave with him, and when they got into the parking lot, Devlan and the rest of us would jump the guy, rob him, and then beat him up pretty bad. We made a lot of money that way, and the cops never caught us.

One day Devlan hatched a new plan.

Back home in Ohio, Devlan had two kids. He decided he wanted the kids to live with him, but his ex-girlfriend who was the mother of his children wouldn't let them.

"I'm going to kill her and get the kids myself," he told me. "I need your help."

"I can't do something like that!" I replied, but Devlan wouldn't take no for an answer. He kept talking about it and continued to make plans.

Eventually, I went to my father and told him.

"Shut up!" he said to me. "You don't know what you're talking about. You're making all this up."

As Devlan continued to bother me about helping him kill his ex-girlfriend, I kept telling him I wasn't going to have any part of that. If he wasn't careful, I warned him, I was going to tell the police.

Eventually, I made that threat one too many times.

Devlan and I got into an argument at the house and before I knew it, his friends started beating me with a couple of baseball bats. As I've said, I was a mean and angry person growing up, and that had earned me respect as a Latin King. With Devlan, I tried to be a lot more submissive, just to keep the peace between us.

Devlan had never seen my other side...until he did.

After deflecting most of the blows from Devlan's friends, I looked up to see that Devlan had pulled out a knife and was moving toward me as if he intended to use it. When I saw that, I went into a rage and leaped forward to try to wrestle the knife away from him.

In the process, it was Devlan who got stabbed.

And later that night, it was Devlan who died.

I was arrested for his murder.

Given my age, I was placed into juvenile detention, and it was there that I awaited my fate. Not once did my father bother to come see me.

I was eventually charged with first-degree murder. When my court-appointed attorney couldn't work out a plea deal, a second attorney was named to my case.

That turned out to be my "dad," as I call, know, and love the man who changed my life and brought me to Jesus Christ.

You know him as Travis Bryan III.

The first time I met Dad, I was sitting on a bench in the hallway of the Brazos County Courthouse. I had been there, alone, for some time, and as I pondered what I thought might happen to me, I began to get scared. My dad later told me that when he walked up to me, I was shaking like a leaf.

When Dad introduced himself, he said, "Shaun, you're going to be okay." No one had ever said something like that to me in my life.

I wound up spending a lot of time with Dad in preparation for the trial. But we didn't just talk about Devlan's death. Pretty early on he asked me, "Do you know Jesus Christ?"

I told him my story at the risk of him thinking I was a really bad person but, he didn't flinch.

"God loves you," he said. "And as a Christian, it's my privilege to love you, too. We're going to get through this together."

I was found guilty, but in the weeks after the trial, evidence came forth that Devlan had died, not as a result of the stab wound I had inflicted, but as a result of his friends "finishing him off." Like I said, his middle name was Lucifer, and I guess his friends felt like he needed to die.

The judge in my case sentenced me to three years at a boys' home near Philadelphia. It was tough, but for the first time in my life I was surrounded with structure and discipline. I got my high school GED there and started playing basketball on the reform-school team.

And all during my stay, my dad and I regularly exchanged letters. He constantly encouraged me to do my best, follow orders, and keep reading my Bible.

During my trial, Dad regularly took time outside the courtroom to begin teaching me about the Holy Word. What I found in the Bible surprisingly made sense to me, and for the first time in my life I began to experience a sensation I'd never known before, something I would have to call peace.

After Philadelphia, I returned to Bryan. I met a young woman, we fell in love, and the two of us got married. After we had our little girl, Sierra, I decided a good way for me to support my family would be to join the army. I wound up getting stationed at Fort Sill outside of Lawton, Oklahoma, and my wife and daughter moved there with me.

I was pleasantly surprised when Dad told me he had spent time in the army at Fort Sill, too.

While I loved the army, it turned out the military wasn't my wife's thing. She had difficulty with the experience, so much so that in 2000, less than two years after we had met, the marriage was annulled. I was crushed to lose my family but found solace in serving my country.

Then the 9/11 attacks occurred. In the aftermath of that, I was deployed to Afghanistan and spent the final six months of my enlistment there.

When they say, "War is hell," they're not kidding. What I experienced in Afghanistan shook many of my Christian beliefs to the core. After I got out, I came back to Bryan, and my dad helped me get a job at a country club working as a greenskeeper. With a chance to make amends, I started spending time with my ex-wife and daughter.

Soon I moved back in with them.

While I was glad to be a daddy to my daughter, things with my ex-wife rapidly went downhill again. We fell back into the same bad habits we had known before. Given the friction between us, I began thinking about rejoining the army. That was the last thing my ex-wife wanted to hear.

We began to argue more and more, and those arguments got more and more ugly as Satan ratcheted up the tension between us.

Finally, one night, after our daughter had been gone to bed, things exploded. My wife grabbed a kitchen knife and tried to stab me. I retaliated by punching her in the face.

She called the police, and I was arrested.

I was humiliated that I had to call my dad from jail.

"I'm in trouble again," I told him.

"What happened?" he asked.

When I explained the situation, again Dad told me not to worry and that "everything will be okay."

Dad felt like he could probably get me off, given that my ex-wife had attacked me first. "It's still not right to hit a woman," he said, "ever." Dad also thought my military record could work in my favor. He met with my ex a couple times, asking her to drop the charges, but she was intent on teaching me a "lesson."

My case went to trial, and I was found guilty. Dad still felt like he might be able to get probation for me. But, when the time came for sentencing, I had a change of heart about what a "just" punishment should be. I had been praying a lot, and it seemed like God was telling me to "Embrace The Cross."

In the courtroom during the sentencing part of my trial, I surprised both Dad and the judge when I said, "I haven't been completely honest with you about what happened between my ex-wife and me."

Frustrated with my life as a man struggling to save his family, I had taken things out on my ex more than I had admitted in court. While I never enjoyed seeing a knife waved in front of my face, the truth was I had antagonized my ex to the point where she felt like a knife was the only thing that could get my attention. I told the judge I still considered myself to be a good father.

"Wait a minute," I said in the next breath. "I have the *makings* to be a good father, but I still have a lot to learn.

"I deserve to go to jail," I continued. "I believe God needs me to go to jail."

Dad was shocked at my courtroom confession, but after it was said and done, I hoped he would be proud of me for following his own advice.

"Always be honest," he had told me from the time we first met. "Never be afraid to tell the truth."

In living up to that charge, I discovered the truth doesn't always set you free. In fact, in my case, the truth put me behind bars.

I was sentenced to four years in prison and sent to one of the units in Huntsville.

While prison time might seem a "death" to most, in Embracing The Cross, I saw my death coming the night I had struck my ex-wife.

Prison, God had told me, would serve as my "resurrection."

And He was right!

One of the things that strengthened my resolve to put my life in God's hands was a conversation I'd had with Dad while I was in Bryan on leave from basic training in the army.

"Through all my failures," I said to him in his office one day, "why do you still love me?"

He smiled and replied, "Shaun, I look at you through the eyes of Christ. I see you as a Christian, but I also see you as a 'New Creation' of the Lord.

"I'll never stop loving you," Dad said. "It's as simple as that."

I've never forgotten those words.

Before I went to prison, Dad asked me, "Shaun, why did you tell the truth?"

I may have startled him with my answer.

"In Matthew 5:25, Jesus says, 'Settle the matter with your adversaries along the way before you get turned over to jail.'"

"You know that verse of Scripture?" he asked.

"That and a lot more, thanks to you."

During my incarceration, I began my personal ministry.

After leaving the Army, I knew I didn't want to work at a golf course the rest of my life, and one of the things which interested me was the possibility of becoming a preacher. In Huntsville, I began holding regular Bible-study classes, and over time attendance at those meetings grew. Given my own background, guys took my story to heart, as well as the story of God's Redemption in my life.

Even the leader of the prison's Aryan Brotherhood, a neo-Nazi prison gang, valued my testimony and began attending my Bible study sessions—along with a few of his friends whose white-supremacist loyalties had led them to jail.

For my good behavior, I was released on parole eighteen months early.

Upon yet another return to Bryan, I met yet another woman, and once again I became a husband. In the process, I adopted her four children from a previous marriage, two boys and two girls. With all my responsibility, Dad thought I needed to get serious about my future.

"Have you given any thought to going to college?" he asked me one day.

In fact, I had.

In the army, I had seen what a difference a college degree can make. The officers were all graduates, while almost all the enlisted men were not. At that point, I had set my sights on continuing my own education someday.

College, though, costs money.

"If you want to go," Dad told me, "I'll pay for your school, but on one condition."

Whatever condition that was, I knew Dad had my best interest at heart.

"I think you should go to a Bible college," he said. "I think that would be best for you."

"To become a preacher?" I asked.

"Not necessarily," Dad replied. "I just want you to get an education so you can give yourself and your family the lives you all deserve."

I agreed, and that's how I wound up at the Jimmy Swaggart Bible College and Seminary in Baton Rouge, Louisiana, where I still live today.

I've known Travis Bryan for nearly twenty-five years. As I look back over that time, I can truthfully say that the man has never judged me, not once. I know he loves me because he loves everyone.

The Bible says we are weak, but He is strong.

My life is sometimes still hard. My second wife abandoned her family and left me to raise our two daughters. I've done that. All of my children are good people with a great love for the Lord. Two of them have graduated from college. One is now attending Texas A&M.

When I come back to Texas to see my daughter, or to see my dad, I sometimes run into members of the Latin Kings, guys I grew up with on the streets of Bryan. They respect the fact I love Jesus, and they look to me now for advice about God.

While in prison, I got several certifications. One was in plumbing, and that's what I do now for a living. I hope to go back to college and get my master's degree in theology.

Is ministry in my future? Maybe. The Bible says that a man plans his steps, but God directs his path (Proverbs 16:9).

All I know is that God has my back, and He's brought me this far.

I wouldn't be where I am today without my dad. I shudder to think of my destiny if he hadn't come into my life…as my court-appointed lawyer.

In prison? I've already done that.

A criminal on the street? Perhaps.

Dead? A good possibility, I think.

Without Dad, I'm certain I wouldn't have had the chance to serve my country in the military. I know I wouldn't have known the joy of being a father and teaching my kids to love God.

And I would have never been able to turn my hardened heart into one eager to serve others and to love the Lord.

I now know what unconditional love means. "*Agape* love," Dad calls it.

My Father in Heaven loves me like that.

And so does my dad, right here on earth.

24

Sharing the Word

Entering Donnie Sullivan's third trial, Billy Carter and I decided to declare him an "indigent client" and seek state reimbursement for the expenses associated with our defense.

With murder charges hanging over his head a third time, Donnie had not worked for more than three years, since the day he was originally arrested in 1991. In the first two trials, his mother, Frances, had paid our fees based on whatever money she could dig up from her back yard...literally. When we told her a third trial would take place, she informed us her "savings" were depleted.

Bless her Mississippi heart.

Our request was approved, and Grimes County picked up our tab. Our fees were far less as "court-appointed lawyers," but by this time, all Billy and I desired was to see Donnie free to resume his quest for "life, liberty, and the pursuit of happiness."

Our Founding Fathers would have wanted nothing less for him.

Among the many receipts we turned in for our legal representation of Donnie were a couple of breakfast checks from a downtown Livingston diner. There, I met with Mike Barber, and over coffee and a couple of tasty breakfast omelets, we talked about Donnie in brief and about Barber's prison ministry at length.

I knew about Barber's long-standing efforts to bring the Word of God into prisons throughout Texas, across the country, and around the world. By the mid 1990s, he'd been preaching the Gospel behind bars for more than a decade.

Barber said he made his first visit to a prison only as a favor to a friend. He was reluctant to do so, but the experience changed his life.

"Travis, you know these people," he said of criminals. "A hard life leads to a hard heart."

He then quoted from Matthew 25:40: "As you did it unto the least of them…, you did it unto Me."

Around that same time, I started my first Bible study in Bryan. Mostly, I met with people I knew, friends and fellow Christians. After I gained some confidence in my approach, I began inviting clients, and occasionally, if on bail or having served his time, one would attend. Their real-world stories and legal challenges rivaled many of the parables to be found in the Bible, and the sessions grew in popularity as a result.

While God may often work in "mysterious ways," sometimes He just sort of slaps you in the face to get your attention. I've long believed that people come into our lives for a reason, and one of those people in my life was W. S. "Dub" Pearson.

I first met Dub around 1980 when he was publisher of *The Bryan Daily Eagle* newspaper. Up to that point, he had been a newspaper man his entire adult life, advancing through the advertising ranks. But shortly after we met, he left the paper and started a sporting goods store in town.

Dub had grown up in New Mexico and had been an all-state basketball player in high school. Our mutual love of sports was rivaled only by our devotion to family and love for God.

Dub and I became true friends after he took a job as a bailiff at the Brazos County Courthouse. He told me he had sold his business and wanted to pursue a "less stressful" occupation.

The primary duties of a court bailiff are to maintain order and provide security in the courtroom. Dub excelled at doing both, always in a friendly and respectful manner—unless the circumstances dictated he conduct himself otherwise. At the same time, the network of friends he made around the courthouse enabled him to pursue a new volunteer opportunity: ministering to prisoners, especially those in state prisons around Texas.

When he first told me about the experience, it was obvious he was having a lot of fun turning lawbreakers toward the Lord.

"Travis, you need to come with me sometime and watch how God touches these people's lives," he said. Always the consummate salesman—both in preaching about Jesus Christ and in promoting his ministry to others—Dub was constantly on me to make a trip to nearby Navasota. It was there, at a correctional facility known as the Wallace Pack Unit, that he had his closest prison ministry. I put him off as long as I could, but when I realized he wasn't going to take no for an answer, I finally agreed to make that trip with him.

Mike Barber had painted a pretty poignant picture about the importance of leading convicts to Christ. So, when Dub Pearson opened that door for me, I suspected God was leading me down an important path.

My first visit to Navasota left me a little bemused. Dub was working on a couple of two-time offenders, and it didn't seem like he was making much headway.

"Yeah, the victories sometime come slowly," he laughed as we left the prison one sunny afternoon. "But the signs of redemption are almost always there. You just have to look closely to find them."

He was right, and soon I realized there was no "mystery" to this particular part of God's plan for me. I've been involved in prison ministry ever since, for more than twenty-five years.

Before he died in 2014, Dub and I visited prison installations throughout central and southeast Texas. One of our most important duties, we felt, was to remind the men behind bars that while they are serving time as punishment for their early crimes, their Heavenly Father has already forgiven them for their sins.

The fortunate ones in jail stay connected to family and friends on the outside. They make the most of incarceration, learning new skills, enhancing their education, and perhaps most importantly, reflecting on their circumstances and the future which awaits them. Those individuals retain a certain amount of trust in others, and many are receptive to the teachings of Christ.

The hardened criminal takes a lot longer to convert. They are slaves to their anger and ego and are unable or unwilling to accept the Unconditional Love of God. That particularly holds true for those in jail for the first time. I've seen many first-time offenders spend too much of their prison existence seething at the "injustice" of their incarceration.

"Fool me once, shame on you. Fool me twice, shame on me." You won't find that in the Bible, but that centuries-old Italian proverb describes a lot of us and how rigorously we hold onto our egos.

Not everyone who has broken the law is in search of redemption. Sometimes, the light of Goodness that God has placed in each of us goes dark. Those with troubled souls must fight against the ways of Satan and reach for the ray of hope that is God's Love.

Some, like Shaun Carney, eventually see that Light.

For the past twenty years, much of my prison ministry work has been devoted to the women serving time at the Bryan Federal Prison Camp. "FPC Bryan" is a minimum-security facility located on the campus of the old Allen Academy here in my hometown.

My grandparents were big supporters of Allen Academy and the students who attended preparatory school there. The facility opened its doors in Bryan back in 1899 as a boarding school for boys. During World War I, military instruction was added to the curriculum.

Many were the Sundays when I was growing up that I'd run into Allen students at my grandparents' home. In the late 1980s, the school moved to the east side of Bryan and adopted a private-school coeducational model.

The FPC Bryan facility is about a ten-minute drive from my house. For many years, I held Bible study sessions there on Saturdays. Now I go every Wednesday evening.

The chapel where we meet used to be the Allen Academy mess hall. As a volunteer through the years, I've worked with several prison chaplains to conduct my ministry at the facility.

I've offered Bible instruction study to hundreds of women.

By and large, the inmates who attend are receptive to my efforts and my teachings. Most are in jail for non-violent crimes, like selling drugs or embezzlement. Some come to my class for the first time and leave after a while, never to return, but most stay. I've had some women who've attended my classes for as many as ten or twelve consecutive years.

Regardless of the crime or punishment, all of these women are broken. My regular attenders are almost always open to God's Word.

My message to them is one of pure Grace, not law. I try to make it clear to the gathering that while they are where they are because of their violation of man's law, God's law is a much different thing.

"God's law is about Love," I tell them. "Love of God and Love for others, especially your enemies."

Most of them get a chuckle out of the "enemies" thing.

"You don't gain acceptance from God by your actions," I tell them. "Christians who understand His teachings don't relate to God in a 'right-or-wrong' fashion. We reach Him and honor Him through the dynamic of 'Death and Resurrection.'

"We must be willing to suffer and die so He can Resurrect, Renew, and Heal us."

Most modern churches don't preach this message to the extent I try to teach it, so when I introduce the concept, newcomers to my Bible study class oftentimes have little idea what I'm talking about.

Paul wrote in 1 Corinthians 2:2, "For I determined not to know anything among you except Jesus Christ and Him crucified." This, I believe, is *the* central tenet of the Bible.

Not "I" the ego, but Christ.

The Christian life is about Grace and God's Love, God's *Unconditional Love*. God loves everybody. This is going to sound blasphemous to some, but God even loves Satan, who was the original "prodigal son." God doesn't like what Satan does, but he loves all his creatures. When I share that in prison, the women shout with glee. Many, at some point in their lives, have been accused of having the "devil inside them," so to hear that God loves them regardless of their sins gives them, I think, a greater sense of hope.

"The Cross," I share, "comes to everyone, good or bad, whether they 'deserve' it or not. In each of our lives, there is death: someone has hurt you, or you've hurt someone you care about. When you feel bad, really bad, you die a little inside, right?"

Most of the time heads nod in agreement. Occasionally, there's an "Amen!" from a member of the group.

"When Christ died, He died for our sins. When He rose from the dead, He ascended into heaven and *began His eternal life* there with God. What follows is our own earthly hopelessness, despair, and ultimately our own death, which begins the Resurrection and Redemption.

"That's God's Plan for us, and it is His Hope for us, too," I tell them.

That message resonates with the women. They appreciate the instruction I bring into their midst. The chaplains love what I'm doing, and prison officials always tell me my efforts make a difference.

I'm currently ministering to one young woman who says she wants to teach the Word when she leaves prison. And I believe she will. She's originally from Africa and moved to America when she was young. She became a Christian before she ran afoul of the law, and she's regularly attended my Bible studies for nearly a decade. She now has a complete understanding of The Cross, and I hope she'll use that knowledge for her own sake and to share with others after she is released.

My favorite time to visit the prison is in the dead of winter. By the time I get there after work, the grounds are mostly dark, illuminated by streetlights placed around the prison grounds. All is quiet.

Entering the classroom inside the chapel building, the group warmly greets me. I get caught up on their lives, and they get caught up on mine. Regardless of how my own day or week has gone to that point, I always feel renewed in their presence.

When we're done and after I've offered prayers and said my goodbyes, I head back out into the cold. Despite the darkness and the chill, a real inner peace comes over me.

I've learned to stop and savor those moments there at FPC Bryan, to sense God's Presence and His Power, and to feel a more intense closeness to Him than I experience almost anywhere else.

God is so, so Good.

25

Judgment Day

I ran across a quote the other day I'd like to share with you:

If it weren't for Jesus, I would not be where I am today, and my life would be without purpose. I've heard kids say they want to be just like me when they grow up. They should know, I want to be just like Jesus.

Baseball star Albert Pujols spoke those words. And he's an Angel. To be exact, Albert Pujols is a Los Angeles Angel and a future baseball Hall-of-Famer. And it turns out I have a connection with Albert.

My co-author, Tim Gregg, helped support Albert's charitable foundation during his years as a member of the St. Louis Cardinals. Tim designed the original website for the Pujols Family Foundation and spent time in the Pujols' home working to promote Albert's wife, Deidre, in her cooking ministry.

I wish I'd thought to spread the word of God through the consumption of food.

In 2009, Albert Pujols won Major League Baseball's Roberto Clemente Award, awarded each year to the player who exemplifies the highest standards and personal values, both on the field and off.

As I looked through the list of recent Clemente award winners, I was struck by how many of those players have an open relationship with Jesus Christ.

The world needs more people like Albert Pujols, individuals unafraid to let themselves be known as men and women serving the Lord.

One of my favorite golfers is Bubba Watson. The two-time major champion can be about as entertaining as they come, both on and off the golf course. But he's a Christian, too. He found the Lord when he was nineteen, renewed his Faith when he got married to his wife, Angie, and now calls golf *"an avenue for Jesus to use me to reach as many people as I can."*

I won't argue with that.

All of us as Christians–and even those who aren't–will someday face a judgment day before our Heavenly Father. But for me, I also consider March 17, 2008, as a "judgment day," in that I was sworn in to be Judge of the 272nd Judicial District Court of the State of Texas, on that day here in Bryan, Texas.

I would be hard pressed to find a day–other than the day I married Becky, or the days our three children were born–that means more to me than St. Patrick's Day of 2008. I didn't intentionally choose that day to become a judge, but my ancestors, along with those of Stephen F. Austin, are of Scotch-Irish descent.

Throughout most of my career in the law, I gave little thought to becoming a judge. But the rigors of my job as a criminal defense attorney finally took their toll and when my predecessor in the 272nd District Court, Rick Davis, asked if I'd be interested in trying to succeed him, I gave the matter some thought and decided I was interested.

Despite the cut in pay I would have to take.

Did I get rich as a defense attorney? No, but the money I did make, thanks to my brother Tim's financial assistance, set up my wife and me to live comfortably in whatever I chose to do after leaving my firm.

State district judges in Texas are appointed by the governor. Rick Perry was governor in 2008, and while I did not know Rick, I knew one of his closest associates, who also is a dear friend of mine.

Phil Adams and I are fellow Aggies who chose to call Bryan, Texas, our lifetime home. Phil is an insurance executive here, and a long-time member of the Texas A&M University System Board of Regents. I asked Phil if he could put in a good word for me with Governor Perry, and he did. That, along with Rick Davis's help got me my judicial appointment and I've held the office since the spring of 2008.

State judges in Texas stand for reelection every four years, but I have run unopposed since becoming a member of the bench.

At my swearing-in ceremony at the Brazos County Courthouse in downtown Bryan, I asked Roland Searcy, the incumbent whom I ran against in my quest to become district attorney 30 years before, to be my "keynote" speaker. Roland and I eventually became great friends and I was honored he was willing to speak on my behalf.

I told Roland I wanted him to challenge me in my new duties with his remarks. He did so by citing from an address by Margaret Marshall, the former Chief Justice of the Supreme Court of Massachusetts.

It was not lost on me that Searcy chose to share wisdom from a female judge.

"The business of law," Searcy told the gathering, quoting Marshall, "is to make sense of the confusion of what we call 'human life,' to reduce it to order but at the same time give it possibility, scope, and even dignity.

"And it is truly the business of law, and it is in great measure the responsibility of the members of the judiciary, to administer and interpret the law to replace the confusion experienced by society with order, hope, and dignity."

Roland, I hope I've met your challenge.

What's the hardest part about being a judge? Occasionally presiding over life-and-death decisions is a moral challenge for me, but it's the law which I'm sworn to uphold.

Another facet of the job which many judges struggle with— myself included—is handing down rulings which won't be looked upon favorably by a large segment, or even the majority of the population.

Judgeships are elected positions and thus, there is an element of politics to the position.

When I suggested the ex-Marine who killed two people may not have received a fair trial in my own courtroom, I was opening myself up to public dissent. Second-guessing the case was risky, but I knew in my heart it was the right thing to do.

A lot of judges are former prosecutors. That's a very common "career move" in our judicial system. Successful prosecutors are thought to make good judges.

Well, I suggest that until you've defended someone charged with a serious crime, you don't really get the complete picture regarding an individual's constitutional rights.

And, as a judge, I see that as my biggest duty: to uphold the rights and liberties spelled out in the Constitution of the United States of America, no matter the outside pressures, influences, or considerations of "political correctness."

It's a matter of "justice for all."

Reflecting back on one's life, as I've attempted to do here, is a humbling experience. I already knew that I'd spent too much of my time on golf courses in an attempt to replicate the success of pros like Bubba Watson. I've never come close to being the golfer my daddy was, but I would have enjoyed seeing him and my son, Austin, go head to head while both were in their prime.

I guess, technically, Austin still is.

I'm not afraid to admit that at the age of seventy-three I'm now a little past my prime. In concluding work on this book–which, believe it or not, has taken more than a year–I've announced my retirement as a district judge. Will that bring an end to my life in law? Probably, but the truthful answer is, "I don't know."

Could I be lured back into the role of a defense attorney? Maybe, but probably not.

What I'm hoping to do with my retirement is spend more time with Becky and help lighten her load as much as I can. I'm also looking forward to spending more time with my boys, since they're now back in town, and make more trips to Colorado to see my daughter and her family.

I suspect I'll also be doing more work in service to the Lord. This book is an attempt at that. In fact, it's the starting point to my own ministry which will be called Faith in Resurrection Ministry. You can learn more about that at the website www.faithinresurrection.org.

I will also continue supporting our local Salvation Army corps.

A year after Daddy died, he received the Jefferson Award for Public Service, a national honor presented by the American Institute for Public Service. I'd like to quote an excerpt from a 2010 story by Crystal Galny, a local news anchor at station KBTX-TV.

It's a name that can be seen all over town, from street signs, to signs welcoming people to the city. It's a name that belongs to Travis Bryan, Junior.

He was a man loyal to the city that bears his family name, and to the bank founded by that family.

"My dad, Travis B. Bryan told me to take care of the customer and I would be taken care of," Travis Bryan, Jr. said.

Bryan served as Chairman of First National Bank for 43 years. During a 2002 interview, he explained his motto for success.

"By treating people the way they like to be treated. That's the name of the game," Bryan said.

"He would never abandon someone in their difficulties if he knew they were still trying. I've seen him loan people money out of his own pocket that he knew the bank examiners would not approve," his son, Travis Bryan III said.

"First National Bank means everything to me, second to Jesus Christ, who is the most important thing in mine or anybody else's life, if they've got any sense," Bryan, Jr. said.

Known for his deep-seated faith, Mr. Bryan served as a Deacon at First Baptist Church. But it was another organization, also known for saving souls, he fell in love with during World War Two. Then went on to lead it locally for 35 years.

"People don't know that he really was the Salvation Army. I've been in his office more than one time to see him as he dealt with people who were in need," Merrill Green said.

"He did everything, and he did it right out of his office. So if people came in and needed help from the Salvation Army, he's the one that would stop everything and take care of that family or those people that came in," State Representative Fred Brown said. Brown served as a board member for the Salvation Army for 15 years.

I currently serve as a board member for the Salvation Army's local corps here in the Bryan-College Station area. Like my father, I believe in the good work of the Army in helping those in need.

As I've recounted in this book, I spent an extraordinary amount of time during the middle part of my life seeking to find both Spiritual Salvation and answers to life's most perplexing questions. I did so through an intense study of the Bible.

For most of my life, I was told by others that's where I needed to look to ease my burdens. An intense lack of inner peace ultimately motivated my search, and I proceeded forward with all the passion and dedication I could muster.

As a veteran criminal defense attorney, I knew the importance of hard work and was willing to do what it took to best represent my clients. I spent much of my free time–after dinner, during weekends, and even on vacation–preparing for the battles which awaited me in court. So I was accustomed to going more than the extra mile, and when I put that same zeal to my study of the Bible, the Truths I found in there gave me a hunger to learn even more.

I don't claim to have all the answers. I also hope I haven't come across as "preachy" or a spiritual know-it-all within these pages. Still, I have a complete conviction that the principles I've shared in this book not only have merit, but also can be a road map to Eternal Salvation.

As I've told friends and acquaintances, some of whom sort of chuckle behind my back at my fervent commitment to God, I can't really explain why I feel so strongly about this, other than I believe God has opened my eyes to one of His Fundamental Truths.

If you choose to share this book with a friend for purposes of helping them find God, mark this page and tell them to begin reading here, or at least make sure they get here before putting the book aside.

Let me revisit a few of the tenets of what I've called here "Embracing The Cross."

Our greatest enemy in life, for each and every one of us, is our own ego, our "self-centeredness," if you will. The Bible teaches that for us to live for Christ, our ego must die. This is accomplished through our participation in the death, burial, and resurrection of Jesus Christ.

Then He said to them all: "Whoever wants to be My disciple must deny themselves and take up their cross daily and follow Me. For whoever wants to save their life will

lose it, but whoever loses their life for Me will save it"
(Luke 9:23-24).

This "Christ-event" described in Luke can be mystically
reenacted in each of our lives. We are called into Fellowship with
the Lord, a union only achievable through the demise of our self-
importance. In taking up the Cross daily, our old self is slowly
dismantled, and we are transformed from a self-centered to a
Christ-centered existence.

> *"I have been crucified with Christ and I no longer live, but
> Christ lives in me. The life I live in the body, I live by faith
> in the Son of God..."* (Galatians 2:20).

One of the reasons the idea of Embracing The Cross has fallen
out of favor in the modern church is that it requires an acceptance
of hardship. We must suffer at the Cross. It is only through this
tribulation that we move deeper and deeper into the Kingdom of
God.

> *"We must go through many hardships to enter the
> kingdom of God"* (Acts 14:22b).

It is only through sharing the suffering of Christ on the Cross that
we can know Him and the power of His Resurrection.

> *"I want to know Christ—yes, to know the power of His
> resurrection and participation in His sufferings, becoming
> like Him in His death, ..."*
> (Philippians 3:10).

The truth is we all suffer in life: through anxiety, physical pain,
stress, conflict, and emotional upheaval. God never intended our
lives to be perfect. He knew Adam and Eve would sin against Him,
thus setting a precedent which the rest of us have followed.

God does not cause our suffering directly, but He does
withdraw His protective "hedge" from around us. He allows Satan
to attack our lives, just as the devil was allowed to bring about the
earthly demise of God's Own Son at Calvary's hill.

A Biblical dramatization of the suffering Satan can bring to our lives comes from the story of Job.

Job was not an evil man. He was a good man, and as we've all experienced firsthand or witnessed in the lives of others, good people suffer at the Cross. When you read the book of Job, you see just a few of the many instruments of suffering Satan has at his disposal. Everything bad that happens to us comes directly from Satan's hand, including death, disease, weather calamities, persecution. and unfair treatment, whether from individuals or from the responsibilities which hold domain over our daily lives, such as schools, employment, and even our government.

This suffering at the hands of Satan is one of the main things that can destabilize the corrupt aspect of our "old self." "Self" cannot love unconditionally the way God does. Self always wants to receive and too rarely wants to give unto others.

Self can attend church regularly, pray with seemingly humble intent, and even witness to others about the "Good News" of Jesus Christ, but when these things are done for the specific purpose of reaching Heaven, they become meaningless in the eyes of God.

Strangely, Satan destroys his own power when he is allowed by God to attack:

> *"Since the children have flesh and blood, He too shared in their humanity so that by His death He might break the power of him who holds the power of death—that is, the devil—..."* (Hebrews 2:14).

The narcissist within us is the devil's greatest tool. Yet, when Satan knocks us down, we wind up falling into God's Blessings. In such despair, control is wrenched from our hands, and our destiny is placed in the Hands of God. In that moment the choice becomes ours. We can choose to remain in Satan's misery, holding onto our old sinful nature, or become a part of our "new nature" by accepting the Unconditional Love offered by God through His Son, Jesus Christ.

Transformation does not occur in our efforts to "keep the rules," even obeying God's Commandments, unless we allow ourselves to die and rise with Christ. Salvation comes through the death and resurrection to be found at the Cross of Jesus Christ.

Or don't you know that all of us who were baptized into
Christ Jesus were baptized into His death? We were
therefore buried with Him through baptism into death in
order that, just as Christ was raised from the dead through
the glory of the Father, we too may live a new life.
For if we have been united with Him in a death like His,
we will certainly be united with Him in a resurrection like
His. For we know that our old self was crucified with Him
so that the body ruled by sin might be done away with, that
we should no longer be slaves to sin—because anyone who
has died has been set free from sin (Romans 6:3-7).

Sadly, most churches have stopped teaching these key elements to be found by Embracing The Cross. While the Cross is the only true gospel, churches present what I think of as a "selfish gospel."

"Believe in Christ, and you'll go to heaven," churchgoers are taught today. While true, this notion only scratches the surface of what God intended to be our true destiny in this world. There is no Transformation without the deep inner working which comes from Embracing The Cross.

Through the Cross, we are given Faith, the Faith of Jesus Christ. When bad things happen to you, when the devil attacks with one of his many devices designed to bring you to your knees in anguish, "Faith through" those times and know that on the other side of every darkest death is the brightness which comes from the New Resurrection.

And when times are good, enjoy the moment, count your blessings, and give thanks to God.

Give thanks to the Lord, for He is good.
    His love endures forever.
Give thanks to the God of gods.
    His love endures forever.
Give thanks to the Lord of lords:
    His love endures forever.
to Him who alone does great wonders,
    His love endures forever.
who by His understanding made the heavens,
    His love endures forever.

who spread out the earth upon the waters,
  His love endures forever.
who made the great lights—
  His love endures forever.
the sun to govern the day,
  His love endures forever.
the moon and stars to govern the night;
  His love endures forever.
to Him who struck down the firstborn of Egypt
  His love endures forever.
and brought Israel out from among them
  His love endures forever.
with a mighty hand and outstretched arm;
  His love endures forever.
to Him who divided the Red Sea asunder
  His love endures forever.
and brought Israel through the midst of it,
  His love endures forever.
but swept Pharaoh and his army into the Red Sea;
  His love endures forever.
to Him who led His people through the wilderness;
  His love endures forever.
to Him who struck down great kings,
  His love endures forever.
and killed mighty kings—
  His love endures forever.
Sihon king of the Amorites
  His love endures forever.
and Og king of Bashan—
  His love endures forever.
and gave their land as an inheritance,
  His love endures forever.
an inheritance to His servant Israel.
  His love endures forever.
He remembered us in our low estate
  His love endures forever.
and freed us from our enemies.
  His love endures forever.

And who gives food to every creature.
His love endures forever.
Give thanks to the God of heaven.
His love endures forever (Psalm 136).

Epilogue

"Go, My people, enter your rooms and shut the doors behind you; hide yourselves for a little while until His wrath has passed by" (Isaiah 26:20).

The COVID-19 pandemic has impacted the world and affected many of us in deeply profound ways. But a call to "shelter in place" is nothing new, going back, as we read in Isaiah, to Biblical times.

There are countless verses within the Bible that speak to plague, wide-spread destruction, and the wrath of God. This is the nature of the Old Testament, where God is depicted as a temperamental, vengeful, and at times, almost "bipolar" almighty being. In fact, I believe the Old Testament is God taking the blame for what He allows Satan to do.

In the New Testament, Jesus reveals that God's True Nature is Love, which is the central premise of the Christian faith.

Many have called the coronavirus a "plague," and while that might be an accurate description, I do not believe the COVID-19 pandemic is punishment from God. Given the global death, sickness, and financial hardship which the disease has caused, little good, at least on the surface, has come about from the coronavirus.

But the Bible teaches a paradox: Life is hidden under death and strengthened under weakness. God turns people over to their own selfish desires for a good purpose: to deliver them from the sinful nature of their own egos.

God sometimes removes His protective hedge and allows the devil to attack as part of His overall plan.

The coronavirus, as it turned out, provided an extraordinary backdrop against which to present the power and the meaning of The Cross.

As Tim and I sought to bring this book to an apt ending, we prayed that God might reveal to us His own purpose for the story we've shared here. Several were the paths we explored, but each led us to a Spiritual or narrative dead end.

The coronavirus, on the other hand, provides an extraordinary backdrop against which to present the power and the meaning of The Cross. Particularly so in my case, as I was directly exposed to someone who told me they had the virus.

That happened to me after I had lunch with a friend following Texas Governor Greg Abbott's order allowing restaurants to reopen. It was only after our meal together that my friend found out one of his relatives with whom he'd recently come in contact had tested positive. The next day after I saw him, he called to tell me he had tested positive, too.

The local health department put me and my entire district court staff on a fourteen-day quarantine. I was tested when a pair of long cotton swabs were forced up my nostrils and into my nasal cavities. Five days later, I got the result.

I had tested negative for COVID-19.

For me in quarantine–and for many of you, too, I'm sure–sheltering in place provided an opportunity to slow down; to stop, sit, and think; to reflect and meditate more deeply on God's Holy Word and to find comfort there for these difficult times.

> *"You will not fear the terror of night, nor the arrow that*
> *flies by day,*
> *nor the pestilence that stalks in the darkness,*
> *nor the plague that destroys at midday"* (Psalm 91:5-6).

The coronavirus may or may not be a portent of the end times. Humankind has coped with the sometimes-unsavory nature of microbes throughout and before recorded history. In our technological and scientific modern times, it is humbling that something so small can loom so large along the human landscape. And that the simple act of separating ourselves from those we do not know, as well as our friends and neighbors, is thought to be a powerful elixir in the quest to restore a healthy order to our everyday lives.

Yet, as the Bible tells us, God seeks unity among us, bringing people together in fellowship.

One place where it is impossible to keep a six-foot barrier between yourself and the next person is within the confines of a jury box. And that is a primary reason why business at the courthouse during the COVID-19 pandemic has slowed to a crawl.

When a friend recently asked me how things were at work, I told her, "We've had to swallow a camel, and we're straining at a gnat." She looked at me somewhat curiously at my comment, so I explained that cases had gotten horribly backlogged, and we were having difficulty keeping the wheels of justice turning.

Mostly because of our inability to conduct a jury trial.

The jury trial is the "hammer" that makes the entire legal system work. Many lawyers, you should know, won't do much until they are faced with having to come to trial.

There's something profound about presenting a case in court, and simply seeing the whites of the jurors' eyes will often make a prosecutor or a defense attorney seek a settlement or plea bargain in a case. You might be surprised to learn that it is physically impossible to seek a jury-rendered court verdict for every single case. The majority of cases on my docket never go before a "jury of peers."

Like much of the rest of the business world, my associates at the courthouse and I, as a result of efforts to social distance, were forced to conduct many of our pre-trial meetings online. Never in my wildest dreams as a judge did I imagine that I'd be spending so much time talking to a computer. Like a lot of you, I grew to appreciate the Zoom web-conferencing app. Somehow, I think Zoom may become an important part of my future ministry, too.

Sure beats riding on the back of a donkey.

Is there an upside to this pandemic? I believe so, because through Faith, there is always a resurrection to every death.

Chances are that by the time you've read this page, our world will have moved past the pandemic and life will have returned to normal, although I'm guessing it may not ever be again what we've known previously as normal before.

And that will be okay. If you think about it, much of the Bible preaches about changing what is "normal" forever.

Consider what Paul had to say to the Corinthians:

> *"So from now on we regard no one from a worldly point of view.*

Though we once regarded Christ in this way, we do so no longer.
Therefore, if anyone is in Christ, the new creation has come.
The old has gone, the new is here!" (2 Corinthians 5:16-17)

I, for one, very much welcome this new creation in a pandemic and post-pandemic world.

One of the websites I visit from time to time is called the *Center for Action and Contemplation.* I immediately liked the name, although I might have put the "thinking" part before the "doing."

The site is the home of the daily meditations of Father Richard Rohr, a Franciscan priest who founded the Center in Albuquerque more than thirty years ago. As the website says, Rohr is a "globally recognized ecumenical teacher."

I'm not always in agreement with Father Rohr's teachings, but frequently, I feel compelled to pass his posts on to family and friends. His message on COVID-19 was one I'd like to share with you here:

We are in the midst of a highly teachable moment. There's no doubt that this period will be referred to for the rest of our lifetimes. We have a chance to go deep, and to go broad. Globally, we're in this together. Depth is being forced on us by great suffering, which as I like to say, always leads to great love.

But for God to reach us, we have to allow suffering to wound us. Now is no time for an academic solidarity with the world. Real solidarity needs to be felt and suffered. That's the real meaning of the word "suffer"—to allow someone else's pain to influence us in a real way. We need to move beyond our own personal feelings and take in the whole.

***

I hope this experience will force our attention outwards to the suffering of the most vulnerable. Love always means going beyond yourself to otherness. It takes two. There has to be the lover and the beloved. We must be stretched to an

encounter with otherness, and only then do we know it's
love. This is what we call the subject-subject relationship.
Love alone overcomes fear and is the true foundation that
lasts (1 Corinthians 13:13).

As I've already mentioned in these pages, America went through a similar opportunity for Spiritual transformation in the aftermath of 9/11. Eventually though, the tide of renewed Hope faded and then vanished completely. I pray the "new creation" which Father Rohr speaks of emanating from our shared COVID-19 experience may indeed be life-changing and long-lasting.

The Real Truth, though, as I see it, is that until Jesus returns as prophesied in the Bible, our earthly existence will always be comprised of yin and yang, ebb and flow, and death and resurrection.

The Apostle Paul, in discussing the message of The Cross in his contributions to the New Testament, often talked about the many times he had faced death. He wrote in 2 Corinthians 11:23, "I have worked much harder, been in prison more frequently, been flogged more severely, and been exposed to death again and again." That process, he went on to say, brings one to a spiritual reality that can't be achieved any other way.

One of the most dramatic life-and-death stories of the Bible is the account of Jesus walking on water. In the version contained in the gospel of Matthew 14:22-32, once Jesus reaches the boat containing His disciples, they become afraid. Fearing that the sight of Jesus atop the water is but an apparition, Peter seeks proof. "Lord," he says, "if it is You, tell me to come to You on the water."

When Jesus does, Peter steps out of the boat and, for a short time, walks among the waves himself. Then he grows fearful, loses his faith, and begins to sink.

Think about that. As Peter sinks, there's a strong possibility that he may die, buried under the "baptismal" water, but Jesus pulls him out. When the two step into the boat, the storm ceases, defining Peter's personal "resurrection."

Peter wanted to believe, and in the moments when he gave up control of his life and bowed to the Will of God, he became a participant in the miracle he saw before him. Losing that Faith became cause for despair.

"Lord, save me," he cried out.

In our lives, when we hit rock bottom, at the bottom of that pit there's a decision to be made. Do we blame God and demand an answer to the question, "Why are You doing this to me?" Or, do we ask for help?

"Lord, save me."

In the wake of the coronavirus pandemic, when mandatory shelter-in-place orders caused millions of Americans to lose their jobs, both literal and figurative death became abundant within our midst. Many of us uttered the words, "Lord, save me."

Thousands died, but millions upon millions were, or will be, resurrected by God. I am certain of that outcome. Those people were given an opportunity to embark into a "newness of life" and subjugate themselves and their selfish desires to find The Cross, Embrace The Cross, and come closer to God.

Growing up, my dad taught me to love the Detroit Tigers. At the time, there were no big-league teams in Texas. The New York Yankees were the preeminent team at the time, and the Tigers' rivalry with them was huge. Daddy loved underdogs, and I suspect that's why he became a Tigers fan. My brother and I were loyal followers, too, analyzing the newspaper's box score of Tigers' games over breakfast and collecting the full complement of Detroit bubblegum cards.

I hadn't thought much about those days until I read about the death of former Tigers' star Al Kaline on April 6, 2020. Kaline played his entire twenty-two-year career with the Tigers. He was the consummate ballplayer in that he could run, throw, and hit with the best of them. After I learned about his passing, which was not a result of the coronavirus, I found myself musing on both his career and my childhood as a fan of his. That nostalgia for my younger years became a frequent companion and source of comfort during the weeks and months of the COVID-19 shutdown.

Out of curiosity, I searched online for more about how nostalgia factors into our lives and ran across the work of Dr. Constantine Sedikides, a professor at the University of Southampton in England. His research has shown that nostalgia can alleviate loneliness, boredom, and anxiety. In addition, it can bring couples closer together and make people more tolerant of strangers. In a *New York Times* article, Sedikides says, "Nostalgia makes us a bit more human," a modern scientific view that is a far cry from centuries before when nostalgia was considered a "neurological disease of essentially demonic cause."

And from what I've seen from my fellow Texans here in the heart of the Lone Star State, I readily concur with Dr. Sedikides' view of the psychological and societal benefits of looking back on our lives with fondness and appreciation.

I'd like to think the tone of my story here is shaped in large part by nostalgia, a part of the great blessing which God has bestowed on me in these the latter days of my earthly life.

And now, I believe, a great change awaits our Christian lives as this most recent "plague" brings about the "new creation."

Someday, it is my belief, every knee will bow and every tongue will confess when humankind is finally confronted with the reality that God is nothing but Love. People have been sitting in churches for years and years being told that, "God loves you, but..."

There is no "but" about it.

God is Love. His nature is Love. His acts are a show of Love. He cannot act in a way contrary to this nature. God does not retaliate, and He does not kill. Instead, He suffers with us, and He takes the blows on our behalf.

In the book of John, Jesus said—and I'm paraphrasing a little here—"If you've seen Me, you've seen My Father. We are one. I don't do anything My Father doesn't tell Me to do. I don't say anything that does not come from Him."

Realizing God is Love will inspire you to truly love others, even as they curse you or persecute you or stand in opposition to you. He is our Father, and we are his prodigal daughters and sons.

So, Love one another. Love God. Believe that God is Love and that He loves you unconditionally. And trust that Heavenly Resurrection is God's reward in the aftermath of death.

If you suffer with Me, you will be glorified with Me
(Romans 8:17).

Discussion Guide

Discussion Guide

Introduction

The job of teaching and preaching, when done well, draws from real life examples in order to illustrate less tangible ideas. Ultimately, this was the practice of ancient wisdom, be it in the form of biblical Proverbs, or the cultures and religions of ancient Sumer, Egypt, Babylon, Greece, or Rome. A life lived is a teacher unlike any other. Today we find all manner of inspirations and lessons in the pages of biographies. Figures already known, such as Nelson Mandela, Mahatma Gandhi, and Winston Churchill all live on, and teach on, through their memoirs. And the same can be said for figures otherwise lesser known, such as Louis Zamperini, John Boyd, and Nellie Bly. Shared experiences from many lives lived can fill volumes of textbooks. And those willing to listen to and learn from the lives of others find themselves to be wiser than their years lived would otherwise indicate.

That's a lot of words, but they illustrate, in part, why there is value in writing and reading personal memoirs, such as this one. Travis Bryan has a story to tell, a life lived. (Actually, he has many stories to tell, as you've seen.) And hidden within that story are lessons learned the hard way, lessons that are being passed down to all who are willing to listen. These lessons range from parenting to marriage, from hard work to changing one's mind, and from matters of football and golf to matters of faith and God.

Embracing The Cross, as a philosophy of life and faith, has permeated Travis's experiences and his message. After all, into everyone's life a little "pain" will surely fall. And the measure of us all is how we respond to the challenges, losses, and failures that surface as we live out our days. The example held up in the Christian faith is that of Jesus Himself who, as Paul describes in Philippians 2:8, "humbled Himself by becoming obedient to death – even death on a cross." That same Jesus spoke to His followers, offering them the true definition of His disciples: "whoever wants to be My disciple must deny themselves and take up their cross daily and follow Me" (Luke 9:23). Embracing The Cross in our daily lives may not always be a popular message, but it is nothing less than the preached and lived-out message of Jesus, the central figure in the Christian faith.

It is Travis's hope that his story will not merely be one to be consumed, as so much entertainment is today. While there would be nothing inherently wrong with that goal, by him or by you, that is not his ultimate purpose. Rather, his hope is that his story will prompt you to consider your own life, to give thought to how you might need to evolve, and to give attention, either for the first time or the thousandth time, to God and His purpose for your life. And that hope is what prompted this Discussion Guide.

For those that may be reading this on your own, the hope is that these additional thoughts and questions will further stimulate your own thinking as you consider how Travis's stories and lessons might intersect with your own life. If you are a writer, perhaps you can use them as prompts for personal journaling. On the other hand, if you are inclined to read this story together with a friend or a few others, then we hope this guide will provide you with ideas that lead to rich conversations stimulated by the story told within this book. Don't forget that the richness of Travis Bryan's story rests in part on the occasional changing of one's mind and the open conversation with and shared experiences among people of differing opinions on key issues.

However you use this story, we hope that it will add Travis Bryan's collected wisdom to your own treasure chest, and that it will benefit your own life in matters of family, work, hobbies, and, most importantly, faith. And I suspect it will add to your repository of knowledge on other matters, too, important subjects, such as Aggie football, Texas history, Texas law, and the lovely cities of Bryan and College Station.

Steve Laufer

Steve is a minister and Bible scholar based in Houston, TX. He has a Ph.D. in Old Testament/Hebrew Bible, and has taught pastoral and preaching development in the U.S., Mexico, Honduras, Thailand, Russia and South Africa.

Chapter 1: Speaking the Truth

The Christian life should be one of continual growth and development. The example of Jesus is also rich in examples of being a peacemaker. Consider the following discussion topics based on Chapter 1:

1. Throughout his story, Travis describes instances where his opinion on debatable issues has changed over time. Here in the first chapter, the subject of women's rights and roles in leadership is touched upon. Are there examples in your own life where you have had a change of opinion over time? Discuss the nature of your previous and current positions, as well as the process you went through in moving from one to the other.

_____

_____

_____

_____

_____

2. Travis was largely vilified for his position and language about Sandra Day O'Connor by people who held a dissenting view. Even today, people on opposing sides of challenging issues often tend to see each other as enemies. How good are you at understanding the points of view of people with whom you disagree? See if you can identify a topic where people in the group disagree. Then, practice discussing the elements of the topic for the purpose of understanding those who hold a different position from yourself. (Note that "understanding" does not necessitate "agreement.")

_____

_____

_____

_____

_____

Chapter 2: The Court of Law

Perceptions can be accurate or inaccurate, but they always are significant to the one perceiving. To that person, they are reality. This is one reality that makes communication so difficult: two different people can be communicating from two totally different perceptions. From your reading of Chapter 2, consider the way that two very different people responded to Travis during his first campaign. And consider the attention that an attorney must give to how he or she is being perceived by a jury.

1. Imagine yourself being accused and going to trial. How does Travis's description of the "drama" that is the American judicial system make you feel? The truth of someone's guilt or innocence is often hard to uncover and can at times be muddy. How does this compare to our understanding of God, who is the ultimate judge for humanity? Does having an unbiased judge who knows everything give you comfort or does it have the opposite effect?

_____

_____

_____

_____

_____

2. Which do you think people value more: discovering the truth or "winning the competition"? If God values justice, as the Bible claims, and if His people should also value and pursue justice, then discovering the truth should always be more important than being proved right or winning a competition. Consider how this dynamic can play out as we discuss various points of theology, practices in differing Christian denominations, viewpoints across different religions, and even conflicting political perspectives.

_____

_____

_____

_____

_____

Chapter 3: Good Samaritan
Many people never attempt to serve in the Kingdom of God because they are afraid they cannot. They feel unqualified or incapable. But the Bible is full of examples of people finding strength to accomplish more than they could on their own when they step out in faith with God in their life. Consider these topics of discussion from Chapter 3:

1. How do you deal with feelings of inadequacy? Some people ignore them or hide from them. Others let those feelings breed fear into their lives. Give consideration to inadequacies or fears in your life, especially those that might prevent actions on your part, such as educational pursuits, career changes or advancements, relationship dynamics, Christian service opportunities, etc. How can Travis's testimony about praying through this challenging trial and his stepping out in active faith encourage you to move forward in facing your own felt weaknesses?

_____

_____

_____

_____

_____

2. The story in this book is that of Travis Bryan's. The reader can clearly see how his experiences have, in part, shaped his perspective on a host of subjects. As he discusses matters of life and death, both in the spiritual domain and the contemporary legal domain, where do you find yourself agreeing with him? Are there places you find yourself disagreeing with him?

_____

_____

_____

_____

_____

Chapter 4: The Father of Texas
Every one of us has a family history that has left its mark on who we are today, even if they aren't all as historically impactful on the state or national level as Travis's happens to be. For example, my ancestors emigrated from Germany to Russia in the 1700s, and again from Russia to the United States around 1900. They were farmers and they were Christian Protestants. And those factors, among others, have left their mark on me.

1. Discuss together some of the positive, generational family characteristics and events of which you are aware that have influenced the person that you are today. Also give some

consideration to any negative or painful traits that have a lingering effect in your life.

_____

_____

_____

_____

_____

2. While generational influencers can be persistent over long periods of time, individuals also have the power, like Stephen F. Austin, to input new characteristics into their family tree. Perhaps you'd like to consider adding new positive elements to the generations of your family to come or maybe to eliminate some negatives that have been passed down to you. In either case, talk about how you would like your lineage of influence to be affected by you. What steps can you take, or continue to take, to make these hopes a reality?

_____

_____

_____

_____

_____

Chapter 5: TB and the Guys
With all of the Austins, Travises, Joels, and Guys making appearances in Chapter 5, I wonder how many readers found themselves squinting their eyes, looking at the ceiling, and trying to form a mental picture to keep the Bryan family tree straight. But isn't this true of most families? You can gain a certain level of understanding from reading or being told about certain nuances, but you absolutely have to be an insider to really grasp everything. I think every family of every type is like that, to a certain extent.

1. Give some consideration to the unique qualities of your own family that you "just have to be an insider" to fully grasp. Share with others some of those qualities and listen to theirs. Seeking to share your own and understand others' families is an important facet of friendship and community.

_____

_____
_____
_____
_____

2. If we transition this dynamic to the world of the Christian Church, what parallels can you identify? How do outsiders perceive the Church in ways that are skewed? What truths might we glean from them? What truths or realities about the Church can you really only experience or understand from the inside?

_____
_____
_____
_____
_____

Chapter 6: Mama and Daddy

I appreciate so much Travis's recognition of his mama's and his daddy's different personalities. Both of them contributed to the person he is today in unique ways, and they both contributed through weaknesses as well as strengths. I was particularly struck by his description of his mother's mental health struggles. This is a challenging issue for people still today. Getting help when you struggle is difficult. Understanding loved ones who struggle when you do not is equally tough.

1. What personal experiences have you had with depression, anxiety, or other mental and emotional illnesses or struggles? They could be struggles you have endured personally, those of a friend or family member, or encounters at work or in your community. How has personal experience shaped the way you think about these unique struggles?

_____
_____
_____
_____
_____

2. A major part of Travis's faith testimony stems from his mother finding peace in the Bible and in the God of the Bible during her depression. Consider how personal storms have driven you either away from or toward God. Can you share any examples of how your faith has been shaped by, or how your connection to God has been influenced by, personal difficulties?

_____

_____

_____

_____

_____

3. If you are in the middle of a personal struggle, have you given consideration to the possibility that in God there might be help for you?

_____

_____

_____

_____

_____

Chapter 7: "Victory or Death"

Sacrifice in our human history is quite often truly inspirational. In our own national history, military conflicts, fights for civil rights, and rescue efforts during disasters are just a few areas that provide a wealth of sacrificial stories. It's interesting how examples of sacrifice such as the "Travis Letter" can inspire such enthusiasm, but when we are called on to suffer our own share of indignities, bruises, shame, and loss, we tend to feel very differently about the nobility of "sacrifice."

1. Travis's first-day-of-school story is not the type of experience you might normally consider a "sacrifice." However, it clearly constituted shame, frustration, and a deal of pain for him as a young student. Not all sacrifices are chosen ones, for the sake of others. Sometimes sacrifices are thrust upon us, and how we process them can dictate whether they are empty losses or experiences that make us grow. Can you think of examples in your own life where personal struggles or loss and how you responded

to them served as a sort of personal sacrifice to your own individual growth?

_____

_____

_____

_____

_____

2. The statement that Travis remembers from his mom is worth some additional thought: "Things are going to happen to you, and you'll eventually be alright. You'll get up the next morning, and you'll be ready to go." To be fair, and depending on the level of pain brought about by the experience, the morning in which you'll be "ready to go" might be the next day or might be a year away. Nevertheless, the wisdom remains the same. What types of experiences or people have you found to be comparable to those chocolate chip cookies in his story? What or who do you find to be good medicine when you just need to gain some perspective, get through the day, and see what the next morning holds?

_____

_____

_____

_____

_____

Chapter 8: Bear Bryant and Doc Sprague
Being from Oklahoma, I read Travis's football chapter with a fair amount of insider appreciation. Travis's co-author Tim and I both share a love for Oklahoma Sooner football, and that of course gives us opinions about the Longhorns, the Aggies, the Big 12, the SEC, and Jack Mildren! (I didn't know he was from Abilene. Thanks, Travis.)

In our sports-enamored society, the athletic arena truly has become a classroom of sorts for all manner of life. The football field is a strong one, but so can be the basketball court, the baseball and softball diamond, the tennis court, and the golf course, as well as a host of others.

1. What lessons about life and character development did you see represented in Travis's recollection of his football years? Can you connect any dots between those lessons and the other biographical details about which you've read so far?

_____

_____

_____

_____

_____

2. Now, turn the magnifying glass on yourself. If you spent time playing sports in your life, what lessons did you pick up doing so? If sports weren't your "thing," can you describe another facet of life in which hard work and perseverance became teachers for you? Maybe it was a job, learning to play a musical instrument, or a particular area of study.

_____

_____

_____

_____

_____

3. The Bible does *not* say that God helps those who help themselves (that was Ben Franklin), but it has plenty to say about the value of hard work and responsibility. Scroll through the book of Proverbs and you'll find numerous examples. God put Adam in the Garden of Eden to work it. We are designed for work: productive, meaningful, life-giving work. Whatever work you spend your time doing, do you see that as part of God's calling on your life and your contribution to his Kingdom?

_____

_____

_____

_____

_____

Chapter 9: Walk-On

Every day is full of countless decisions. Many are relatively unimportant in the grand scheme of your life. What clothes do you wear? What are you going to have for lunch? But every day also has decisions surrounding what kind of person you are going to be or what kind of person you are going to become. And sometimes single decisions come our way that shift everything from that point forward.

1. If we start with Travis's decision to stop playing football and focus his energy on golf, we see an example of a decision that shifts everything that comes after. Travis mentioned that this was a decision that he regrets, while he also has shared a lot in his story so far about the importance of golf in his and his family's life. Changes in our lives sometimes require us to let some things go in order to gain or to grow in other areas. Can you think of decisions like this in your past? Discuss the types of things that had to be abandoned, as compared to the ways that those decisions helped you to grow.

_____

_____

_____

_____

_____

2. Shifting gears to Coach Stallings, discuss your observations about the coach's tactics and character during Travis's personal experiences with him, as opposed to Stallings's own assertions in his memoir. While we may have to surmise just a bit, the indication is that Coach Stallings at some point became aware of changes in himself that he wanted to see take place. And in order to make those changes a reality, he had to make small decisions every day in order to make those changes a permanent reality.

_____

_____

_____

_____

_____

3. This process is very much like the Christian process of discipleship. The example we follow is Jesus Himself, but the kinds of changes necessary to become more like Him necessitate small

decisions every day. Spend some time talking through your current
state of discipleship and what decisions you are making or would
like to make as you continue your own personal spiritual growth.

_____

_____

_____

_____

_____

Chapter 10: The Best We Had to Give

In general, Western thinkers, and Americans in particular, think
about individual rights and prosperity first and group rights
second. This is not a universal reality, however. Travis's description
of military service during the Vietnam conflict and the many he
knew who served and died is a strong example of the opposite
priority: country first. Still, the American dream causes many to
prioritize community and country only after self and family.
Perhaps this is why Travis's thoughts about corporate resurrection
in this chapter is so engaging to me. Throughout much of the
book, this idea of Embracing The Cross is applied to the
individual, and for good reason. But it is not only individuals that
should learn from mistakes, welcome the storm, and grow as a
result. Organizations should do this. So should cities, states, and
countries. As should churches.

1. What do you recall of the "before and after" effects of the
Vietnam conflict? Or the 9/11 tragedy? Or the COVID-19
pandemic? Did you see the best of humanity at times? Why do you
think (if you do) these national disasters have such positive effects,
and why do you think the positive effects tend to only be
temporary? If you disagree, please explain.

_____

_____

_____

_____

_____

2. While we may not all be able to influence gradual corporate change on the national or global scale, we can seek to influence an "Embracing The Cross" mentality in corporate groups to which we do belong. Discuss how you might be such an influencer in your family, your church, your work environment, and your city.

_____

_____

_____

_____

_____

Chapter 11: Embracing The Cross

Dying to self; turning the other cheek; Embracing The Cross— none of these practices are common in the typical American context. Which makes them all the more striking when they are lived out in front of other people! Give strong consideration to the examples in Chapter 11 of seeking to live out Jesus's words, "he must deny himself, take up his cross, and follow Me" (Matthew 16:24).

1. Can you identify an example from your past where you were clearly to blame for a bad situation, but you sought to blame somebody else? What is it about ourselves that makes it hard to admit when we are wrong? As Travis affirms, there is something profoundly powerful about an accused owning up to his or her wrongdoing and striving to learn from past mistakes.

_____

_____

_____

_____

2. Confession and repentance are the twin hallmarks of the beginning of salvation. After all, nobody can find salvation if they do not recognize their need to be saved. How does Travis's use of the idea of "Embracing The Cross" resonate with your understanding of the Christian life?

_____

_____

_____

_____

_____

3. Did you notice that choosing to live a life Embracing The Cross is a decision that is begun in one moment, but has to be committed to over and over throughout our lives? Long after Travis's initial decision to follow Christ, he still has to fight to embrace the Christ-like life. Spend some time discussing the two examples from his time at Pebble Beach. Give particular consideration to the positive result of his turning the other cheek and seeking to bless someone who would have otherwise cursed him. Where in your life might you be challenged to do likewise?

_____

_____

_____

_____

_____

Chapter 12: "Mad Dog"
There's a lot to consider in this chapter about failure, perseverance, and faith. Many undergraduate and graduate students would empathize with the notion that some school requirements are really just there to weed out the students who can't cut it. Or, in other words, to identify those who have the perseverance necessary for the job. Not every lesson is learned from textbooks, lectures, or research papers.

1. The failures in Mad Dog's class that Travis discussed were surely embarrassing. He talks at length about feelings of defeat. But somewhere in the process of law school, Travis managed to think outside the box, call on his network of human resources, and ask for help. The help he received for the mock trial class was clearly a pivotal moment in his life. Give some thought to similar struggles or failures you've experienced in your life. What happened after? Did you give up? Did you try again? How many tries? What resources did you utilize in your life to help with the process?

_____

_____

_____
_____
_____

2. The episode of the bar exam is important for the purpose of framing our struggles. After all, the first two questions that created the "failure" were followed by a host of questions that Travis knew! Failures are only true failures when we refuse to learn from them and advance ahead of them. Even when the failures are significant, the idea of Embracing The Cross is paramount to our lives. Why do you think it's hard for so many to acknowledge failure and learn from it? What is it about our self-worth that is tied up with the competition to be "right"? If we can never let ourselves be wrong, we can never learn from our failures.

_____
_____
_____
_____

3. The notion of hearing from God is a mysterious and personal experience. But generally, people who have a sense of direction from God have some things in common: They believe in God, they know something about God's revelation of Himself in the Bible, and they seek wisdom from Him. These can be at all manner of levels, but people don't usually hear unless they are listening, and they don't usually listen unless they believe. What experiences have you had in discerning direction or wisdom from God? What practices or factors were present in your life that made such an experience possible?

_____
_____
_____
_____

Chapter 13: The Tyler, Texas Wedding Brawl

I would have _loved_ to have been a spectator at that wedding! If only cell phones had been invented at the time, this book might have provided some YouTube links to some killer wedding videos! But sadly, we're just left with mental images from our authors' story-telling. This chapter provides a very intriguing contrast between the wedding in Tyler, annulled inside of one year, and the Bryans' wedding, still going strong almost fifty years later. And what is true of marriages is often true of all human relationships: some can stand the test of time, and some just can't. All relationships are challenging, but not all are equally challenging.

1. Start by giving some consideration to the many friendships you've likely had in your life. How would you describe the differences in those that have lasted versus those that have not? In some cases, circumstances can be a strong factor, but give special consideration to other relational factors, such as personality, problem-solving skills, ability to work through conflict, things you have in common, etc.

_____

_____

_____

_____

_____

2. Friendships are a good test case because we usually have a much larger sample size. Next, let's consider family. We only have two parents. Some might have another parental figure or two. When it comes to spouses, the number is small: sometimes zero, sometimes one, sometimes two or three. And kids and grandkids might add a few more relationships to the mix, but most likely still a limited number.

_____

_____

_____

_____

_____

3. What parallels do you notice in the friendship dynamics discussed in Question 1 and the family relationships you have throughout your life? Do you have estranged relationships with parents, spouse(s), or children? What factors (including personal

characteristics) contributed to that estrangement? What family relationships do you have that are strong and healthy? To what do you attribute that health?

_____

_____

_____

_____

_____

Chapter 14: Attorney for the Defense

So the law was our guardian until Christ came, that we might be justified by faith. Now that this faith has come, we are no longer under a guardian (Galatians 3:24-25). This is pretty significant theology, presented in the form of personal testimony. Today, if you asked one hundred people at random what they think a person must do in order to be received by God and to gain eternal life, the overwhelming majority will give an answer related to "being good." Even in circles where the theology of salvation by grace through faith is acknowledged, the reality of "acceptance via performance" is so deeply ingrained in us that we can act or live differently than we think!

1. To be fair, there are many relationships in our society where a person's evaluation is based on performance. The work environment is a big one. Some friendships also qualify. And in some cases, family relationships can function this way. Spend a few minutes thinking about where you have seen and experienced these types of relationships in your life and community. We may not say it overtly, but where do our behaviors implicitly communicate, "you are okay only inasmuch as you do good"?

_____

_____

_____

_____

2. No parent is perfect, but the experience of a parent relating to their child is the absolute best example for us for considering the different kind of relationship that Travis correctly identifies as how

God relates to His children. If you are not a parent, perhaps you have experienced a similar dynamic in a teacher/student, coach/athlete, or older sibling/younger sibling relationship. A parent's love for the child is not based on how good the child is. (Or at least that's true in healthy parental relationships.) Their love is based on the relationship itself. A parent loves their son or daughter simply because they are his or her son or daughter. It is very true that human relationships can be damaged over time. And children can hurt their parents, sometimes even deeply. But the overwhelming majority of parents can say that they love their kids, regardless of how they succeed or how they screw up. How have you experienced this in your life?

_____

_____

_____

_____

_____

3. Spend some time talking about how you process a relationship with God, real or potential, in light of these contrasting ideas of law and grace. Do you view God as a heavenly Judge, dressed in robes, waiting to determine your fate? Or do you view Him as a heavenly Father, loving His children unconditionally? (The reality of the Bible is that God is both. But even the great heavenly Judge loves His own children unconditionally.)

_____

_____

_____

_____

_____

Chapter 15: "Donnie Did It," Part 1
Innocent until proven guilty—that's a phrase known by most every American. We value it as the cornerstone of our justice system. But, as Judge Bryan has already pointed out earlier in his memoir, the courtroom can be just as much of a drama where the actors play their parts. And whichever side's actors act better typically has a leg up on the verdict. But what about cases that become public outrages? There are of course the big ones, the kind that might

land a true crime TV series. And then there are similar ones that might not become national news, but can definitely incite local communities. When the outraged masses get behind a claim, justice had better hold on to its hat because outraged crowds want vindication, they want a scapegoat, and all of a sudden defendants can find themselves guilty until proven innocent. (This was very much the case with Jesus on that fateful holiday weekend in Jerusalem.)

You'll have to read a few more chapters to find out what happens with the Donnie Sullivan case, but for the moment, let's consider this comparison of "innocent until proven guilty" and "guilty until proven innocent."

1. First of all, try to think about a time when you were accused of something that you did not do. Share how the scenario played out. Was your innocence ever proven? Or was there no proof at all, and so people just had to make up their own mind? How did it make you feel knowing that someone thought you guilty in a case where you were not?

_____

_____

_____

_____

_____

2. What is a valuable and reputable principle in our courts, however, does not translate to the heavenly court. As a follow up to our previous discussion about the Law, the Apostle Paul points out that every single one of us has broken God's law. In Romans 5:12 he writes, "Therefore, just as sin entered the world through one man, and death through sin, in this way death spread to all people, because all sinned." In other words, we are all guilty! We are all sinners, and we all await trial before God, guilty as charged. Discuss how this applies to you personally.

_____

_____

_____

_____

This is an important concept to grasp: we are not good, trying to keep our position with God; rather, we are sinners without a position to keep! And this is why the sacrificial death of Jesus, being God's Son, is so critical to the Christian faith. God Himself took the place of sinners, paying the price for their crimes, and imparting His own righteousness on to them, so that if they are children of His, they stand before Him as innocent! Instead of "innocent until proven guilty," the children of God are "seen as innocent even though they *are* guilty!"

3. Spend some time talking about your understanding of the Christian notion of salvation. Give consideration to the role of Jesus in this process, how a person can respond to God and choose to become a disciple of Jesus and a daughter or son of God.

_____

_____

_____

_____

_____

Chapter 16: Embracing the Cross . . . Examination

As I was first reading this chapter on cross-examination, I was struck by how many of the lessons are applied to other areas of life. In our media and social-media driven world, there are more opinions out there for mass consumption than any time in human history. And the ongoing result seems to be increasing division, dogmatism, and outrage. Cross-examining a perspective or worldview might be very similar to cross-examining a witness: It requires careful listening, considering the character of authorities, watching for blind spots (in others and in yourself), and identifying your own weaknesses. These practices may not lead to a changed mind, in yourself or in a conversation partner, but they can lead to more thoughtful and civil exchanges, as well as an enhanced appreciation for people with different perspectives than one's own.

1. "Some attorneys are too busy thinking of their next question to actually pay attention to the answer to their last one." If you're like I am, you've been in conversations with people where you probably felt the same. They're not listening to me, they're just

waiting for their next turn to talk. Careful listening is a vital skill in coming to understand and appreciate another's theological position, political opinion, or personal experience. So is asking good questions. Discuss some ways that a lawyer's practice of cross-examination might benefit you in growing healthy relationships between you and your family, friends, and colleagues.

_____

_____

_____

_____

_____

2. Analyzing blind spots and weaknesses are two more significant communication tactics. And, frankly, they are tactics that need to be developed and practiced more often. A trial attorney has to pay attention to where their own position is weak, and they must consider their own blind spots, lest the opposing attorney take advantage of them. In the world of embattled opinions, we would do well to practice the same. Doing so enables us to be peacemakers and to be kind and compassionate to those with whom we may disagree. As a case study, let's consider the authority of the Bible. Most Christians will agree that the Bible has a divine nature and is authoritative for human living. But many others, and possibly some of you readers, will have some value for the Bible, but might stop short of giving it any authority in your life. Spend some time discussing both positions, giving special consideration to blind spots and weaknesses that both adherents might not recognize. (If this topic is a bit out of the purview of your group, feel free to select another theological, religious, political, or community subject to apply this exercise, hopefully one that won't lead to too much heated conversation.)

_____

_____

_____

_____

_____

Chapter 17: "Donnie Did It," Part 2

Isn't it incredible how much a person's life can hinge on a testimony? And the recollections of these Sullivan trials have numerous testimonies, all of which held the life of an individual in their hands: from the videographer, to the ex-wife, to the new resident of the house. Testimonies matter because one person's experience or expertise has a validity all its own. But, the testimony *has* to be honest, and it *must* be accurate!

1. Can you think of an experience that you shared with a close friend or family member in which your two recollections differed from one another's? What were the bases for the differences? Discuss the reasons why people may see events through different lenses.

_____

_____

_____

_____

_____

2. What is true in the courtroom is also true in the religious world: The testimony of individuals matters a great deal. More people are engaged in religious communities because of the personal experiences shared by a friend, neighbor, or coworker, than by elaborate theological arguments. Being able to share your own experience as you have encountered God, walked with Him through seasons of your life, and learned about Him and from Him to grow your own spirit are all imperative to the Christian community. Spend some time sharing your own personal testimonies about your most recent experiences living your life "with Christ."

_____

_____

_____

_____

_____

Chapter 18: The Spiritual Nature of Golf

The language of "negative capability" was new for me upon reading Travis's thoughts on golf, but the concept is all too familiar: the ability to keep functioning with confidence even when you don't know where you are or where you're going. I can only imagine this "negative capability" has kept many a person driving around aimlessly lost, instead of consulting a map or asking for directions. And though there is something to be said for allowing others to help you, there is also something to be said for having a spirit of perseverance and grit.

1. The Christian life should be a life involving mystery. After all, Christians claim to worship a God big enough to create the universe and wise enough to know all that is knowable. But in most cases we only like to talk about questions to which we know the answers. Or we pretend that every question about God and faith has an easy answer. But are you able to push on in your faith, even when faced with the unanswerable questions? Spend some time considering what questions simply remain a mystery to you and may always be mysterious. Talk about the nature of "negative capability" in a scenario like this one.

_____

_____

_____

_____

_____

2. Embracing The Cross is described in this chapter as "laying up" on a golf hole; playing out of a penalty stroke; the art of remembering and rediscovery. All of these concepts speak to the truth of learning in the midst of trial and difficulty. Has God taught you some important lessons through failure? Have you found yourself "rediscovering" facets of yourself as you walk with Him? Share some thoughts on these ideas.

_____

_____

_____

_____

Chapter 19: "Donnie Did It," Part 3

I really valued the structure of this chapter, painting a picture of three key players in the trial sitting around reminiscing and sharing opinions from different points of view. It speaks to how different experiences helped to create different perspectives, even though the events and evidence in question were all the same. The shifting witness of Becky Sullivan introduces an intriguing twist to the third trial and also points us in the direction of "shifting testimonies."

1. What factors do you see in the book that might have contributed to the changing nature of Becky's testimony? Are there other factors that you might infer, even if they are not overtly mentioned? In what context is this shift a positive? In what context is it a negative?

_____

_____

_____

_____

_____

2. Testimonies in the courtroom are a great case study for the Christian practice of "testifying." Much of the work of the Christian Church is giving testimony about our salvation and what God is doing in our lives and in our world. So, how have you seen your testimony about God shift over time? Has it developed, or has it largely remained the same? In what way is a constant testimony a good thing here? In what way is it a bad thing?

_____

_____

_____

_____

_____

Chapter 20: The Apples of My Eye

Healthy relationships are reciprocating relationships. Consider the many ways that Travis recounts giving to and serving his wife, his children, and his grandchildren. And then consider the many ways that those same people gave back to him. In the economy of God's Kingdom, service and generosity are imperatives. These qualities only become problems when one person is generous to others, but others are not generous to him or her.

1. Spend some time discussing the nature of sacrifice in family relationships, particularly as it pertains to your own sacrifices made. What motivates you to give in such capacity? (And don't just say "love!" Dig deeper than that.) Have you been in relationships, whether family, friend, or work, where you sacrificed a great deal, but the other party did little or nothing?

_____

_____

_____

_____

_____

2. Now reverse the coin and give some time to discussing the people in your life who have made relationship sacrifices for you. How have those sacrifices shaped you, and how have they impacted that relationship? Do you believe that you have done or are doing your part in reciprocating the sacrificial nature of Christ-like relationships with those who have been generous with you?

_____

_____

_____

_____

_____

Chapter 21: "Mumme-fied"
It may be that not every reader is a parent or grandparent, but I would guess that most readers have an opportunity to invest in the younger generations in some capacity. There are a lot of lessons shared by Travis in this chapter, many of which he "learned the hard way." Being a parent myself, I'm really glad that my perfection is not a requirement for my kids to turn out pretty well. Keeping the many interactions between Travis and Joel in mind, give consideration to the following questions:

1. Let's evaluate Travis in this story first. Where would you identify some positive parenting tactics in this chapter? And what are some situations that you might have handled differently?

_____

_____

_____

_____

_____

2. The point of any discussion guide is to get the reader to apply the book's content to his or her own life. So with that in mind, where do you see some of Travis's positive actions in your own interaction with children or grandchildren? Can you identify some of the lesser qualities exemplified in this chapter in your own parenting style? (Trying to temper down one's competitive nature as it pertains to your kids' world is *incredibly challenging!*) Lastly, what lessons can you take from this chapter? How can you work to implement changes in how you parent, or grandparent, or teach school, or coach kids, or work with children or youth at your church?

_____

_____

_____

_____

_____

Chapter 22: Modern-Day Parables
This chapter provides an excellent exercise in evaluating one's own experiences with God and faith, and crafting from them stories that illustrate key spiritual truths to others. Start off this discussion by trying to identify one or two comparable stories of your own. If you need some help remembering such incidents, try considering the following:

1. In Travis's "Jailhouse Conversion" account, the impact on the lives of others started with Travis initiating a tough conversation with a colleague about a tough subject. Maybe you can think of a time in your life where a single conversation started an avalanche of effects that turned out to be "God-inspired."

_____

_____

_____

_____

_____

2. In "The Purple Camaro," Travis was reminded about God's provision and empowerment to overcome difficult obstacles. But those opportunities would never have surfaced had he not been willing to help out a friend in need, even when he felt unqualified. Maybe you can think of a time where you stepped into an uncomfortable environment, for the sake of someone in need, and found God's help to be more than sufficient for the difficult task at hand.

_____

_____

_____

_____

3. In "The Voice of God," Travis found direction for his task by spending time reading the Bible. When he felt ill-prepared for the task, he turned to the Bible, and in it he found God speaking to him, not only from its pages, but also from the circumstances of his trial. Maybe you can think of an occasion where words or passages from the Bible revealed a "too close for coincidence" experience, prompting you to recognize God's voice speaking to you in multiple formats.

_____

_____

_____

_____

Chapter 23: Shaun Carney

When the New Testament talks about the people of God being a royal priesthood (1 Peter 2:9), it isn't just talking about vocational pastors and missionaries. The identity of the Church, with Jesus as its Head, is that every member has a part to play. Every Christian has a calling. And every career has "missionary" potential.

1. Throughout the book, and in this chapter in particular, we see how Travis practiced law *as a missionary!* Give some reasons, practices, and ways of thinking that have been on display in this book that have contributed to this ministry mindset in our subject. What do you notice in Shaun's story about Travis being persistent with his ministry? What does success look like in this particular missionary endeavor?

_____

_____

_____

_____

_____

2. Being a lawyer surely brings some interesting opportunities across one's path. But every career, every job, every pursuit has similar opportunities. Spend some time considering such opportunities past or present in your own world. Maybe you capitalized on some of them, and maybe you missed some. Either way, talk about how you can be more mindful of the chances that God gives you in every environment to make an impact on the lives of others for the sake of God's Kingdom.

_____

_____

_____

_____

_____

Chapter 24: Sharing the Word
There's something ironic and beautiful about an attorney and judge also investing part of his life in prison ministry. And, I suppose, the picture is entirely appropriate. It brings full circle the idea discussed in the previous chapter that one's career *is* one's calling to ministry. But this ministry is something that Travis is a part of that's above and beyond. It takes the skills and experiences of his job that have created unique gifts and passions and connects them to a significant Christian mission endeavor.

1. Have you given any thought to how your own education, work experiences, and life experiences have created unique ministry gifts in you? Spend some time talking about how your own pathway through life has uniquely equipped you for Christian mission work. And if you've never considered what areas of ministry and service you might be "fit" for, brainstorm some ideas with your group.

_____

_____

_____

_____

_____

2. God loves us no matter what our sins happen to be. That message, taken for granted by many long-time Christians and church-goers, is *still* good news to so many people who have never heard it. And many people who *have* heard it have never had the kind of love claimed for God actually modeled to them by Christians. Is this a message that you've heard so often, you think "surely everyone already knows this"? How can you reposition the value of this good news in your mind to make it more readily available to people that you encounter in your life?

_____

_____

_____

_____

_____

Chapter 25: Judgment Day
If you were not already aware that Travis Bryan considers this memoir as a testimony of faith, his final chapter definitely leaves no doubt. As he brings his personal story to a close, he has chosen to wrap things up with a full-scope presentation of the Christian gospel or, as he calls it, the idea of Embracing The Cross. As American Christians living in what is quite possibly the most comfortable and wealthiest environment for Christians in our history, the message that this journey of faith will call us to embrace hardship, difficulty, shame, discomfort, and more is not often a popular message. (In fact, I find great irony writing much of this study guide under COVID-19 shut-down and quarantine! The

debates about our comfort versus discomfort as they pertain to appropriate responses to this situation are a perfect example of this matter.)

"Then He said to them all: 'Whoever wants to be My disciple must deny themselves and take up their cross daily and follow Me. For whoever wants to save their life will lose it, but whoever loses their life for Me will save it. What good is it for someone to gain the whole world, and yet lose or forfeit their very self?'" (Luke 9:23-25).

1. Taking up one's cross does *not* sound to me like an easy task. Embracing The Cross does not sound easy, either. Can you think of times in your life where you had the option to take up your cross, or embrace the cross, and you avoided doing so? Can you describe a time where you had the same choice and you chose to embrace the cross and follow the example of Jesus? How did that experience help shape who you are today?

_____

_____

_____

_____

_____

2. Travis asserts that many churches are reluctant to proclaim the full nature of the gospel, especially the components that speak of difficulty and hardship. What have your experiences been with this dynamic? Have you visited or been part of churches that presented the gospel in a manner different from Travis's biblical portrayal? Or perhaps you have been part of churches that swung the pendulum too far in the other direction, making the gospel harsh or overbearing. Most importantly, how do we as individuals communicate the good news of Jesus in a balanced and holistic way? What elements *must* be included?

_____

_____

_____

_____

_____

Epilogue

I was visiting with my two high school sons about the current COVID-19 situation. In doing so, I reminded them of how they've heard stories about World War II, the Vietnam conflict, the assassination of President Kennedy, the explosion of the space shuttle Challenger, and the 9/11 World Trade Center destruction. And then I pointed out how they are now living through their generation's defining "trauma." But unlike the past several in recent memory, this one is extending for months. It is much more like the Vietnam conflict in that way. We discussed how this experience will shape their generation. We talked about how things might be different and how the Church might be different. And, to Travis's point, I also believe there will be a resurrection on the other side of this experience, just like the others mentioned.

1. The timing with which you read this book will dictate how you think about the COVID pandemic and its effects on the world. In your current situation, how do you see the effects on the Church taking place? These may be past, present, or future. But the exercise reminds us that the people of God are always evolving to be the ambassadors of God's Kingdom in whatever global context they happen to find themselves. So, has the Church evolved? Is it evolving? Will it evolve? Or better yet, how does the Church need to evolve in order to continue carrying out its mission in our ever-changing world?

_____

_____

_____

_____

_____

2. The importance of loving people, especially people with whom you have differences, continues to be a shifting target. Crises such as the COVID pandemic, struggles over race relations, theological differences within the Church, and differing political perspectives are all constant sources of division. Keep in mind that Jesus' twelve disciples included a tax collector who worked for the Roman government and a zealot who, like a religious extremist, wanted to overthrow the Roman government. Jesus didn't try to separate

such differing opinions, but rather tried to bring them together, that they might learn to live in peace with one another. Spend some time discussing how the Christian concept of God's love relates to division wherever it appears in the world. What kinds of attitudes do Christians need to present on sensitive subjects? In what contexts should they speak, and in what contexts should they hold their words for another time?

_____

_____

_____

_____

_____

Works Quoted

Chapter 1 "Telling the Truth"
"I believe in the Bible and that God created woman to be man's helper…" July 11, 1981, *The Bryan Eagle*. Used by permission.

Chapter 3 "Good Samaritan"
"Driver found dead after apparent try to start vehicle." December 12, 1978, *The Bryan Eagle*. Used by permission.
"Man's beating death may be linked to robberies." December 13, 1978, *The Bryan Eagle*. Used by permission.
"Helpful habits probably led to killing." December 14, 1978, *The Bryan Eagle*. Used by permission.

Chapter 8 "Bear Bryant and Doc Sprague"
"Carl Sprague, the 'Original Singing Cowboy,' had the pedigree to prove it." *The Encyclopedia of Country Music: The Ultimate Guide to the Music*. Oxford University Press. 1998. https://books.google.com/books?id=XsiL49XFbnkC&pg=PT2 018&lpg=PT2018&dq=%22encyclopedia+of+country+music% 22+carl+sprague&source=bl&ots=11YRMh_ZCO&sig=ACfU3 U15E49OPzEoNUOZSjRWo9_oRWcaEQ&hl=en&sa=X&ved =2ahUKEwjL25bwxZvqAhWQG80KHWLdCxoQ6AEwAXoE CAsQAQ#v=onepage&q=%22encyclopedia%20of%20country %20music%22%20carl%20sprague&f=false Used by the kind permission of the Country Music Hall of Fame and Museum.

"Carl Sprague lived in Bryan, Texas, from 1920 until his death." Williams, Dennis. *The Handbook of Texas Music*. Published by the Texas State Historical Association, Denton, TX. 2012. https://books.google.com/books?id=CE8xiT3pV6QC&pg=PT1 439&lpg=PT1439&dq=%22Carl+Sprague+lived+in+Bryan,+Te xas,+from+1920+until+his+death.%22+handbook+of+texas&s ource=bl&ots=hClzoNSSQQ&sig=ACfU3U2Uq5dTj0GS3p9M LxxJVA5KOO3BeA&hl=en&sa=X&ved=2ahUKEwjAo5Omx5 vqAhWMaM0KHXv2BZkQ6AEwAHoECAMQAQ#v=onepag e&q&f=false

Used by permission of the Texas State Historical Association.

Chapter 9 "Walk-On"
"As a young football coach there were plenty of times when I
didn't have the best judgement." Stallings, Gene and Cook, Sally.
Another Season: A Coach's Story of Raising an Exceptional Son. Little,
Brown and Co. 1997.
https://books.google.com/books?id=_B_zZfxI3w0C&pg=PA65
&lpg=PA65&dq=As+a+young+football+coach+there+were+pl
enty+of+times+when+I+didnt+have+the+best+III.+another+
season&source=bl&ots=-
qJPSnusG_&sig=ACfU3U2JRxC0nMXPF-
YkSWOedUpDQpGZjA&hl=en&sa=X&ved=2ahUKEwj7hpvjy
ZvqAhWUB80KHcC8BJ0Q6AEwAHoECAUQAQ#v=onepage
&q&f=false Used by permission.

Chapter 14 "Attorney for the Defense"
"Bill's Personal Journey." ChristIsLifeMinistries.com.
http://www.christislifeministries.com/bill-s-journey.   Used   by
permission.

Chapter 18 "The Spiritual Nature of Golf"
"The bond between a caddie and his golfer is a spiritual thing." *The
Authentic Swing: Notes from the Writing of a First Novel.* Pressfield,
Steven. Black Irish Entertainment LLC: New York. 2012.
https://books.google.com/books?id=3R7hAAAAQBAJ&pg=P
A25&lpg=PA25&dq=The+bond+between+a+caddie+and+his
+golfer+is+a+spiritual+thing.&source=bl&ots=TcB9nymnO7&
sig=ACfU3U09DZWkwjqfb27Dr68LLt0pIQg_4A&hl=en&sa=
X&ved=2ahUKEwiUnpjQzJvqAhVYvJ4KHUTkCJUQ6AEwA
HoECAsQAQ#v=onepage&q=The%20bond%20between%20a
%20caddie%20and%20his%20golfer%20is%20a%20spiritual%20
thing.&f=false

"...the ability to keep functioning with confidence..." Ibid.
https://books.google.com/books?id=3R7hAAAAQBAJ&pg=P
A36&lpg=PA36&dq=%E2%80%9Cthe+ability+to+keep+functi
oning+with+confidence%E2%80%9D+the+authentic+swing&s
ource=bl&ots=TcB9nymtW5&sig=ACfU3U2-

mPaLIINuxfsYN_3anTv
v3YSKw&hl=en&sa=X&ved=2ahUKEwju_ruTz5vqAhUSqp4K
HQ2iDX0Q6AEwAHoECAQQAQ#v=onepage&q=%E2%80
%9Cthe%20ability%20to%20keep%20functioning%20with%20c
onfidence%E2%80%9D%20the%20authentic%20swing&f=false

The Legend of Bagger Vance is the story of a man, who after years of
resisting, finally listens to his own inner voice." Ibid.
https://books.google.com/books?id=3R7hAAAAQBAJ&pg=P
A112&lpg=PA112&dq=%E2%80%9Chis+own+inner+voice%
E2%80%9D+the+authentic+swing&source=bl&ots=TcB9nymt
R0&sig=ACfU3U0dmAfWnkkBmjGZXi8jb4ACkbBlkA&hl=en
&sa=X&ved=2ahUKEwjZ4aj5zpvqAhUHsZ4KHT6vC0cQ6AE
wCnoECAoQAQ#v=onepage&q=%E2%80%9Chis%20own%2
0inner%20voice%E2%80%9D%20the%20authentic%20swing&f
=false
All used by permission of Steven Pressfield.

Chapter 21 "Mumme-fied"
"The No. 17-ranked Texas A&M Football team worked out for
two hours in full pads Tuesday on the artificial turf practice field
adjacent to Kyle Field." 12thMan.com

Chapter 25 "Judgment Day"
"If it weren't for Jesus, I wouldn't be where I am today." Pujols,
Albert.
https://www.pujolsfamilyfoundation.org/discover/faith/

"Golf is just an avenue for Jesus..." Calloway, Phil. *Under Par:
Celebrating Life's Great Moments On and Off the Golf Course.* Harvest
House Publishers. 2020. P. 138. Used by permission

"It's a name that can be seen all over town, from street signs, to
signs welcoming people to the city." Galny, Crystal. KBTX-TV,
April 22, 2010. Used by permission.

Epilogue
"Nostalgia makes us a bit more human." Tierney, John. *The New
York Times*, Science. July 28, 2013.

https://www.nytimes.com/2013/07/09/science/what-is-
nostalgia-good-for-quite-a-bit-research-shows.html.   Used   by
permission from Constantine Sedikides.

"We are in the midst of a highly teachable moment." Rohr, Fr.
Richard, OFM. Copyright © 2018 by CAC. Used by permission of
CAC. All rights reserved worldwide.

Acknowledgments

I would like here to thank the people who helped me gain whatever spiritual, personal or professional success I may have achieved: my mother and daddy, Norma and Travis Bryan, Jr, who took me to the First Baptist Church, Bryan, every Sunday as a youth; my mother who let me know clearly that all solutions to life's problems could be found within the pages of the Holy Bible; my daddy, who was the greatest role model a boy could ever have; these Bible teachers who taught me the secrets of pure grace, the Exchanged Life, and the mystery of the cross: the great Apostle Paul, Col. R. B. Thieme, Jr., Bill Loveless, Bob George, Witness Lee, Andrew Murray, and Michael Gorman. And the two men who were most important in my legal education to become an effective trial lawyer: Angus S. McSwain, Dean of the Baylor Law School, and Matt Dawson, my Practice Court professor.

I have been and continue to be crucified with Christ. It is no longer I who live, but Christ who lives in me; and the life I now live in the flesh I live by faith, the faith of the Son of God, who loved me and gave Himself up for me (Galatians 2:20, my paraphrase).

I learned the philosophy of the entire Bible can be summed up in these simple words: "Not I, but Christ."

And finally, I am so grateful to my aunt, Grace Ann Norman Carr, who continues to this day to be my number one encourager to continue and persevere to teach people God's Word of the Cross.

As for this book, I have tried to recreate events, locales, and conversations from my memories of them. In order to maintain their anonymity in some instances, I have changed the names of individuals and places. I may also have changed some identifying characteristics and details, such as physical properties, places of residence, and occupations. Any mistakes are inadvertent and are mine alone.

Index of Scriptures

About the Author

Tim Gregg is a former award-winning radio sportscaster and long-time marketing and public relations consultant. A University of Oklahoma graduate, Tim has written several books, including *Moon Shots: Reflections on a Baseball Life* with Texas A&M graduate and three-time World Series champion Wally Moon; *Dear Jay, Love Dad: Bud Wilkinson's Letters to His Son* with Jay Wilkinson; *RELLIS Recollections*, the history of the Texas A&M University System's RELLIS Campus from conception as Bryan Army Air Field to today; and *South College Avenue "Time, Circumstance, and History:" Images from the Storied Roadway around which a Town and a College Grew*. Tim and his wife Nancy Currie-Gregg live in College Station, Texas, where Nancy teaches engineering at Texas A&M University after a 30-year career at NASA in which she flew four times on the Space Shuttle.

For more information, please visit:

www.faithinresurrection.org

Made in the USA
Middletown, DE
22 February 2022

61473702R00176